Online Evaluation of Creativity and the Arts

This book makes an important, useful, and well-timed contribution to the digital humanities, as a forerunner in the emerging area of digital evaluation.
—*Owen Gallagher, National College of Art and Design, Ireland*

Social media have dramatically popularized practices of evaluation, especially of cultural products and artistic expressions. The practices of "liking" and rating any shared content such as music, blogs, film, videos, photographs, artwork, and performances are ubiquitous in today's digital environments. As a result, creative producers are increasingly developing reputations and careers through a complex blend of online social reputation management and distribution platforms and more long-standing forms of marketing channels and professional evaluation. In this context, *Online Evaluation of Creativity and the Arts* seeks to examine the newly emerging forms of evaluation, such as contests, competitions, ranking, commenting, liking, and rating, which are taking place in digital environments. In doing so, this book investigates the criteria and assessment practices tied to the evaluation of creativity and artistic works and further questions what is at stake when digital environments heighten the role of amateur and peer criticism to the level of expert critiques. While exploring potential informal learning opportunities and offering incisive critiques on the emerging norms and standards of evaluation, the essays in this book cover a wide range of artistic and creative practices.

Hiesun Cecilia Suhr is Assistant Professor of Digital Media at Miami University–Hamilton and Affiliate Faculty in the Department of Art at Miami University–Oxford, OH.

Routledge Studies in New Media and Cyberculture

1 **Cyberpop**
Digital Lifestyles and Commodity Culture
Sidney Eve Matrix

2 **The Internet in China**
Cyberspace and Civil Society
Zixue Tai

3 **Racing Cyberculture**
Minoritarian Art and Cultural Politics on the Internet
Christopher L. McGahan

4 **Decoding Liberation**
The Promise of Free and Open Source Software
Samir Chopra and Scott D. Dexter

5 **Gaming Cultures and Place in Asia-Pacific**
Edited by Larissa Hjorth and Dean Chan

6 **Virtual English**
Queer Internets and Digital Creolization
Jillana B. Enteen

7 **Disability and New Media**
Katie Ellis and Mike Kent

8 **Creating Second Lives**
Community, Identity and Spatiality as Constructions of the Virtual
Edited by Astrid Ensslin and Eben Muse

9 **Mobile Technology and Place**
Edited by Gerard Goggin and Rowan Wilken

10 **Wordplay and the Discourse of Video Games**
Analyzing Words, Design, and Play
Christopher A. Paul

11 **Latin American Identity in Online Cultural Production**
Claire Taylor and Thea Pitman

12 **Mobile Media Practices, Presence and Politics**
The Challenge of Being Seamlessly Mobile
Edited by Kathleen M. Cumiskey and Larissa Hjorth

13 **The Public Space of Social Media**
Connected Cultures of the Network Society
Thérèse F. Tierney

14 **Researching Virtual Worlds**
Methodologies for Studying Emergent Practices
Edited by Ursula Plesner and Louise Phillips

15 **Digital Gaming Re-imagines the Middle Ages**
Edited by Daniel T. Kline

16 **Social Media, Social Genres**
Making Sense of the Ordinary
Stine Lomborg

17 **The Culture of Digital Fighting Games**
Performances and Practice
Todd Harper

18 **Cyberactivism on the Participatory Web**
Edited by Martha McCaughey

19 **Policy and Marketing Strategies for Digital Media**
Edited by Yu-li Liu and Robert G. Picard

20 **Place and Politics in Latin American Digital Culture**
Location and Latin American Net Art
Claire Taylor

21 **Online Games, Social Narratives**
Esther MacCallum-Stewart

22 **Locative Media**
Edited by Rowan Wilken and Gerard Goggin

23 **Online Evaluation of Creativity and the Arts**
Edited by Hiesun Cecilia Suhr

Online Evaluation of Creativity and the Arts

Edited by Hiesun Cecilia Suhr

Routledge
Taylor & Francis Group
NEW YORK AND LONDON

First published 2015
by Routledge
711 Third Avenue, New York, NY 10017

and by Routledge
2 Park Square, Milton Park, Abingdon, Oxon OX14 4RN

Routledge is an imprint of the Taylor & Francis Group, an informa business

Library of Congress Cataloging-in-Publication Data

Online evaluation of creativity and the arts / edited by Hiesun Cecilia Suhr.
pages cm — (Routledge studies in new media and cyberculture ; 23)
Includes bibliographical references and index.
1. Communication and the arts. 2. Creative ability—Social aspects.
3. Art criticism. 4. Social media. I. Suhr, H. Cecilia (Hiesun Cecilia), 1979–editor of compilation.
NX180.C65O55 2015
700.28′7—dc23
2014013423

ISBN: 978-0-415-74985-5 (hbk)
ISBN: 978-1-315-79583-6 (ebk)

Typeset in Sabon
by Apex CoVantage, LLC

Printed and bound in the United States of America by Publishers Graphics, LLC on sustainably sourced paper.

Contents

Figures and Tables

FIGURES

TABLES

Acknowledgments

This book was originally conceived as a result of a research award from the Digital Media and Learning Competition 4, supported by the MacArthur Foundation. This generous funding allowed me to pursue my two overlapping research goals: (1) understanding the emergence of online evaluations of musicians by exploring digital badges as a credentialing system; and (2) more broadly applying this online evaluation phenomenon by expanding its scope to other creative and artistic fields. To effectively facilitate the second aim, a working group was formed with the following members: Joseph Reagle, Kelly Page, Ernabel Demillo, Brooke Duffy, Linda Vigdor, Mary Nucci, and Bridget Conor. We met in person and virtually to share and engage in lively conversations. I sincerely thank all participants of this working group, as each member shared their ongoing projects and allowed one another to strengthen and enrich their ideas by providing invaluable feedback. All of these exchanges also helped me conceive of the broader framework for this book.

As the book project evolved, other researchers who were working on similar issues found their home in this book. I would like to sincerely thank all contributors to this volume for their chapters, as well as Ramon Reichert for further offering comments on my latest introduction. I thank anonymous reviewers of this book proposal who offered initial feedback on the overall vision of the project, as well as acquisition editor Felisa Salvago-Keyes at Routledge for efficiently facilitating the process. My gratitude goes out to DML directors, David Goldberg and Mimi Ito, for their guidance and support, and Ellen Seiter, editor of the Digital Media and Learning MacArthur Foundation report at MIT Press, for her critical and helpful feedback, since significant parts of my chapter on Indaba Music came directly from this report. I also thank Rachel Hildebrandt and Rebekah Hildebrandt for assisting me with the editing of this collection. Finally, special thanks goes to my incredible parents and my colleague and dear friend, Yujung Nam, for truly lifting my spirits with their endless support and many prayers.

An original version of Helen Kennedy's chapter "No Learning, No Spec: Spec Work Competitions and the Spec Movement" was published as "Against Amateur Economies: Spec Work Competitions and the Anti-Spec Movement" in *Cultural Studies Review, 19*(1).

1 Introduction

Toward an Interdisciplinary Understanding of Online Evaluation of Creativity and the Arts

Hiesun Cecilia Suhr

The journey of creative artists in their attempts to build reputations is often tortuous, since the evaluations and judgments related to creative productions are prone to heated controversy and contention. Most importantly, a career in the arts commonly grants no sustained promise in terms of success or income. Much of this unpredictable reality is especially true for amateur or aspiring artists, but it is in no way exclusive to them. Even trained creative artists (with degrees) do not always follow preconceived pathways to build reputations. The construction of reputations for creative artists is directly connected with making a living, since distributors, audiences, and consumers consider reputation as a critical factor in their decisions to support their endeavors (Becker, 1982). In this vein, creative labor[1] has been considered precarious (Deuze, 2007; Gill & Pratt, 2008; Hesmondhalgh & Baker, 2008). In the creative fields, uncertainty and unforeseen pitfalls can potentially transform invisible courses into concrete destinations.

Regardless of this reality, we have recently seen a surge of amateur cultural producers creating and sharing their works in today's digital environments.[2] They are not only gaining recognition, but more doors now seem to be opened for them to compete with one another and build their own careers, either by directly selling their own cultural products or through other opportunities. The rampancy of amateur creative productions in digital environments has also fostered the activities tied to the evaluation process, such as rating, ranking, commenting, competing, and "liking." In music communities, social and digital media networking sites have had a far-reaching impact, as exemplified by the recent controversy around Al Walser's effort to market his music for a Grammy nomination on *Grammy 365*, a private social networking site for voting members of the Recording Academy (Del Barco, 2013). Music contests are ubiquitous; Paramountsong.com unsigned-only music competitions, international songwriting contests, Indaba Music contests—all of these boast that winning songs can provide opportunities to artists, producers, and record label managers in the form of a variety of prizes. Visual arts communities are no exception to this trend. Many contests are now tied to the acts of "liking," rating, and commenting. For instance, Youbethejudgeartcontest.com is one of many examples of art communities organized into digital environments. This site allows "everyday" people to judge which artworks deserve to win grand prize packages worth over $10,000. Pixoto.com similarly hosts weekly photography contests for members with prizes worth up to $150 for images chosen by voting members within the community.

Crowdsourcing contests have also been on the rise in design communities, along with sites that share portfolios for ratings and comments. Game designers exchange design ideas and collaborate through feedback and contests on BoardGameGeek.com. The ability of users to share their ideas and videos has turned this site into one characterized by constant ratings and rankings. YouTube, most commonly known for distributing amateur as well as traditional media content, is also serving as a viable platform for makeup artists to showcase their tutorials; the popularity of these videos cannot be underestimated, and the number of "views" on YouTube is not inconsequential. On this platform, one popular makeup artist, Michelle Phan, has even scored a deal with Lancome, a major cosmetics company (Gold, 2010).

As evinced in quotidian examples, digital environments can potentially provide a springboard to help build reputations or create opportunities and platforms for professional artists. In this respect, this book explores various creative communities and their online evaluation cultures. The goal of this book is to critically understand developing themes and to further expound on the evaluation cultures' potential, as well as limitations and challenges. The contributors to this collection each tackle a different creative field, including art, music, photography, design, fashion blogging, game designs, and makeup tutorials. Together, they capture the nuanced issues therein from a wide range of methodological and theoretical viewpoints.

CREATIVE PRODUCTIONS IN THE DIGITAL ERA

With the rise of participatory culture (Jenkins, 2009), the scholarly discourses surrounding creative productions have increased in a variety of contexts; subsequently, these discourses have engendered various buzzwords and key terms, such as "D-I-Y," "user-generated content"(Cha, Kwak, Rodriguez, Ahn, & Moon, 2007; Hesmondhalgh, 2010; Martens, 2011; van Dijck, 2009), "co-creative labor" (Banks & Humphreys, 2008; Banks & Potts, 2010), "crowdsourcing" (Howe, 2008), "fan labor" (Jenkins, 1992), and "peer productions" (Benkler & Nissenbaum, 2006).

For some scholars, digital environments are positive developments, since they seem to open doors for amateurs and everyday consumers to partake in cultural productions, thereby fostering creativity. In particular, Benkler and Nissenbaum (2006) note that not only do the benefits of peer production exist in terms of offering opportunities through collaboration, but peer production further "serves as a context for positive character formation" (p. 395). A similar lauding of amateur creativity can be seen in the context of fan productions (Jenkins, 2006), through which fans take part in the process of creation. Such activities have been labeled and hailed as a form of "democratic" participation. In a similar vein, do-it-yourself productions have also been studied in terms of how these types of activities foster creativity and new types of learning in the informal context (Ito et al., 2009; Kafai & Peppler, 2011).

Against this backdrop, the positive views of some scholars have been challenged by other scholars (Andrejevic, 2009; Martens, 2011; Turner, 2009). The detractors' arguments are usually tied to the concept of free labor, as conceived by Terranova (2004). This concept seeks to capture the ambivalent meaning of work. One works voluntarily, but these efforts can be simultaneously exploited and unwaged (p. 74). Andrejevic's (2008, 2009) case studies on fan labor in the cocreation of television scripts is a case in point, whereby the democratic potential for interactivity and participation masks potential exploitation. Most notably, Kreiss, Finn, and Turner (2011) observe that peer production pertaining to digital collaboration not only may end up serving the commercial sector but may actually encroach on people's private autonomy as the boundary between private and public lives blurs.

A similar tone of concern and caution was raised through the creative collaborations that have taken place in many crowdsourcing contests. The notion of crowdsourcing, as coined by Jeff Howe (2008), a contributing editor of *Wired* magazine, relates to the outsourcing of jobs for an open call in order to solve a particular creative problem. This trend has been of growing interest to scholars from varying fields, as they strive to unpack problem-solving efforts through crowds and their relation to the market (Brabham, 2008, 2012; Kittur, 2010). People who participate in these contests have noted intrinsic and extrinsic gains, such as simple pleasure, leisure activities, or earning an income (Brabham, 2012). Still, these crowdsourcing contests have been problematized through a critical lens that focuses on creative individuals' working conditions. For instance, Massanari (2012) problematizes various aspects that challenge the graphic design professions in terms of ambiguous intellectual property, the failure to educate designers, and the meager compensation that undermines the profession in general.

In surveying various discourses surrounding creative production, the utopian views are repeatedly problematized, especially those that valorize the notion of "democracy," under which rubric work relations and commercial interests thrive and prevail in the guise of user empowerment. Massanari (2012) argues that the issues can be understood from a professional or aspiring creative artist's perspective, for whom stakes are different than for the everyday user of the web who may be simply passing the time. If choosing to not participate is presumably one of the solutions to escape the exploitations of everyday consumers, how can creative artists build their portfolios, share their works, and compete in opportunities to further their career goals, as well as build their reputations?

Problematizing these phenomena in terms of the creative individual who is seeking an opportunity or work of any kind requires an outlook that goes beyond judgments limited to labels of right or wrong. The complexity of working conditions for creative artists has already been explored in Hesmondhalgh and Baker's (2010) study of the television industry, the recording industry, and the magazine industry. In this study, they note that self-exploitations are common, and the experiences of creative workers are most aptly described as "highly ambivalent" (p. 17).

Ito (2010) also examines the unique cultural expectations and norms that take place in anime music video scenes, the remix videos made by Japanese animation fans. She asserts that unlike the kinds of fans that want to appropriate mainstream standards or expect financial incentives, these fans establish their own standards and creative values by resisting commercialism. Although I would argue that the stakes are different for fan producers and aspiring or professional creative artists, as evinced in Ito's study, sometimes recognition within a certain subculture community and intrinsic pleasure are the driving force. Through my casual encounters with artists and musicians, I am also reminded of the rich and profound motivations of artists. One memorable discussion I had was with a New York City–based painter at an art exhibition in Brooklyn. Upon discussing the potential exploitations of emerging and aspiring artists, his responses resonated deeply with me and baffled me momentarily. He stated that artists are not oblivious of this, but sometimes this is the choice one makes. In considering the discourses surrounding creative individuals and the digital economy, we seem to ignore that complex motivations exist. Beyond intrinsic pleasure or recognition, artists can knowingly and consciously consent to certain conditions or rules through a decision to either maintain or resist change. Some artists choose not to continuously weigh potential gains and losses, not because they lack critical thinking abilities, nor due to their naiveté. Instead, they are driven by a profound inner urge to keep their creative inspiration intact. When intrinsic pleasures or romantic views of artists turn into myths or platitudes, we may potentially overlook the very experiences and feelings that drive the creative fields.

Along this vein, the question becomes, if a researcher or scholar is unable to replicate the same intrinsic experience as an artist, how can he or she critique these practices from a creative producer's perspective? How could the efforts to foster amateur, ordinary creativity, as well as professional artistry, not be discarded in problematizing these practices? A similar point was raised by Banks and Humphreys (2008) when they argued for moving beyond the two diverging discourses based on utopian and dystopian views: "The extraction of economic value from social relationships is a dynamic and emergent process which also transforms the practices of business and capital" (p. 402). The concept of "user cocreative labor" emerges from the authors' ethnographic research into Auran Games; this notion recognizes the intricate work relationships that transcend the empowerment versus exploitation dynamics. As evinced here, creative artists' issues are often located on uncertain ground, especially if the argument focuses on the gains and losses in the field of digital cultural production (Suhr, 2012).

To this end, the challenges of navigating these controversial boundaries still remain, and by no means does this book collection claim to resolve them completely. Finding solutions to these challenges will require intentional effort to incorporate the voices of artists as part of research data. Although this book does not serve as a radical departure from previous discourses surrounding creative productions, it seeks to bridge them by focusing on the emergence of evaluations and the reputation economy of creative artists in the digital era.

To move along this vein of thoughts, van Dijck's (2009) commentary sheds further light on the trajectory of the scholarly inquiry at hand. In his discussion of YouTube, where evaluation occurs frequently through popularity and algorithms, he notes that "rankings and ratings are vulnerable to manipulation, both by users and by the site's owners" (p. 45). This is a key point to keep in mind, as these manipulations of evaluative measures cannot be seen as always one-sided or explained only through power dynamics. After all, the users themselves are not entirely outside of the culture. The crux of the issue requires unpacking the evaluation process from an immanent stance. This involves "not the deployment of conventional understandings and standards in ordinary or even more reflective discourse, but the assessments of the rationality or worth of conventional understandings and standards by somehow drawing on resources internal to the society or culture which they are a part" (Sabia, 2010, p. 687).

MAPPING INTERDISCIPLINARY APPROACHES TO CREATIVE EVALUATIONS

Understanding the new terrain of evaluation in digital environments is no simple task, as the topic of creativity and evaluation is interdisciplinary at its essence. The discourses regarding the evaluation of creativity not only have had a long-standing history but are linked into multiple disciplines, such as arts criticism, music criticism, film criticism, media criticism, and aesthetics, to name a few. Taking a brief moment to explore the traditional and formal critique process regarding these topics is useful, since the concern and controversy over arts criticism has not disappeared in the digital age. For instance, the discussion of whether "only specialists can assess the quality of art, or whether the taste of the general public also has some merit" extends to the current discussions regardless of its different context (Haan, Dijkstra, & Dijkstra, 2005, p. 59). This is because artists and creative producers have always had an interesting relationship with critics and criticism, since criticism has long been a staple of most artists' careers. As long as art critics have been influential, the concerns over art criticism have also existed, as reflected in *The Crisis of Criticism,* in which Berger (1998) problematizes the roles and the validity of the criticism of art. For some scholars, such as Jarvie (1967), upholding objectivity in art criticism is important; Jarvie contends that "criticism is pointless unless it has some objectivity, unless there are arguments which count, and unless we can gain from it something like an increase of knowledge (or appreciation, or insight)" (p. 83). In a similar vein, the dichotomy of subjective versus objective criticism also extends to professional/expert and amateur/public criticism of taste. The tension that arises between amateur judgment versus expert opinions has also been discussed in the context of film and book criticism (Holbrook, 1999, 2005; Holbrook, Lacher, & LaTour, 2006; Verboord, 2010). Much of Holbrook's research sought to explain the intersection between ordinary people's tastes in film versus expert preferences and to further ascertain whether or not consumers' opinions were inferior to those of the experts.

The issues tied to professional and amateur tastes in the digital era also have a long-standing history in the discipline of philosophy, as Levinson (2010) points out:

> What should be the relationship between what one as an individual prefers in the realm of art and what is objectively artistically superior? To what degree should the former be aligned with the latter? Might there be a conflict between these two apparent values, that is, on the one hand, one's own taste in art and, on the other, what is truly better art? If there is such a conflict, in what way might it be resolved or reduced?
> (p. 225)

Levinson notes the paradox that lies between preserving one's personal tastes and changing one's personal tastes in the name of aesthetic perfectionism. In doing so, he shares his doubts on the wholesale value of art critics:

> Might not an ideal critic apt for identifying and judging of artistic quality in a given art form or genre be incapable, or less capable, of identifying and judging of such quality in other art forms or genres, ones quite removed from those in which he or she displays clear competence? And, if so, how can such an ideal critic make comparative judgments of artistic value across all art forms and genres, so as to serve the action-guiding purpose that such critics are charged with fulfilling?
> (p. 228)

For Levinson, the ideal critic cannot exist, nor should one pursue the ambition to be such, since it can lead to the demise of one's aesthetic individuality. However, even if one were to achieve such a status, the issue of taste would result in an "objective" good taste and negate the personal aesthetic experience. This deep tension creates a greater distance between aesthetic individualism and universal standards for aesthetic tastes.

If the criteria of evaluation are based on a combination of popular votes and judges' selections, a contestation of subjectivities related to personal tastes ensues. The meaning of the subjectivity of personal tastes is slightly different from aesthetic tastes. Personal tastes here may seem like individual tastes, but often personal tastes leave no room for argument, as they widely and unapologetically escape what is considered the high/low, good/bad, and moral/immoral dichotomy.

Aesthetic tastes do not have such leeway, since they invoke many heated arguments and philosophical discourses aimed at unpacking and defining the criteria related to assessment. Most notably, Kant's (1951) notion of the judgment of aesthetic tastes comes to the forefront of the controversy. A paradox exists because the judgment of tastes assumes an ultimate objective standard which is connected to universalism, but taste also has a subjective quality, as in the concept of refined taste. If there is an objective measure for the "beautiful" aspect of art, this concept does not rely on any logical faculty but on a communal sensibility, "a sensus communius" (Kant, 1951, p. 135). The contentious quest to determine the ultimate standard for aesthetic tastes continues; yet, in the digital environment such process can be located in the context of everyday aesthetic practices, where casual discussions of tastes/standards/quality and subjectivity often occur in a discursive way.

Although the digital environment is decentralized, the impulse to create hierarchy is still present, as ranking and ratings are commonplace. The discussion about this hierarchy reminds us of the controversial high- versus low-art dichotomization by Horkheimer and Adorno (2002). Although this dichotomy was charged with "moral panic," due to the seeming alignment of aesthetics in conjunction with ethics and elitism in the context of the hierarchy of tastes (DiMaggio & Useem, 1978; Gans, 2008), such a view increasingly became irrelevant over the years. With abating interest in the notion of quality, values, and aesthetics, the focus has shifted to the wider approaches to understanding popular culture (Lynch, 2005; Mukerji & Schudson, 1991). As the debate about high culture and mass culture gradually became moot, some scholars made attempts to put aesthetics back in the framework of cultural studies (Bérubé, 2005; Suhr, 2009; Webb, 2002). In particular, the contributions to *The Aesthetics of Cultural Studies* (Bérubé, 2005) were written by scholars who wrestled with the fraught relationship that cultural studies has long had with the notion of universal aesthetics.

If the notion of aesthetics was considered elitist due to its top-down hegemonic imposition, a reverse power dynamic also exists when the emphasis tilts more toward the valorization of ordinariness. As stated by Webb (2002), "The cultural studies 'take' on the aesthetic field doesn't necessarily or effectively problematize its elitist features; what it tends to do instead is tip the cultural studies' hat to Reason, and in the process overlook the everyday experience of appreciating art" (p. 152). While one of the reasons behind this lack of attention to the everyday appreciation of art is presumably due to understanding and relating tastes with hierarchy and class, another underlying reason is that this reverse hegemonic imposition is neither popular in nature nor easily understood. The discussion of artistic tastes and standards can be very contentious and divisive, and the esoteric journeys taken by most artists are something to which very few people can relate.

In further problematizing this oversight, Webb (2002) precisely points out the shortcomings of the cultural studies field:

> Cultural studies writings tend not to take into account the identity of art objects and artists qua art, or as aesthetic experience. Unlike art historians, literary critics and aestheticists, cultural theorists focus on developing a critique of the field and its practice, rather than engaging directly with the works themselves.
>
> (p. 149)

In support of Webb's claim, the broader, underlying goal for this book is to reignite the scholarly conversation regarding quality and values related to creativity by focusing on the criteria and various conditions concerning evaluations. Yet, tapping into the discussions of evaluation is not an easy task, since a similar dilemma was also expressed by Hesmondhalgh (2007) when he noted how cultural studies researchers and sociologists have adopted varying stances in regard to the relevance of aesthetics. In this vein, he further questioned whether they "should make their own interventions into aesthetic evaluation" (p. 509). What does it mean to study evaluation from this context, when ordinariness is valued and an active conversation about quality seems to disavow an egalitarian status?

A critical intervention is needed at this juncture to help further understand tastes, aesthetics, quality, and value in the context of everyday digital environments. At the same time, an effort must be made to eschew the creation of a new hierarchy. Most recently, concerns have been raised in the context of the digital realm. Verboord (2010) explores how consumers in Flanders and the Netherlands wrestle with varying types of book critiques, such as ordinary, peer, and expert. He concludes that "internet-related information-retrieval practices have a limited effect on the perceived legitimacy of critics" (p. 623). In a more recent article, Verboord (2013) incisively raises a timely question: "Has the internet really democratized cultural evaluation?" (p. 2). On a related note, to what extent should we uphold the democratization of arts or creative evaluation? Does the democracy here only relate to everyday people's participation or also to that of machines? In digital media studies, beyond the inclusion of newly emerging cultural intermediaries, the complex issues of evaluation, assessment, and artistic reputations are heightened by the digital technology, algorithms, and social dynamics affected by these mechanisms. To this end, understanding evaluation practices can expand beyond the hierarchy of tastes and can incorporate many perspectives.

To achieve this, it is useful to account for evaluation's manifold interpretations and definitions. First, one must understand what evaluation means. Sefton-Green and Sinker (1999) compare evaluation to assessments in the context of creativity:

> [E]valuation is the term often used to describe informal judgments made by teachers about individual students or pieces of work. Evaluation will often include an extended or discursive response, but can include a grade or mark. Sometimes evaluation is used as a diagnostic term—to make sense of an individual's progress—although this is also called formative assessment. On the other hand, assessment is used to refer to formal summative assessments, both terminal examinations or teacher based marking, either required by law or the internal reporting system of a particular school or institution.
>
> (p. 4)

According to Sefton-Green and Sinker, evaluation has more informal nuances in the context of pedagogical environments. However, evaluation takes place beyond schools, such as in the industry and artist communities, and the criteria whereby an artwork is evaluated in a pedagogical context may be different from the one used in the industry, or they may overlap to some extent. In a pedagogical setting, evaluation often takes place via the teacher as an authority, although self-evaluation and peer evaluation are often part of the critiquing process. In this book, evaluative environments often displace the central authority, but different types of authority may be present (here the emphasis on the market/commerce is prominent). Often a blend of evaluation measures takes place, allowing experts as well as other cultural intermediaries to be in charge of evaluations. However, the person in charge of an evaluation does not necessarily remain unaffected by other aspects, especially the culture in which she takes part.

While evaluation suggests judgments on creative quality, this book does not seek to inform readers about what should or should not be considered good or superior in terms of artistic and creative standards. The focus is, instead, on capturing evaluative practices as a cultural phenomenon by examining the prominent and emerging trends of online evaluation. For instance, online evaluation cannot ignore the aspects that are solely unique to digital environments. Hearn's (2010) study on rating and ranking raises a similar point; she maintains that much online feedback relies on "affective conditioning" and on reputations that are being built as a result of "market discipline" (p. 421).

In this collection, contributors echo this observation in their respective chapters regarding the exploitative dimensions, market discipline, and different types of conditioning based on the reciprocity and feedback loop. As authors in this collection tap into this ground, readers will recognize recurring patterns that come out of this new context, and they will discover how social dynamics affect the evaluative criteria and standards, as well as other facets that are simply too difficult to isolate as independent domains. Many influences and subjectivities prevail in this new ground. The meaning of "new" can be somewhat problematic, as this ground and its environment are constantly shifting due to the creation and alteration of the rules and criteria.

Online Evaluation of Creativity and Arts: A Comparative Chapter Overview

As briefly articulated before, the emerging trend of online evaluation does not just pertain to judging the merits of cultural products but rather involves a focus on the interplay of many interrelated facets. All of the chapters in this collection intersect with at least one of the five aspects related to online evaluation, and they further address what constitutes a prominent evaluation technique in a select creative community. On some occasions, the authors also challenge what it means to evaluate—thereby broadening the preconceived notions about fixed definitions of evaluation. In this section, I broadly survey these aspects while introducing how each chapter connects with the others.

The first aspect pertains to the advancement of digital technology. Clearly this trend shows a new way to approach or think about evaluation in the digital era. The cultural lens of the algorithm has risen in the context of Web 2.0 (Beer, 2009). Not only do algorithms determine what is hot or trending, most discussed, or most popular, but they are also considered mechanisms whereby information becomes knowledge through the representation of what is deemed the most relevant (Gillespie, 2014). In social networking sites, these algorithms are commonplace in determining the popularity and values of creativity via ranking systems; to borrow the term by Gerlitz and Helmond (2013), we have encountered the advent of "The Like Economy." Although ranking implies establishing an order, does this order shape itself organically in digital environments, or are there calculated efforts to produce this order? Along this line of inquiry, Alessandro Gandini's case study on Klout.com, Chapter 9, addresses how algorithms can measure the reputations of creative professionals. In this chapter, he raises a critical question underpinning what it means to have an online influence and what criteria determine this authority. By examining Klout.com, Gandini notes how algorithms do not provide an accurate measure of this influence, since they are based on pure quantity. Gandini problematizes the quantitative elaboration of data that includes "likes," comments, and social "buttons," which primarily produce partial data. Gandini's case study of Klout also allows us to question the operation of algorithms, not just as inhuman objects, but as human-coded mechanisms that function at the intersection of human and inhuman hybridity.

In a similar vein, my chapter on Indaba Music contests, Chapter 8, explores three prominent methods of evaluation on Indabamusic.com: voting, peer assessments, and the subjective decisions of select judges. While populism is one of the prevailing characteristics of online evaluation, it has been criticized for valorizing self-promotion activities on social media. The merits of peer assessments have also been questioned for a seeming lack of genuineness, while the subjectivity of musical tastes plagues the arbitrary decisions of judges. In addition, I highlight the emergence of algorithms in music evaluation and their role in creating further exposure during the course of contests. To this effect, the algorithm is conceptualized as a form of evaluative surveillance, whereby monitoring takes place not within a top-down framework but via several different power dynamics. These include the participation of users in tandem with the notion of "participatory surveillance" (Albrechtslund, 2008). As a whole, I argue for the need to reconceptualize the music evaluation from an astatic standpoint, as evaluation entails polysemy.

Perhaps the most prominent theme that anchors many case studies in this collection is the social dimension, which is the second aspect of online evaluation. The social dimension in digital environments poses a stark contrast to Becker's (1982) seminal work *Art World,* where collectivity and collaboration are highlighted as integral social activities and experiences in the production of arts. Instead of relating social contacts solely with various kinds of networking, in a digital context, the social activities are often based on noise-making, and they require an adoption of social protocols. For instance, if the criteria for evaluating creative content are based on only the number of views, which is the case on YouTube, finding ways to raise the viewing numbers will dominate the politics. This can, unfortunately, engender corruption in the system; for example, recently, several major music labels contrived efforts to increase their number of views on YouTube (Gayle, 2012). On the other hand, if the rules for determining talent are based on peer endorsement or votes, the efforts focus on gaining the attention of fellow users of the social media services, and this may result in active networking.

Most of the authors in this collection agree when it comes to the negative side effects of social networking in evaluative and judgmental environments. This is evinced by Joseph Reagle in Chapter 2, which focuses on photography. According to Reagle, social protocols and norms within the Photo.net community have been manipulated by the users. In his in-depth study on Photo.net, he delineates how photographers have wrestled with the evolving criteria for judging photography. He raises important questions regarding the quantification of aesthetics, further problematizing whether evaluations should be open or anonymous. Perhaps the most extreme example of the negative side effects of social protocols is the practice of "revenge rating." He notes how some people are acrimonious to the point of being vindictive in rating others. Overall, Reagle's chapter documents various pitfalls and challenges as the criteria for photography goes through a hegemonic struggle between site administrators and users.

Similarly, Brooke Duffy's chapter on fashion blogging, Chapter 3, explores how users on the Independent Fashion Bloggers network wrestle with the politics of gaining more comments on their blogs. The emerging norms in this community are directly linked with mutual support; support in this case has been interpreted as leaving only positive feedback. To this extent, the very notion of community building is problematized in the context of evaluations. If supporting one another is synonymous with providing positive comments at all times, what merits do the evaluations have? Duffy reflects on these lines of inquiry to further understand how having to gain these comments intersects with self-marketing and building one's potential career as a fashion blogger.

Often the activities of critiquing or providing feedback on each other's blogs are driven by receiving the same types of comments or ratings in return—thus, the nature of peer criticism often becomes rather formulaic and contrived. Intersecting with previous discussions on reciprocity, Ramon Reichert's case study on YouTube makeup tutorials, Chapter 6, echoes related points through his discussions of feedback loops and response systems from audiences. In this chapter, beyond the scope of evaluation as a method of grading and critiquing, he views evaluation as a form of discipline and rationalization. He also introduces a unique perspective by arguing that the YouTube makeup tutorials are a type of self-evaluation practice. In noting authenticity as an important marker of these videos, this chapter explores the issues that emerge at the epicenter of the evaluation culture, such as the blurring of private and public, "presentation" versus "observation," and production and reception demarcations. In doing so, Reichert inserts the YouTube makeup videos into the framework of film aesthetics, and he conceives of YouTube videos as "a permanent, nonlinear, and heterogenic culture of perception." To this end, it is important to note that not only are evaluative measures fluid and astatic, but the actual process of creative production related to YouTube makeup videos relies on instability.

The issue of social activity is also highlighted in Gandini's case study of Klout, where he notes how reputation is measured through the activity of the users, regardless of the quality of that activity. Being social, once again, is a prime indicator of one's work and reputation. Similarly, the social manipulation or positive exchanges of feedback are also highlighted in the Indaba Music chapter. Linda Vigdor's chapter on visual art, Chapter 5, prominently showcases these types of affective, simple social interactions based on "likes" (explored further in the discussion of pedagogy). Overall, the social element in the context of evaluation has a new meaning, which is equated with ingratiating practices.

The third aspect of online evaluation pertains to power and politics. The question of granting power to elevate or authorize one's status as an artist was studied by Bourdieu (1993), who maintained that those who have "power to consecrate" artworks convey value (p. 42). In a digital context, the power is not necessarily exercised to grant artistic status, but rather to convey a "professional creative status," whereby the notion of "professional" is often equated with employment. In a digital context, *the power to mystify the professional status* is very critical. As Foucault (1982) argues, "Power is exercised only over free subjects, and only insofar as they are free" (p. 777). By extension, the concept of power is tightly interwoven into the policy and rules related to contests. However, Foucault's notion of power is not solely linked to coercive measures: "By this we mean individual or collective subjects who are faced with a field of possibilities in which several ways of behaving, several reactions and diverse compartments, may be realized" (p. 777). His concept of power can be extended to understanding how social media services operate, as many activities involve the voluntary and sometimes enthusiastic actions of participants. To this effect, digital environments are places where power can be more covertly exercised. Helen Kennedy's chapter exploring the anti-spec movement, Chapter 7, is a prime example of how professional designers are dealing with an asymmetrical power relation between themselves and the organizers of competitions. Contrary to the utopian view that amateur creative producers benefit from the contests through new work opportunities and professional status, Kennedy's study on spec competitions shows how the status of professional designers is vulnerable, as these competitions exploit amateurs through meager wages and unfair treatment. The site she examined reveals an increasingly alarming reality for professional artists, as their work conditions are undermined and devalued. Most importantly, this chapter demystifies what it means to be "professional designers" within the context of design competitions. Beyond the power dynamic between competition organizers and users, the tension between amateurs and professional designers is heightened, similar to that which exists between amateur critics and professional critics.

The fourth aspect pertains to the deep tensions that rise between creativity and the commercial market. This underlying obfuscation of the creative versus commercial dichotomy has long sustained the tension within the creative culture industry. As Roberts (2010) notes,

> In the context of this clash of objectives and processes, much of the research work on media production focuses on the struggle of wills between the creative and the commercial. The power of this basic conflict to shape the sector is revealed in structural and managerial features apparently evident in companies and in the cultural industries.
>
> (p. 766)

If the tension between the creative and commercial poles is an existing struggle within the culture industry, how can the digital era reconceptualize this struggle, or does it simply maintain the status quo?

In the digital era, the creative/commercial binary has seemingly been blurred—but at closer observation, the boundaries are still intact, since many sites or contests are sponsored by commercial interests, and often winners are chosen based on a client's choice rather than on artistic merit or creativity. This trend is evident in many crowdsourcing competitions for designs, as well as music competitions, especially the Indaba Music contests explored by me. The logic of the market and commerce affecting the criteria for creativity is problematized by Aaron Trammell's chapter, Chapter 4, on a game design competition site called BoardGameGeek. In this chapter, contrary to the utopian view of a grassroots creative community in which authentic exchanges of design ideas are shared and collaboration thrives, Trammell underpins how markets construct the criteria and standards for judging the game designs. He explores the challenges that work against the fostering of grassroots creativity when competition techniques are appropriated and adopted from a market-centered approach. To consider creativity rising out of the market context as comparatively inferior to the one that exists outside the borders of the market may bring up a number of points. Essentially, the fundamental question of what we regard as creativity comes to the fore. As Banks and O'Connor (2009) insightfully point out: "If everything can be creative—a management model, a kidney dialysis machine, package holidays—then wherein lies the specific value of the cultural/creative industries?" (p. 367). In comparing different sets of criteria for game designs, Trammell argues that the standards pervasive on BoardGameGeek only reproduce the status quo. To this extent, what is celebrated are the different guises that permit the repetition of known lucrative measures, reflecting the ongoing discussions of profit in the context of the culture industry. The underlying theme of reproducing the traditional structures of cultural production in grassroots communities is also echoed in other chapters, most notably in Duffy's chapter on fashion blogging.

Finally, the last dimension addressed in this book is the intersection between the pedagogical implications of evaluation and the informal evaluations taking place in digital environments. In broad terms, to what extent can evaluations yield learning opportunities? Do these activities enhance the experience of learning about one's work through feedback or exposure to others' work? The forerunners in these pedagogical inquiries have been those involved in the ongoing efforts of the Digital Media and Learning Research Hub, the members of which are trying to better understand how casual and everyday online activities can be seen as a new type of learning opportunity. Much of the learning we describe in this book applies to emerging, groundbreaking forms of education, such as peer-based learning, digital learning, self-learning, and connected learning. Peer-based learning is most prominent in the music, photography, and gaming communities, as numerous social networking sites and competition sites drive their contents through peer feedback.

Another type of conceptualization of learning is "digital learning," which defies the typical top-down approach symptomatic of traditional learning environments and takes into account the interactive, shared experience. Davidson and Goldberg (2009) note that

> digital learning is not simply about interaction . . . but of interaction that, because of issues of access, involves cocreation with myriad strangers who have the anonymity to respond as they wish, candidly. From

> such a process, we learn and continue to learn from people met only virtually (if at all) and whose institutional status and credentials may be unknown.
>
> (p. 7)

In the evaluation process, learning can be viewed from many perspectives. What do creative producers learn as they consider their feedback in connected learning spaces? What do evaluators learn as they evaluate, rate, and comment on creative productions? Do they gain any benefit as they learn about different opinions related to artistic and creative contents? In sum, evaluation and learning can exist in tandem, as a poorly expressed or negative evaluation can hinder the learning process. Rather than viewing these emerging evaluations as one-dimensional in their impact, this book highlights interactivity and connectivity as pivotal places to examine whether informal learning can take place.

The authors in this collection have taken a variety of approaches to understand how evaluative practices in digital environments facilitate learning experiences. For example, Vigdor, in her chapter on visual art, brings up the challenges of learning in digital spaces. She highlights the emerging issue of online evaluations pertaining to art communities through comparing two critique sessions at the School of Visual Art and two online visual arts communities (DeviantArt.com and Wetcanvas.com). In comparing the two kinds of critiques, the crit session consists of constructive criticism that leaves room for critical thinking, while online feedback focuses on only reductionist affirmation practices. This reality echoes the previous discussions on the reciprocity of positive (or negative) comments and ratings (see fashion blogging, Indaba Music, Photo.net, etc.). To this extent, Vigdor's chapter notes that while participatory culture has opened up democratic evaluation, much of this practice is reduced to valorization of simple affirmations, such as "liking" practices. What is at stake is not only the inferior discourses of art criticism but also the undermining of learning experiences. In a similar vein, Kennedy takes a clear stance on how competitions are not conducive to learning due to several of the aforementioned problems. In a rather ambivalent position, music communities (such as Indaba Music), fashion blogging communities, and Photo.net have recognized the potential whereby learning can take place. Nonetheless, the emergence of various prominent trends can clearly inhibit learning. In his chapter on YouTube, Reichert conceptualizes self-reflective learning through which makeup artists learn and adapt to others' perceptions of them on the YouTube platform. In this vein, learning about oneself is not necessarily a practice of autonomy but rather a customization of oneself in a socially negotiated context. Many of these issues will never be resolved if researchers focus solely on questioning whether online evaluation practices provide learning experiences or not (or facilitate beneficial learning). Just because learning potential and experiences exist does not automatically make evaluations fair and just. In short, while evaluation and learning aspects dovetail with one another, they are not mutually exclusive in terms of benefits and strengths.

Taken as a whole, a number of important contributions and themes emerge in this collection. As the evaluation of creative production increasingly holds weight in the digital era, evaluations not only are affected by the merits of creativity or the arts, but are intricately interwoven with the normalization of life and the development and adaptation of certain lifestyles. For some scholars, evaluations may seem to function as a form of social control, while others are concerned with the skewed or misleading creation of reputations. Another dominant issue is the demystification of the status and conditions of professional artists in the digital era. In general, the authors share similar concerns about the nature of evaluations, but by no means do they all unequivocally predict the persistence of such practices in the future. The contributors' analyses represent only the emergent conditions of the present, and thus they remain as a snapshot of rapidly evolving criteria and the culture of online evaluations.

NOTES

1. By "creative labor," I am referring to both the time and effort required to develop one's craft, whether one is a writer, a musician, an artist, or a designer. This concept also relates to the emergent conditions of doing self-promotion, competing in contests, and other activities that pertain to being a creative artist. Jenkins and Deuze (2008) note that many individuals pursuing creative work in the media industries are contingently employed and independently contracted.
2. By "digital environment," I am referring to all online, Internet environments, as well as those used by digital devices.

REFERENCES

Andrejevic, M. (2008). Watching television without pity: The productivity of online fans. *Television & New Media, 9*(1), 24–46.

Andrejevic, M. (2009). Exploiting YouTube: Contradictions of user-generated labor. In P. Snickars & V. Patrick (Eds.), *The YouTube reader* (pp. 406–423). Stockholm: National Library of Sweden.

Albrechtslund, A. (2008). Online social networking as participatory surveillance. *First Monday, 13*(3). Retrieved from http://firstmonday.org/article/view/2142/1949

Banks, J., & Humphreys, S. (2008). The labour of user co-creators: Emergent social network markets? *Convergence: The International Journal of Research into New Media Technologies, 14*(4), 401–418.

Banks, M., & O'Connor, J. (2009). After the creative industries. *International Journal of Cultural Policy, 15*(4), 365–373.

Banks, J., & Potts, J. (2010). Co-creating games: A co-evolutionary analysis. *New Media & Society, 12*(2), 253–270.

Becker, H. (1982). *Art worlds.* Berkeley and Los Angeles: University of California Press.

Beer, D. (2009). Power through the algorithm? Participatory web cultures and the technological unconscious. *New Media & Society, 11*(6), 985–1002.
Benkler, Y., & Nissenbaum, H. (2006). Commons-based peer production and virtue. *Journal of Political Philosophy, 14*(4), 394–419.
Berger, M. (1998). *The crisis of criticism.* New York: The New Press.
Bérubé, M. (2005). *The aesthetics of cultural studies.* Malden, MA: Blackwell.
Bourdieu, P. (1993). *The field of cultural production: Essays on art and literature.* New York: Columbia University Press.
Brabham, D. C. (2008). Crowdsourcing as a model for problem solving: An introduction and cases. *Convergence: The International Journal of Research into New Media Technologies, 14*(1), 75–90.
Brabham, D. C. (2012). Crowdsourcing: A model for leveraging online communities. In A. Delwiche & J. J. Henderson (Eds.), *The Participatory Cultures Handbook* (pp. 120–129). New York: Routledge.
Cha, M., Kwak, H., Rodriguez, P., Ahn, Y-Y., & Moon, S. (2007, October). *I tube, you tube, everybody tubes: Analyzing the world's largest user generated content video system.* Paper presented at the proceedings of the 7th conference on Internet measurement of the Association for Computing Machinery Special Interest Group, San Diego, CA.
Davidson, C. N., & Goldberg, D. T. (2009). *The future of learning institutions in a digital age.* Cambridge, MA: MIT Press.
Del Barco, M. (2013). Why Al Walser got a Grammy nomination and Justin Bieber didn't. *NPR Music.* Retrieved from www.npr.org/blogs/therecord/2013/02/07/171308797/why-al-walser-got-a-grammy-nomination-and-justin-bieber-didnt
Deuze, M. (2007). Convergence culture in the creative industries. *International Journal of Cultural Studies, 10*(2), 243–263.
DiMaggio, P., & Useem, M. (1978). Social class and arts consumption. *Theory and Society, 5*(2), 141–161.
Foucault, M. (1982). The subject and power. *Critical Inquiry, 8*(4), 777–795.
Gans, H. (2008). *Popular culture and high culture: An analysis and evaluation of taste.* New York: Basic Books. (Originally published 1999)
Gayle, D. (2012). YouTube cancels billions of music industry video views after finding they were fake or 'dead.' *MailOnline.* Retrieved from www.dailymail.co.uk/sciencetech/article-2254181/YouTube-wipes-billions-video-views-finding-faked-music-industry.html
Gerlitz, C., & Helmond, A. (2013). The Like economy: Social buttons and the data-intensive web. *New Media & Society,* epub ahead of print, doi: 10.1177/1461444812472322.
Gill, R., & Pratt, A. (2008). In the social factory? Immaterial labour, precariousness and cultural work. *Theory, Culture & Society, 25*(7–8), 1–30.
Gillespie, T. (2014). The relevance of algorithms. In T. Gillespie, P. J. Boczkowski, & K. A. Foot (Eds.), *Media technologies: Essays on communication, materiality, and society* (pp. 167–194). Cambridge, MA: MIT Press.
Gold, G. (2010). Lancome signs Michelle Phan, YouTube makeup star. Retrieved from http://main.stylelist.com/2010/02/10/lancome-michelle-phan/
Haan, M. A., Dijkstra, S. G., & Dijkstra, P. T. (2005). Expert judgment versus public opinion—evidence from the Eurovision song contest. *Journal of Cultural Economics, 29*(1), 59–78.
Hearn, A. (2010). Structuring feeling: Web 2.0, online ranking and rating, and the digital 'reputation' economy. *Ephemera: Theory & Politics in Organization, 10*(3/4), 421–438.
Hesmondhalgh, D. (2007). Audiences and everyday aesthetics: Talking about good and bad music. *European Journal of Cultural Studies, 10*(4), 507–527.

Hesmondhalgh, D. (2010). User-generated content, free labour and the cultural industries. *Ephemera: Theory & Politics in Organization, 10*(3/4), 267–284.

Hesmondhalgh, D., & Baker, S. (2008). Creative work and emotional labour in the television industry. *Theory, Culture & Society, 25*(7–8), 97–118.

Hesmondhalgh, D., & Baker, S. (2010). 'A very complicated version of freedom': Conditions and experiences of creative labour in three cultural industries. *Poetics, 38*(1), 4–20.

Holbrook, M. B. (1999). Popular appeal versus expert judgments of motion pictures. *Journal of Consumer Research, 26*(2), 144–155.

Holbrook, M. B. (2005). The role of ordinary evaluations in the market for popular culture: Do consumers have "good taste"? *Marketing Letters, 16*(2), 75–86.

Holbrook, M. B., Lacher, K. T., & LaTour, M. S. (2006). Audience judgments as the potential missing link between expert judgments and audience appeal: An illustration based on musical recordings of "My Funny Valentine." *Journal of the Academy of Marketing Science, 34*(1), 8–18.

Horkheimer, M., & Adorno, T. W. (2002). *Dialectic of enlightenment: Philosophical fragments* (E. Jephcott, Trans., G. S. Noerr, Ed.). Redwood City, CA: Stanford University Press.

Howe, J. (2008). *Crowdsourcing: Why the power of the crowd is driving the future of business.* New York: Crown Business.

Ito, M. (2010). The rewards of non-commercial production: Distinctions and status in the anime music video scene. *First Monday, 15*(5). Retrieved from http://firstmonday.org/ojs/index.php/fm/article/view/2968/2528

Ito, M., Baumer, S., Bittanti, M., Cody, R., Herr-Stephenson, B., Horst, H. A., . . . Pascoe, C. (2009). *Hanging out, messing around, and geeking out: Kids living and learning with new media.* Cambridge, MA: MIT Press.

Jarvie, I. C. (1967). The objectivity of criticism of the arts. *Ratio, 9,* 67–83.

Jenkins, H. (1992). *Textual poacher: Television fans & participatory culture.* New York: Routledge.

Jenkins, H. (2006). *Convergence culture: Where old and new media collide.* New York: NYU Press.

Jenkins, H. (2009). *Confronting the challenges of participatory culture: Media education for the 21st century.* Cambridge, MA: MIT Press.

Jenkins, H., & Deuze, M. (2008). Convergence culture. *Convergence: The international journal of research into new media technologies, 14*(1), 5–12.

Kafai, Y. B., & Peppler, K. A. (2011). Youth, technology, and DIY developing participatory competencies in creative media production. *Review of Research in Education, 35*(1), 89–119.

Kant, I. (1951). *The critique of judgement.* New York: Hafner Press.

Kittur, A. (2010). Crowdsourcing, collaboration and creativity. *XRDS, 17*(2), 22–26.

Kreiss, D., Finn, M., & Turner, F. (2011). The limits of peer production: Some reminders from Max Weber for the network society. *New Media & Society, 13*(2), 243–259.

Levinson, J. (2010). Artistic worth and personal taste. *Journal of Aesthetics and Art Criticism, 68*(3), 225–233.

Lynch, G. (2005). *Understanding theology and popular culture.* Malden, MA: Wiley-Blackwell.

Martens, M. (2011). Transmedia teens: Affect, immaterial labor, and user-generated content. *Convergence: The International Journal of Research into New Media Technologies, 17*(1), 49–68.

Massanari, A. L. (2012). DIY design: How crowdsourcing sites are challenging traditional graphic design practice. *First Monday, 17*(10). Retrieved from http://firstmonday.org/article/view/4171/3331

Mukerji, C., & Schudson, M. (1991). *Rethinking popular culture: Contemporary perspectives in cultural studies*. Berkeley and Los Angeles: University of California Press.

Roberts, J.P. (2010). Revisiting the creative/commercial clash: An analysis of decision-making during product development in the television industry. *Media, Culture & Society, 32*(5), 761–780.

Sabia, D. (2010). Defending immanent critique. *Political Theory, 38*(5), 684–711.

Sefton-Green, J., & Sinker, R. (1999). *Evaluating creativity: Making and learning by young people*. New York: Routledge.

Suhr, H. C. (2009). Severing the disjuncture between cultural studies and aesthetics: New ways to engage aesthetics in the study of social networking sites. *Rhizomes, 19*. Retrieved from www.rhizomes.net/issue19/suhr.html

Suhr, H. C. (2012). *Social media and music: The digital field of cultural production*. New York: Peter Lang Press.

Terranova, T. (2004). *Network culture: Politics for the information age*. Ann Arbor, MI: Pluto Press.

Turner, G. (2009). *Ordinary people and the media: The demotic turn*. London: Sage.

van Dijck, J. (2009). Users like you? Theorizing agency in user-generated content. *Media, Culture & Society, 31*(1), 41.

Verboord, M. (2010). The legitimacy of book critics in the age of the Internet and omnivorousness: Expert critics, Internet critics and peer critics in Flanders and the Netherlands. *European Sociological Review, 26*(6), 623–637.

Verboord, M. (2013). The impact of peer-produced criticism on cultural evaluation: A multilevel analysis of discourse employment in online and offline film reviews. *New Media & Society*, epub before print; doi: 10.1177/1461444813495164.

Webb, J. (2002). Cultural studies and aesthetics—pleasures and politics. *Critical Studies, 20*(1), 147–157.

2 Revenge Rating and Tweak Critique at Photo.net

Joseph Reagle

INTRODUCTION

In today's world, most anything can be posted online, rated, liked, and ranked. Flickr (founded in 2004), Tumblr (2007), and Instagram (2010) exemplify this Web 2.0 penchant for the sharing and evaluation of images. Yet, these sites were not the first to support these practices among photographers. For instance, PhotoSIG.com has been operating since December 2001 and has long supported photographic critiques among its contributors (Xu & Bailey, 2012).

In this chapter, I focus on the evaluation of photographic works at Photo.net, another early site, begun in 1993. It started as a few discussion boards on a personal website, and it now describes itself as "a site for serious photographers to connect with other photographers, explore photo galleries, discuss photography, share and critique photos, and learn about photography" ("Photography Community, Including Forums, Reviews, and Galleries from Photo.net," 2012). Indeed, the discussions at Photo.net about the practices, meanings, and abuses of digital evaluation anticipate discussions about all manner of contemporary digital evaluation. Hence, I claim that Photo.net is a seminal site of practice and discourse about digital evaluation. In the following pages I describe Photo.net's origins and how the community grappled with the issues of numeric ratings (what range should be used?), anonymity (are blinded reviews better?), manipulation (how to prevent people from "mate-rating" friends and "revenge-rating" enemies?), genres (why are nudes so much more popular?), and critique etiquette (is it okay to tweak another's image in Photoshop?). I relate these issues to a few, more recent, examples of online evaluation beyond photography. Most importantly, I offer six characteristics of evaluation learned from Photo.net that continue to be broadly relevant in the age of digital evaluation. In light of these, I argue that it is hard to quantify the qualitative; and when people do so, quantitative mechanisms often beget their own manipulation.

BACKGROUND

Philip Greenspun and Photo.net

Unlike the *founding* of Tumblr in 2007, it is better to describe Photo.net as *starting* in 1993. This was before venture capitalists spoke of "social media" and platform "launches." At the web's start, people were building and experimenting with this new medium, and sometimes personal projects took on a wider significance. Such was the case for Philip Greenspun. In the early 1990s Greenspun was a student in MIT's storied "course 6" (electrical engineering and computer science). Greenspun completed his master's degree in 1993 and planned to continue on with a doctorate. Yet, he was not a quiet, computer-obsessed nerd, toiling away alone in a back room. Greenspun was brash and reflective and had interests outside of computers. He traces his interest in photography back to the use of his mother's camera as a 10 year old. Later, "as an MIT undergraduate, surrounded by remarkably unphotogenic classmates, I didn't haul out my Minolta SRT-102 too often, but I did take a photo class in which we learned to use the 4 × 5 view camera and darkroom" (Greenspun, 2012). Even on the computer front, he saw himself as outside the mainstream and grew increasingly frustrated that others at MIT did not share his enthusiasm for Internet-based applications (Greenspun, 2000b). He was also fond of travel and Samoyeds, a large, white, fluffy breed of dog; their visages frequented his publications and his own profile picture for many years. In 1993, having completed one stage of graduate work, chafing under others' indifference to the web, and mourning the recent loss of George, his 65-pound Samoyed, he decided to "take the trip we were going to take together, Boston to Alaska and back, rather than wait until I finished my Ph.D" (Greenspun, 1993).

Greenspun's online writing precedes the term "blog." In fact, 10 years before launching his own blog in 2003, he had famously established the web as a compelling, nontechnical medium with his personal site Greenspun.com. It was here that he posted the journal of his trip, *Travels with Samantha*. (Samantha was the Macintosh PowerBook 170 that accompanied him on his journeys.) This travel diary changed how people looked at the still nascent web. Tim Berners-Lee invented the web so that particle physicists from the CERN (European Organization for Nuclear Research) could better collaborate, but Greenspun showed that it could also be a medium for prose and photography. As Greenspun (1996) writes, *Travels*' 210 pages of text and 250 photographs won the "Best of the Web '94 and became one of the 10 most heavily trafficked sites on the Internet. More than a thousand people each day read at least part of the book." It was "born of the world's indifference to the World Wide Web and then paradoxically grew to prominence with the Web" (Greenspun, 2000a).

Hence, Greenspun's work was characterized by the intersection of his technical work, writing, photography, and the community arising out of all of this. At MIT, he started the Scalable Systems for Online Communities group, which then was spun off into ArsDigita, a profitable venture which developed online community applications. On his personal site, Greenspun.com, he hosted hundreds of varied discussion boards (LUSENET, 2012). He continued to publish online: personal reflections, photographs, and more technical works such as "Database Backed Web Sites" (Greenspun, 1996) and *Philip and Alex's Guide to Web Publishing* (Greenspun, 1998). (Alex was his Samoyed dog at the time, and he appears on the cover with Greenspun.)

The approaching millennium brought big changes. At ArsDigita, Greenspun and the other founders were ousted by their venture investors (Greenspun, 2000b). While the domain name Photo.net had been registered and had served pages related to an MIT research group since 1993, Greenspun began adding photographic content in 1997 (Greenspun, 1997). Furthermore, the loss of ArsDigita and the bursting of the dotcom bubble coincided with the migration of the photography forum on Greenspun.com to Photo.net, the last of which was moved in 2002 (Administrators, 2002; Luong, 2002). At this point, in June of 2002, Brian Mottershead, who appears frequently in the following discussions, was hired as publisher and editor of Photo.net to help make it an independent and viable commercial enterprise.

Greenspun became more active again in 2006, but perhaps only to prepare the site for sale. In 2007, the site was sold to NamedMedia. As one photographer noted, what began as Greenspun's personal home page "developed into one of the largest photographer communities online," and one largely free of advertising. Instead, *subscribers* paid for membership, meaning they received extra perks, including more storage space for their photos. The "downside of this was a feel of stagnant technology, but the upside was a noise free environment from advertising" (Goldstein, 2007). Today, the site is still active; it describes itself as "an online community with hundreds of thousands of active members and many more casual viewers visiting daily. We started in 1993 and strive to be the best peer-to-peer educational system for people who wish to become better photographers" ("About Us," 2012). While the site's administrators make efforts to keep current, such as the inclusion of social media sharing buttons (Root, 2011), it does have a dated feel and can be slow to respond. Other than the pokiness, some members might consider its old-fashionedness a virtue that distinguishes it as a venue for "serious photographers" exchanging critique and learning. Its users tend to be a bit more traditional than the "filter-happy" mobile phone photographers who make use of sites like Instagram. (Photo.net does, however, have an "iphone" mobile photography category with many beautiful images.)

Greenspun himself continues to blog, take photographs, and write equipment reviews on Photo.net. (However, his last posting to the site's discussion forum was in 2009 ["Forum Contributions by Philip Greenspun," 2012].) His entrepreneurial efforts, while drama-filled, earned him moderate wealth. In addition to reviewing expensive cameras, he now flies and reviews small aircraft. While the photograph on his home page often featured a picture of himself with his dog, it now includes a picture of a smiling father and young daughter.

APPROACH

In the 1990s, I too was a student at (and later employee of) MIT, an advocate of the web, and interested in photography; I have been a reader of Photo.net (on and off) since that time. However, the discussions below are collected from a systematic review of the "Photo Critique and Rating" forum from 2000 to 2005, and I include discussion of changes at the site up to 2010. My findings are based upon a naturalistic inquiry (Lincoln & Guba, 1985; Thomas & Jones, 2006) into digital evaluation practices at this site. I reviewed approximately 500 discussion topics within this period, paying attention to those related to evaluation and those that generated significant discussion. My analysis consisted of iteratively coding (and recoding) the content of these sources into various categories, a type of "theoretical sampling" or "emergent design" (Glaser & Strauss, 1967, p. 72; Lincoln & Guba, 1985, p. 209). Drafts of this analysis were shared with members of the community for corrections and feedback.

ANALYSIS: EVALUATING DIGITAL PHOTOGRAPHY

For more than two decades, Terry Barrett's (1996) *Criticizing Photographs* has provided an accessible and comprehensive "introduction to understanding images." In the five editions since 1990, Barrett's sensible exploration of the description, interpretation, and evaluation of photographs has enabled many students to "better appreciate photographs by using critical processes." These critical processes include describing photographs, including their subject matter, form, medium, and style. Also, interpretation, "whenever attention and discussion move beyond offering information to matters of meaning," can be from varied perspectives (e.g., comparative, formal) (pp. 1, 38). One can further consider the type of photograph (e.g., descriptive, interpretive), the context (internal, original, external), and the criteria one uses in evaluating photographs. Nowhere does Barrett discuss ratings, rankings, or modifying others' images as a type of critique. Yet, these are characteristic practices of digital evaluation.

Of course, the premise of sharing and critique is that one learns to be a better photographer, that members are "working to help each other improve." People exchange tips and give each other critique and advice, and the very act of sharing is spoken of in terms of learning. For instance, one talented and popular photographer's portfolio includes multiple expressions of gratitude, such as "I learned so much by perusing through your photos" followed by "thanks for sharing" (Pinto, 2005). In addition to these subjective statements, one might also look to quantifiable assessments of performance. In an analysis of over 6 years of data at the related site PhotoSIG, Anbang Xu and Brian Bailey (2012) found that participation at PhotoSIG did, overall, lead to improvements in the average ratings photographers received. However, as we shall see, ratings are not always a transparent metric of quality.

Quantification

In 1983 sociologist George Ritzer published an article arguing that the McDonalds' "rationalization" of food production could serve as a useful model for understanding changes in larger society. That is, McDonalds succeeded because of efficiency, technology, calculability, predictability, and control; these same forces are now shaping our lives at work, in school, and even when on holiday. Indeed, "calculability," a drive toward quantifiable measures, is a defining characteristic of contemporary "rational" society. Why? Ritzer notes that quality is "notoriously difficult to evaluate," yet computers are good at counting.

How do we assess the quality of a hamburger, or a physician, or a student? Instead of even trying, in an increasing number of cases, a rational society seeks to develop a series of quantifiable measures that it takes as surrogates for quality. This urge to quantify has given great impetus to the development of the computer and has, in turn, been spurred by the widespread use and increasing sophistication of the computer (Ritzer, 1983, p. 103).

Hence, we ought not be surprised that Photo.net, a site begun at MIT, would both innovate upon and suffer the consequences of *calculability.* In December 2000, Photo.net took a definitive step in its history, transitioning from a collection of fora for discussing photography into a site in which photos could be rated and ranked (O'Neill, 2005). Photo.net's system was simple and ad hoc. One could rate a photograph according to its *aesthetics* or *originality* on a 10-point scale (Stefan Ballard in rajeev, lisa, audrey, & philg, 2001). While one could also leave a text comment, the innovation of allowing others to quantify the quality of a photograph would be an ongoing source of confusion and controversy. Indeed, by the following August, the site's administrators posted the first message on the "Photo Critique and Rating" forum asking for "suggestions for what to do with the photo ratings systems" (rajeev et al., 2001).

Some of the responses asked about the motivation of the system: "What is the point of this rating system anyway?" (Joe Oliva in rajeev et al., 2001). Advocates for the system responded that it informed the "top rated" pages, helping users find photographers they might like. Yet, others noted the numbers could be an affront. Of course, while one could always "lighten up and ignore it," some felt that the numeric scale was too much:

> Currently all photos are given a rating of 1–10 in two categories—"cleverness" and "aesthetics." I am sure these two categories have meaning to the people who manage Photo.net, but I do not think they mean the same thing to every visitor who logs in here. I also think 1–10 is too big of a spread—a "7" might seem like an average/good score to me, but to someone else (especially a student enrolled in one of our grade-inflated universities), a 7 might seem terribly low.
>
> (Stefan Ballard in rajeev et al., 2001)

Interestingly, research on surveys indicates that this concern is well founded, as there are often problems with skew and consistency when fewer than five or more than nine items are used (Cox, 1980; Preston & Colman, 2000). To avoid these problems, perhaps labels could be used instead? "Let people indicate easily, on all pictures, whether they 'hate it', 'it's ok', 'I love it', and leave it at that" (Wayne Melia and Jonathan Watmough in rajeev et al., 2001). In time, a seven-item scale was adopted, but it too had its problems. Ratings were now compressed around 5 and 6, leading one contributor to ask if rating with decimal fractions would be useful (Kelly, 2004). Another contributor agreed, "The difference between 5 and 6 is dramatic." An average of 6 might land you close to the first few pages of "top rated" photos, whereas with a 5 "you are at the very end . . . like number 2000 or so. At the very least a 5.5, 6.5 and even 4.5 would be nice" (Vincent K. Tylor in Kelly, 2004). Others responded that this was a "bad idea" because a wider, 10-item scale had already been tried and abandoned. Others recommended that people stop worrying about the difference between a 5 and a 6: "Come on guys, are you the types who go to little league games and have to be evicted?" (John Falkenstine in Kelly, 2004). Additionally, some thought the labels at either end of the scale were overly pejorative, suggesting that the words "Very Bad (synonymous with, You Stink) and Excellent (You are the Best)" could be exchanged with "words like Min. and Max.," such that "people might not take low ratings so harshly and others might feel a bit less like massive jerks for giving say a 2/7 [in aesthetics/originality]" (Turner, 2004).

Some worried that the average (mean) of the ratings was not sufficient; it was susceptible to "aberrant ratings" which could be remedied with the reporting of the median and mode of ratings (Counts, 2004). Or, since textual comments were preferred to numeric ratings, perhaps the ranking system should simply use the number of comments (Joe Boyd in rajeev et al., 2001). Also, given that many of the top-rated photos only have a few ratings, perhaps they should be omitted "until the photo has received enough ratings to make the average meaningful?" (M, 2004).

Of course, one could always leave textual comments. These were almost always appreciated over numeric ratings. As an example, an image of some apples lit by candlelight received varied, reasonable critiques. One commenter wrote, "I think that the subject placement is good and that the lighting works well. The light fall-off in the corners is very effective. On the negative side, it's a fairly boring image which fails to excite me in any way." This was followed by a comment that "I must be more easily excited . . . because I find this quite stimulating to the eye. Great use of available light sources. I too have used candle light on some of my photos and I like the result here." Yet, this photo's ratings became the subject of a discussion about revenge: when the photographer of the apples rated someone else's image as a 2/2, "in less than 20 minutes I received a 2/2 on one of my photos from the same photographer." In the subsequent discussion about revenge rating, some members stressed that ratings should not be taken seriously. Another member wrote that while the "photo is well crafted enough to appear in any magazine," it "deserves neither the perfect 7/7 scores it received nor the obviously punitive 1/1 ratings dumped on it" (Lex Jenkins in Dejkam, 2003).

Hence, the expressed skepticism of numeric ratings is understandable. In response to the original 2001 call for help, many responded that numeric ratings should be "ditched" or "scrapped" in favor of comments (Jeremy Burton and Steven Kembel in rajeev et al., 2001). "Comments are a preferred way of giving feedback on peoples' artwork. There is an inherent silliness in assigning quantitative ratings to artistic expression" (Larry Walker in rajeev et al., 2001). Over the course of years, people also suggested that ratings somehow be linked to comments. For instance, "If someone leaves anything lower than, say 3, make it mandatory to leave comments, not just a numerical rating" (Acer Iddibhai in rajeev et al., 2001). However, mandatory comments would then likely prompt an influx of "photo sux" comments. In fact, this fear has been borne out in more recent evaluation systems. Laura Gibbs wrote about her experience in a massive open online course (MOOC) and the demoralizing comments that arose from mandatory peer feedback. She noted that there were plenty of one-word evaluations (e.g., "ug," "terrible") as well as a comment that consisted of the words "one," "two," through "thirty" so as to conform to the minimum word-length requirement (Gibbs, 2012).

In September 2010, after 10 years of experimentation and contention, Photo.net administrators enacted a wide-sweeping series of changes to the rating system. Most surprising of all, "We've finally given up on the 'Aesthetic/Originality' two number ratings system."

> The concept was good in theory, since many people take beautiful though unoriginal images, but it never worked out in practice. Virtually nobody did anything but rate two of the same number (5/5, 3/3, etc.) for every rating. In addition, having a system that worked "in theory"

> but not in practice tended to give people the impression that there was more in-depth information to be gleaned out of the ratings system than there was in reality (Root, 2010).

At Photo.net the community learned that numeric ratings for aesthetic judgments could be a bruising innovation: while a tempting idea, *it is difficult to quantify the qualitative* (characteristic 1). No matter how often administrators and others told people to not take them to heart, to ignore them, to focus on beauty and learning rather than rank, people are seduced by numbers.

Manipulation

There are ironic consequences to Ritzer's (1983) McDonaldization theory. Its features (such as efficiency and calculability) often become ends in and of themselves. This, then, creates systems in which any means possible are used to achieve those (now) arbitrary ends: "We might say that rational systems are not reasonable systems" (pp. 102, 106). This insight has been shared by other scholars, most notably economist Charles Goodhart (1975), who noted that in monetary policy, "any observed statistical regularity will tend to collapse once pressure is placed upon it for control purposes." This "collapse" likely arises from what social scientist Donald Campbell (1976) wrote the following year: "The more any quantitative social indicator is used for social decision-making, the more subject it will be to corruption pressures and the more apt it will be to distort and corrupt the social processes it is intended to monitor" (p. 49). These related insights are now known as eponymous "laws" that are most concisely expressed by anthropologist Marilyn Strathern. In the 1990s, she noted that the "proliferation of procedures for evaluating performance" in U.K. higher education was detrimental to learning, because "when a measure becomes a target it ceases to be a good measure" (Strathern, 1997, p. 308). One can see evidence of this in Photo.net's evolving rating system.

At Photo.net, what prompted the early call for "suggestions for what to do with the photo ratings systems"? Member Vuk Vuksanovic described the emergence of rating manipulation and revenge rating: "Someone has decided to go through the folders of certain people and systematically deposit scores of 1 on all the pictures. I am one of those targeted and suspect it's some kind of revenge related to my recent criticism of certain members who'd created false accounts to rate their own work." As another member noted: "The whole ratings business has turned into a giant pissing contest, with numerous people abusing the system to (I can only assume) see their name in lights on the top-rated photographers list and top-rated photos list until the next idiot comes along with a dozen mediocre snapshots which they and their friends all give '10/10' scores to" (Vuk Vuksanovic and Steven Kembel in rajeev et al., 2001). This type of behavior is now seen throughout the web and is referred to as "karma whoring." The origins of this phrase likely arose from the geek discussion site Slashdot within the same time period

("Karma Whore," 2013). There, users accumulate karma for positive contributions, including posting content and comments, and moderating others' contributions. However, some users attempted to gain karma using tactics that were of little or negative value. This problem is recognized today at the popular site Reddit, which asks its users not to "mass downvote someone else's posts. If it really is the content you have a problem with (as opposed to the person), by all means vote it down when you come upon it. But don't go out of your way to seek out an enemy's posts" ("Reddiquette," 2013).

Hence, in addition to the difficulty of quantifying the qualitative, the Photo.net community learned that *quantitative mechanisms beget their manipulation* (characteristic 2). In addition to the proposals for "scrapping" ratings or requiring comments, members suggested ways to counter manipulation. An obvious step would be to forbid self-rating (Brian E in rajeev et al., 2001). This could also be complemented by what I label minimum thresholds and rate limits. With a *minimum threshold*, raters must post a minimum of their own photos before rating the photos of others (Vuk Vuksanovic in rajeev et al., 2001). Under *rate limiting,* one limits how often a member may rate, or submit a photo for rating (Joe Boyd in rajeev et al., 2001). However, limitations are not necessarily the best way to create a robust rating system. Indeed, broad participation from the whole community is needed to counteract those intent on abuse. Hence, if broad participation leads to a more honest system, one could promote reciprocity by permitting only those who have rated to be rated. However, requiring raters to post their own images and rate others' images presumes that everyone on the site (a) takes a lot of photos (some simply enjoy viewing and discussing them) and (b) feels confident enough in their own skill to evaluate others (Rodriguez, 2003). Other proposals relied upon the distinction between general members and subscribers. Unlike recent social media sites where most services are free—and supported by advertising—subscribers *paid* for their accounts, meaning they received storage space for their photos. Presumably, subscribers (paying members) were less abusive, and their privileges should exceed that of regular members (Peter Daalder in Myers, 2005).

Few of these remedies were immediately adopted, though the problems they attempted to address would return, as would their discussion. For instance, in 2003, after noting many photos with a single high rating, a member asked: "Why are users allowed to rate their own photos?" "A quick check has shown that a disappointingly large number of these have been rated by the photographer themselves. This should be changed!!" (Spitz, 2003). Site administrators did experiment with a few changes, the most important of which was that ratings would no longer be anonymous.

Anonymity can permit one to speak honestly, without fear of retribution. Conversely, it can permit one to speak dishonestly, without concern for accountability. In the digital age, the degree to which a person and an account is linked can be a purposeful decision or an endemic problem. At Photo.net, it was both. What I refer to as *blinding* is the disassociation of a comment or rating from its source. Blind review is a common technique across disciplines, from the sciences to the arts, so as to encourage honest evaluation. What I refer to as *puppetry* is the creation of multiple accounts. "Sock puppet" accounts are problematic across online communities, as many of these throw-away accounts can be used by a single person to skew community deliberations (Wikipedia, 2012).

Much like the rating scales, both types of anonymity (i.e., blinding and puppetry) have long been discussed and experimented with at Photo.net. Indeed, anonymity was thought to be the source of many of the problems at the launch of the rating system in December 2000: "People created bogus accounts to rate themselves and their friends high, and their adversaries low." In response to these problems, in August 2001, ratings were made public "so that people could see abuse and report it to abuse@Photo.net, and so that people would be embarrassed to pump up their own ratings so much that it would be obvious" (Brian Mottershead in 2003, quoted in O'Neill, 2005). Hence Photo.net instituted what I call *reviewer blinding*. (In 2004, *photographer blinding* was proposed—but not implemented—such that the identity of a photographer would be revealed only after a cooling-off period. The hope was that this would lead to impartial evaluation on the basis of the work rather than the photographer [Nichols, 2004].) While revenge rating still happened (Dejkam, 2003), it tended to be on a smaller scale. However, the new system gave rise to a new problem, ratings inflation, and new attempts at remedying that problem.

As we have seen, once one sets out down the road of calculability, of quantifying the qualitative, manipulation soon follows. Given that calculability is seen as worthwhile, in this case to populate the top-rated photo page, its proponents naturally turn to further quantification and adjustments to the system. This is exemplified in a proposed remedy from 2001. Given Photo.net's origins, it should "establish [a] cross-rating algorithm to auto-identify abusers (I'm sure there are some smart people at MIT that would love to put their collective noodles on this project)" (Brian E in rajeev et al., 2001). However, *fixes to manipulation often have unintended consequences that are also susceptible to manipulation* (characteristic 3).

Once identities were associated with ratings, "mate rating" became more common. Rather than the reciprocal down-rating pervasive during the period of anonymity, people reciprocally up-rated during the period of identity. (Similarly, at PhotoSIG, Xu and Bailey [2012] found that the average of reciprocated ratings was higher than nonreciprocated ratings.) This was amplified in that people could leave positive ratings not only to prompt reciprocally friendly ratings, but to gain more storage space from Photo.net, an incentive offered to encourage participation.

> I have been quite disappointed in the way certain users of the site have been, in my opinion, blanket critiquing photographs. A certain user whom I will not name here has been giving the 'very nice image,

> thanks' with a 6/6 rating at a phenomenal rate. It seems as though they are just trying to get more space without subscribing. I personally would like to get more constructive criticism of my photographs even if it is negative.
>
> (Patel, 2004)

This "mate fishing," as I call it, certainly pays off. The ratings of the person you refer to have skyrocketed with the reciprocal payback (Mark Lucas in Patel, 2004). Another "fix" to the revenge rating was that sub-5 ratings had to be accompanied by a comment (Bengtsson, 2002). Even in 2002, members noted that this asymmetry would likely cause problems:

> I note that you now only can give ratings below 5 if you have written a comment. I like that, in the way that more people will add comments. But it feels a bit unsymmetric. [W]hy should I be allowed to give high ratings without telling what's so good about the image? I think this 5 and up system without comments will lead to overratings.
>
> (Bengtsson, 2002)

Bengtsson further proposed an interesting idea: if you comment, you can rate through the whole scale (1–10); but without a comment, one's ratings were attenuated (4–6) (Bengtsson, 2002). Others argued that everyone should always leave a comment (Elaine Roberts in Bengtsson, 2002). Of course, this would likely depress ratings altogether or lead people to leave terse, poor-quality comments.

In any case, the lack of anonymity and the requirement to justify a negative rating quickly led to rating inflation, and the community soon lost any sense of the relative merits of older works. Administrator Brian Mottershead (2002) noted that when using the new feature of perusing top-rated photos by date, what "becomes obvious when the longer periods are selected is that most of the highest-rated photos are still recent photos."

Last summer, the average rating was a little over 5, and it has increased steadily so that the average rating is over 7. This means that the further in the past a photo received its ratings, the lower its average will tend to be. A photograph that would have appeared in the "Top 40" last year, with an 8.5 average, would be nowheresville today. Thus, the stars of last summer, whose photos for the most part still are on the site and of course are just as good as ever, have more or less disappeared from view (Mottershead, 2002).

The inflation persisted into the following year, prompting a member to (ironically) note that "of the 300 highest rated Photo.net images OF ALL TIME, 113 of them were posted in 2003! It is amazing that such better photographers are being attracted to the site now. What is the secret?" Because the system was now suspect by many, "it seems that the bulk of the site has stopped using the rating system altogether." New images might receive a few ratings within the first 3 days of their posting, but then activity ceases.

So an image with 20 "friendly" ratings shoots to the top of the pack and then just sits there because no one else thinks the rating system is worth saving or users have given up on it working. The change in the default page worked for a while, but the same groups flock to the images upon their release and shoot them to the top of those pages as well (Bulger, 2003).

Hence, *any particular "fix" to manipulation will have its own, not necessarily intended, consequences and is also susceptible to manipulation.*

To counter the mate rating and inflation, blinded ratings returned in 2004, but with a twist. Now, one could see the average rating for one's photo, as well as the people who rated it, but not the specific ratings of any particular rater. Interestingly, this strategy was later adopted by a site for reviewing people. While many people-review sites have been poorly conceived and executed, KarmaFile, launched in 2011 as a place to "review your coworkers," is fairly savvy. Those reviewed have the ability to see their raters and aggregate scores, but they cannot link a specific rating to a particular person (KarmaFile, 2013a, 2013b). In 2005, Mottershead noted that this system "works much better than the previous set of rules for bringing the best photos to the fore"; site subscriptions, submitted photos, and photo ratings had all increased (Brian Mottershead in Miller, 2005). Of course, not everyone was pleased. "I miss the old way of rating photos. Someone would give you a rating. Good or bad I was always going to that person's portfolio and have a look. That would give me extra meaning" (Baba, 2005). Also, by this point, some members were cynical that the rating system would ever be satisfactory.

> Another day, another proposed change to fix the ratings system problems. The more things change, the more they stay the same. I have come to believe that the only solution worth considering is primal scream therapy. Next time you get lowballed, give it a shot. It's not going to change a damn thing, but it might make you feel better.
>
> (Baba, 2005)

Another change deployed in 2004 was that comments and ratings were made distinct processes. The gallery would have two parts: one for critique, where a photograph could receive a rating or comment, and the other for exhibition. "The comments on photos in the 'Exhibition' section will be guestbooks, and photographers will be able to moderate comments on their own photos in that section (meaning delete them). But they won't be able to do that with photos in the 'Critique/Competition' section." Additional ideas proposed back in 2001 (e.g., rate limits, thresholds, member/subscriber distinctions, reciprocity) were also deployed. The ability to upload photos to the critique section within a given time was limited, with a higher threshold for subscribers. Thresholds could be increased through greater participation (comments and ratings given) and how "favorably the photos are received (views/ratings received)" (Brian Mottershead in Root, 2004).

Finally, by this point in time, Photo.net (and many other sites) had deployed mechanisms (even if not developed at MIT) to "auto-identify abusers" (Brian E in rajeev et al., 2001). Account creation was now mediated by a CAPTCHA: Completely Automated Public Turing test to tell Computers and Humans Apart. It was now harder to create sock puppet accounts because automated programs could not easily recognize distorted text in an image. Similarly, the site could now automatically detect some types of rating abuse and remove those ratings at regular intervals. Of course, abuses still occurred and some members asked for more fixes. For instance, CAPTCHA could be extended to rating pictures itself: "I am not sure of the practicalities of such a system but entering a 3 or 4 digit code to have your rating accepted is something I would be more than happy to do!" (David McCracken in Myers, 2005). Still, the site had to be careful not to make it too difficult for new users; recently registered members tended to be enthusiastic and "have always been responsible for the majority of ratings. . . . If you set up obstacles for new people to rate photos, you would reduce the number of ratings dramatically, and increase the influence of mate-raters, etc." (Brian Mottershead in Myers, 2005). A few years later, an intermittent CAPTCHA system was deployed for ratings (Root, 2007).

Despite all the clever automations and features, people could still find ways to game the system. That is, instead of learning to become better photographers, they learned to become better manipulators. For instance, given that one could now make a photo available for comment *or* ratings, one could tactically toggle this so as to achieve a high rating: "It seems you submit a photo, get 3 or 4 7/7 ratings, then withdraw the photo from getting more ratings, and presto, one stays at the top and gets a lot of views" (Holtrop, 2005). Another member responded that this was actually an old trick, and: "It's working as designed (or rather, it's broken as designed)."

Yet, the idea of choice, of letting users decide what kind of feedback they could get, was a popular one. Hence, in the large reforms of 2010, choice was finally brought to bear on the old bugbear of anonymity. Josh Root, Photo.net's administrator, noted that members were unlikely to give feedback if they feared it would prompt an attack. "Lacking any way to discern which critique requests were from people who would accept honest critique and which were from those who would not, many simply stopped critiquing at all" (Root, 2010). Hence, a new feature permitted users to opt in to receive anonymous critiques from others. "This allows people to be a bit more free with their words without the fear of getting harassed in return or upsetting a friend or any of the other reasons that cause people to leave mindless 'nice shot' critiques rather than helpful feedback" (Root, 2010).

Genre and Meta Moderation

It did not take long, once the rating system had been established, to notice a trend. Photographs of nude women were more popular than photographs of flowers. "It seems clear to me that the general population (on Photo.net) has, for example, a negative bias toward flower shots. Flower images receive low ratings and few comments, it seems, whether they have any artistic merit or not" (Vardy, 2004). It is quite possible that the ratings system itself, especially the originality variable (O-score), was responsible. When it came to the genre of flowers, landscapes, and such, what is the meaning of originality, and what number ought to be applied? Remember the proposal that the poles of the scales be changed from very bad/good to minimum/maximum? This prompted a response about the likely confusion this would have for the genre of flowers.

> [S]o that would mean that a photo exhibiting "any" originality, even if it ill-serves the photo, should get a high O-score and all flower shots, being so ubiquitous, get a low O-score? and I don't understand what minimum aesthetics would be compared to maximum; the photo either looks good (or better) or just okay. . . . [A]t least from "very bad" to "very good" gives one room to make specific interpretations of each photo.
>
> (Peggy Jones in Turner, 2004)

On the other hand, the preponderance of nudes in the top-rated pages (TRPs) was at times puzzling, "another one of PN's mysteries," as well as a topic of jest (Carl Root in Schoen, 2004). Yet, given that the community likely consists of many white male heterosexuals, one ought not be too surprised. For instance, upon checking the top 30 nudes from 3 consecutive days in 2013, all subjects appeared to be women and white. Nudes have been so pervasive in the top rankings that in addition to being able to view "all" categories, one can also view an "all (no nudes)" category.

However, in 2004, site administrators experimented with changing the default view on the top-rated photos page. As mentioned, earlier proposals had suggested that photos should be ranked according to the number of comments they received. While this was eventually implemented, by July 2004 the default view was actually changed back to the average rating. This prompted a member to note that "now that average is the default rather than number of ratings, the number of nudes has dropped from 25 to 3 in the top 100" (Schoen, 2004). The resulting discussion about what to do about nude ratings prompted humorous replies, such as "I don't think anyone should be nude when they rate photos," as well as guesses as to what could be going on (MacGregor Anderson in Schoen, 2004). For instance, given that the number of nudes up for rating is small relative to all other photos, perhaps they receive *more* ratings per image" (James O'Neill in Schoen, 2004). Site administrator Brian Mottershead offered his own theory: the popularity of nudes on the TRPs was likely due, in part, to the new nude category and a "reinforcing feedback loop."

The photos on the first page or two of the default TRP naturally get even more ratings just from being there, which just entrenches their position near the top of the TRP and "dramatically increases the number of ratings they get overall, compared to other photos. . . . Make something else the default, such as average, which does not depend on number of ratings: the nudes still get more ratings than before by virtue of the new category for them, but most of them don't get extra ratings from being near the top of the default TRP" (Brian Mottershead in Schoen, 2004).

Mottershead thought that by using the average, TRP photos would still see some benefit from people being "reluctant to rate a photo on the first page low because it has a bit of halo from having made it to the first page," but the self-reinforcement would be lessened. Member Carl Root was not quite so optimistic. He agreed that this explanation was plausible, but he recognized that changes often have unintended consequences that are also susceptible to manipulation. This change of showing photos on the basis of their averages would then privilege a different constituency: "I don't think that the 'average' is as benign as it looks at the moment, however. In the past, it attracted photomontages and other heavy [Photoshop] alterations in much the same way 'rates' attracted nudes. The photographers who specialize in those images will be back as soon as they see this change" (Carl Root in Schoen, 2004). That is, *quantification (and how one implements it) privileges some things over others* (characteristic 4).

A few months later in 2004, another member noted another possible source for the popularity of nudes. In an attempt to identify members who seemed to give informed ratings, the site designated some members as "curators." The intention was that these were members who were active ("rated more than 100 photos in the last 30 days") and rated within a reasonable distribution ("an average between 4 and 5.5, with not too high a percentage of 1–2, or 6–7 ratings") (Brian Mottershead in Bartosik, 2004). In the online world, this is often referred to as "meta" moderation or rating. However, some members thought that this feature, like many, "while implemented with the best of intentions, became a joke not very long after its inception" (Steve Marcus in Bartosik, 2004). And, for some reason, the curators strongly preferred nudes. In response to someone asking if simply giving a lot of average ratings would make someone a curator, Mottershead responded: "The 'curators' are people who have rated a lot recently, with a reasonable distribution of ratings—meaning a reasonable average and not too many at the extremes. Why people fitting this profile should have a preference for nudes is completely beyond me" (Brian Mottershead in Bartosik, 2004). This prompted another member to disclaim this preoccupation with engineering the ratings system:

> Sheeeesh. . . . What I do not 'get' and never shall is WHY this site's powers that be have this obsession with means and reason and oh so many things average?! Not to put too fine a point on it but for crying out loud (really), why not simply let the ratings speak to which photos are most popular amongst all viewers?! And just let it ride.
>
> (James Vincent Knowles in Bartosik, 2004)

In the wide-sweeping reforms of 2010, the idea of "curators" was revisited by way of "helpful users." Given that writing "in depth comments takes time, thought, and energy" and people do this "out of the goodness of their heart and their willingness to help other photographers," helpful comments can now be "rated" as such. Helpful members are then recognized via a "special user icon" and their images will have "extra visibility in various areas of the site" (Root, 2010). This sequence of decisions and discussions highlights one more characteristic (number 5) of digital evaluation systems: *fixes to rating systems often take the form of more elaborate, automated, and meta quantification.*

Tweak Critique

Ansel Adams is famous for his beautiful black and white portraits of the American landscape. He was known for the care he took in capturing an image on a negative (using a large format camera) and in rendering a print (e.g., dodging so as to make some areas lighter and burning others so as to make them darker). Within photographic lore, he is often quoted as saying: "The negative is comparable to the composer's score and the print to its performance. Each performance differs in subtle ways." But with software, the changes need no longer be subtle. At Photo.net the question of how much is too much was common, and members debated whether the amount of manipulation was within the purview of critique. One member noted that while his personal philosophy was to "leave the photos as close to the original as possible," he still felt others' "comments should be restricted to originality and aesthetic and not delve into retouching and RBG curve twisting" (Archer, 2004).

Additionally, the novel affordance of digital imaging is that, unlike in the dark room, the composer and conductor need not be the same person. So far, my focus has been on difficulties of ratings and rankings—following the discussion on the ratings and critique forum. However, the online realm does offer significant benefits. A photographer has access to enormous amounts of information, discussion, and examples. She can reach (potentially) many more viewers. And she can connect with others with similar (even if specialized) interests. Also, with the aid of a graphics editing program, any critic can render his or her own performance of an image for comparison. Consequently, one member asked, "Is it generally considered good or bad form to offer a tweaked version of an image submitted for critique?"

> Initially, I would never have presumed to offer an alternative view of an image. Then, a member here offered me a revised crop on one of my own photographs that improved the image significantly. Frankly, I was grateful for the input and realized that the tweaked version spoke more eloquently than words ever would have. So, thereafter, I began to post some tweaked versions (usually just cropping/alignment/color balance stuff).
>
> (Minicucci, 2005)

However, some at Photo.net, especially newcomers, did not welcome such "performances" of their compositions. In the discussion following Minicucci's question, most of the participants noted it was an acceptable practice at Photo.net. Some argued that one has little control of one's content on the Internet, so if you are concerned, do not post anything. Others noted that they choose to attempt to civilly opt out by asking others not to alter their images. Many responded that they appreciate helpful tweaks: "It's kind of like book editing. No writer should ever resent a good editing" (John Crosley in Minicucci, 2005). Indeed, Photo.net is fairly novel in encouraging this type of critique, and the practice is explicitly permitted in its terms of service if it is done as part of commentary and discussion (J.S. and Bob Atkins in Minicucci, 2005). Hence, characteristic 6 of digital evaluation is that *digital works can be "tweak critiqued": photos are not only evaluated or commented upon, but demonstratively altered.*

CONCLUSION

From the reported discussions at Photo.net, one can identify a handful of characteristics of evaluation in the digital age.

1. It is hard to quantify the qualitative: there was much experimentation with rating and ranking systems.
2. Quantitative mechanisms beget their manipulation: people "mate" rated friends, "revenge" rated enemies, and inflated their own standing.
3. "Fixes" to manipulation have their own, often unintended, consequences and are also susceptible to manipulation: non-anonymous ratings led to rating inflation.
4. Quantification (and how one implements it) privileges some things over others: nudes were highly rated, more so when measured by number of comments, not so with photos of flowers.
5. Any "fixes" often take the form of more elaborate, automated, and meta quantification, such as making some users "curators" or labeling them as "helpful."
6. Digital works can be "tweak critiqued": photos are not only rated and commented upon, but demonstratively altered (e.g., cropping).

Despite the challenges of some of these characteristics, many people have benefited from their participation at Photo.net. I found numerous productive discussions about what constitutes useful evaluation and feedback. For instance, the thread "Getting the confidence to critique" was full of useful tips and reminiscent of the sound advice in Terry Barrett's *Criticizing Photographs*: one should study works one likes and dislikes; consider the subject, lighting, and depth of field of a work; practice explaining one's own reaction objectively; read others' comments; and ask yourself which comments you find most useful (Mark Grant, Carl Root, Ben S, Wilson Tsoi, and Seven Stuartson in Parton, 2005). However, for better or worse, Ritzer's "urge to quantify" is the dominant logic of digital evaluation. As Mottershead noted, "The rating system on Photo.net is very addictive" (Brian Mottershead in Vechnyak, 2005). While he spoke of this addiction as a user of the site, the site itself was also always chasing the latest "fix." The evolution of the rating system at Photo.net anticipates and reflects similar challenges faced elsewhere online. I would like to think the systems we have now are more accurate and fair than the ad hoc experimentation of Photo.net's early history. Even so, the lessons learned at Photo.net are still relevant to even the most advanced forms of digital evaluation: they are imperfect, biased, and prone to manipulation.

REFERENCES

"About Us." (2012). *Photo.net*. Retrieved from http://photo.net/info/about-us

Administrators. (2002). Migration of LUSENET photography forums. Photo.net Help and Feedback Forum. Retrieved from http://photo.net/site-help-forum/003069

Archer, B. (2004). The philosophy behind Photo.net? Photo.net Site Help > Photo Critique and Rating. Retrieved from http://photo.net/site-help-forum/0076Ob

Baba, A. (2005). Old rating system better!! Photo.net Site Help Forum > Photo Critique and Rating. Retrieved from http://photo.net/site-help-forum/00DKWN

Barrett, T. (1996). *Criticizing photographs: An introduction to understanding images* (2nd ed.). Mountain View, CA: Mayfield.

Bartosik, M. B. (2004). And you curators can sing? Photo.net Site Help > Photo Critique and Rating. Retrieved from http://photo.net/site-help-forum/009Ee7

Bengtsson, D. (2002). The new rating system. Photo.net Site Help > Photo Critique and Rating. Retrieved from http://photo.net/site-help-forum/003PWq

Bulger, S. (2003). Rating inflation update. Photo.net Site Help > Photo Critique and Rating. Retrieved from http://photo.net/site-help-forum/004wpu

Campbell, D. (1976). *Assessing the impact of planned social change* (No. 8). *Occasional paper series*. Dartmouth College Public Affairs Center. Retrieved from https://www.globalhivmeinfo.org/CapacityBuilding/Occasional%20Papers/08%20Assessing%20the%20Impact%20of%20Planned%20Social%20Change.pdf

Counts, J. (20042). My idea for improving ratings. Photo.net Site Help > Photo Critique and Rating. Retrieved from http://photo.net/site-help-forum/009f6k

Cox, E. P. (1980). The optimal number of response alternatives for a scale: A review. *Journal of Marketing Research, 27,* 407–422. Retrieved from www.jstor.org/stable/3150495

Dejkam, A. (2003). Rating in revenge. Photo.net Site Help > Photo Critique and Rating. Retrieved from http://photo.net/site-help-forum/005RVe

"Forum contributions by Philip Greenspun." (2012). *Photo.net*. Retrieved from http://photo.net/shared/forum-contributions?user_id=23069&all=t

Gibbs, L. (2012). Continuing problems with peer feedback. *Coursera Fantasy*. Retrieved from http://courserafantasy.blogspot.com/2012/08/continuing-problems-with-peer-feedback.html

Glaser, B., & Strauss, A. (1967). *The discovery of grounded theory: Strategies for qualitative research*. Chicago: Aldine.

Goldstein, J. (2007). Photo.net purchased by NameMedia. JMG-Galleries. Retrieved from www.jmg-galleries.com/blog/2007/10/22/photonet-purchased-by-namemedia-inc/

Goodhart, C. (1975). Problems of monetary management: The U.K. experience. *Papers in Monetary Economics*. Vol. 1. Sydney: Reserve Bank of Australia.

Greenspun, P. (1993). Travels with Samantha. *Greenspun.com*. Retrieved from http://philip.greenspun.com/samantha/samantha-II

Greenspun, P. (1996). The book behind the book behind the book . . . *Greenspun.com*. Retrieved from http://philip.greenspun.com/wtr/dead-trees/story

Greenspun, P. (1997). Photo.net. Archive. Retrieved from http://web.archive.org/web/19971014093619/http://www.photo.net/photo/

Greenspun, P. (1998). Philip and Alex's guide to web publishing. *Greenspun.com*. Retrieved from http://philip.greenspun.com/panda/

Greenspun, P. (2000a). Amazon.com: Travels with Samantha. Books. Retrieved from www.amazon.com/Travels-Samantha-Philip-Greenspun/dp/1588750019/ref=sr_1_1?ie=UTF8&qid=1354914210&sr=8–1&keywords=travels+with+samantha

Greenspun, P. (2000b). ArsDigita: From start-up to bust. *Waxy*. Retrieved from http://waxy.org/random/arsdigita/

Greenspun, P. (2012). Philip Greenspun—photographer biography. *Photo.net*. Retrieved from http://photo.net/photodb/user?user_id=23069

Holtrop, M. (2005). A new trick to stay at the top of top rated? Photo.net Site Help Forum > Photo Critique and Rating. Retrieved from http://photo.net/site-help-forum/00BkgF

"Karma Whore." (2013). Know your meme. Retrieved from http://knowyourmeme.com/memes/karma-whore

KarmaFile. (2013a). How the KarmaFile peer review system works. *Karmafile*. Retrieved from http://karmafile.com/how-it-works

KarmaFile. (2013b). Popular questions about KarmaFile. *Karmafile*. Retrieved from http://karmafile.com/feedback

Kelly, L. (2004). Fractions of a point in the ratings? Photo.net Site Help > Photo Critique and Rating. Retrieved from http://photo.net/site-help-forum/0091u2

Lincoln, Y.S., & Guba, E.G. (1985). *Naturalistic inquiry*. London: Sage.

Luong, Q.T. (2002). A personal perspective on the move of the LF forum to Photo.net. Largeformatphotography. Retrieved from www.largeformatphotography.info/lf-photonet.html

LUSENET. (2012). All forums within LUSENET. *Greenspun.com*. Retrieved from www.greenspun.com/bboard/all-forums.tcl

M, N. (2004). Minimum no. of ratings for TRP display. Photo.net Site Help > Photo Critique and Rating. Retrieved from http://photo.net/site-help-forum/0094x3

Miller, C. (2005). Another rant about ratings. Photo.net Site Help Forum > Photo Critique and Rating. Retrieved from http://photo.net/site-help-forum/00CPs2

Minicucci, P. (2005). Critique etiquette. Photo.net Site Help Forum > Photo Critique and Rating. Retrieved from http://photo.net/site-help-forum/00BNwY

Mottershead, B. (2002). Feedback requested on normalizing ratings. Photo.net Site Help > Photo Critique and Rating. Retrieved from http://photo.net/site-help-forum/003ZCG

Myers, J. (2005). This is getting ridiculous! Photo.net Site Help Forum > Photo Critique and Rating. Retrieved from http://photo.net/site-help-forum/00AeJT

Nichols, T. (2004). What would happen if those posting the photographs could be temporarily anonymous? Photo.net Site Help > Photo Critique and Rating. Retrieved from http://photo.net/site-help-forum/008imD

O'Neill, J. (2005). How to fix my biggest complaint with rating system. Photo.net Site Help Forum > Photo Critique and Rating. Retrieved from http://photo.net/site-help-forum/00Btpr

Parton, N. (2005). Getting the confidence to critique. Photo.net Site Help Forum > Photo Critique and Rating. Retrieved from http://photo.net/site-help-forum/00AuI4

Patel, K. (2004). Annoyed with blanket critiquing. Photo.net Site Help > Photo Critique and Rating. Retrieved from http://photo.net/site-help-forum/00AC2O

"Photography community, including forums, reviews, and galleries from Photo.net." (2012). *Photo.net*. Retrieved from http://photo.net/

Pinto, F. (2005). Photos. *Photo.net*. Retrieved from http://photo.net/photos/franciscocpinto

Preston, C. C., & Colman, A. M. (2000). Optimal number of response categories in rating scales: Reliability, validity, discriminating power, and respondent preferences. *Acta Psychologics, 104*, 1–15. Retrieved from www.le.ac.uk/psychology/amc/optinumb.pdf

rajeev, lisa, audrey, & philg. (2001). Photo rating suggestions. Photo.net Site Help > Photo Critique and Rating. Retrieved from http://photo.net/site-help-forum/001YnO

"Reddiquette." (2013). Reddit. Retrieved from www.reddit.com/wiki/reddiquette

Ritzer, G. (1983). The 'McDonaldization' of society. *Journal of American Culture*, 6(Spring), 100–107. Retrieved from http://iss.sagepub.com/content/11/3/291.abstract

Rodriguez, R. (2003). Should members with no photos cretique. Photo.net Site Help > Photo Critique and Rating. Retrieved from http://photo.net/site-help-forum/006auQ

Root, C. (2004). The new comment note under RFC images. Photo.net Site Help > Photo Critique and Rating. Retrieved from http://photo.net/site-help-forum/008hfV

Root, J. (2007). New Captcha verification for rating system . . . Photo.net Help and Feedback Forum. Retrieved from http://photo.net/site-help-forum/00NFG8

Root, J. (2010). Summarizing the recent changes to the ratings/critique system . . . Photo.net Help and Feedback Forum. Retrieved from http://photo.net/site-help-forum/00XHXv

Root, J. (2011). New Facebook/Twitter/Google+/Stumbleupon sharing buttons on Photo.net. Photo.net Help and Feedback Forum. Retrieved from http://photo.net/site-help-forum/00ZDuh

Schoen, D. (2004). Nude ratings and the avg. vs ratings issue. Photo.net Site Help > Photo Critique and Rating. Retrieved from http://photo.net/site-help-forum/008whW

Spitz, M. (2003). Self-ratings. Photo.net Site Help > Photo Critique and Rating. Retrieved from http://photo.net/site-help-forum/004xFl

Strathern, M. (1997). 'Improving ratings': Audit in the British university system. *European Review, 5*(3), 305–321. Retrieved from http://journals.cambridge.org/action/displayAbstract?fromPage=online&aid=5299904

Thomas, G., & Jones, D. (2006). Reinventing grounded theory: Some questions about theory, ground and discovery. *British Educational Research Journal, 32*(6), 767–795. Retrieved from www.jstor.org/pss/30032707

Turner, B. (2004). Change ratings word association from, very bad/excellent to min./max.? Photo.net Site Help > Photo Critique and Rating. Retrieved from http://photo.net/site-help-forum/007Rlk

Vardy, M. (2004). Biases on PN . . . Photo.net Site Help > Photo Critique and Rating. Retrieved from http://photo.net/site-help-forum/009Vuj

Vechnyak, V. (2005). Who gave me this rating??? Photo.net Site Help Forum > Photo Critique and Rating. Retrieved from http://photo.net/site-help-forum/00B1mV

Wikipedia. (2012). Sockpuppet (Internet). Wikimedia. Retrieved from http://en.wikipedia.org/?oldid=529941789

Xu, A., & Bailey, B. P. (2012). *What do you think? A case study of benefit, expectation, and interaction in a large online critique community*. Paper presented at conference "Computer Supported Cooperative Work '12," Association for Computing Machinery, Seattle, Washington. Retrieved from https://wiki.engr.illinois.edu/download/attachments/181174318/p110-xu.pdf?version=1&modificationDate=1324601059000

3 Link Love and Comment Karma

Norms and Politics of Evaluation in the Fashion Blogosphere

Brooke Erin Duffy

INTRODUCTION

Discourses of participatory politics and destabilized communication hierarchies have flourished over the last decade, set against the backdrop of newly emergent technologies, economies, and structures of media. Indeed, digitally enabled forms of creative production—ranging from blogs to online fan communities to user-generated content sites—have been celebrated for upending the top-down flow of mediated communication and opening up spaces for "empowered" consumers to participate in the production and distribution of culture (e.g., Bruns, 2008; Jenkins, 2006; Rosen, 2006). Such themes of consumer empowerment and interactivity have provided strong narrative undercurrents for mediated coverage of fashion bloggers, an online subculture of (mostly female) content creators who publish fashion- and style-related images, information, and personal commentary. Thus, fashion blogging has been hailed for "democratiz[ing] style" and "allowing regular Janes like you and me to become part of the international fashion conversation" (Brown, 2011, para. 3; Givhan, 2007, para. 3).

Perhaps not surprisingly, fashion blogs are often constructed in opposition to more exclusionary, hierarchical, and "professional" forms of cultural production, especially women's magazines. This distinction has been amplified in widely publicized media debates centering on which faction—fashion bloggers or magazine editors—wields more collective power over audiences, designers, advertisers, and more. Although some writers (i.e., Duffy, 2013; Rocamora, 2012) suggest that the blogger versus magazine editor debate reaffirms a false dichotomy, this distinction is nonetheless productive for interrogating the discursive construction of the fashion blogosphere. A sense of community is central to this construction; bloggers frequently remark on the inspiration, encouragement, advice, and even friendship afforded to them by their participation in formal and informal blogging circuits. This chapter presents a case study of the norms and politics of commentary in the largest fashion blogging community, the Independent Fashion Bloggers network (IFB; http://heartifb.com). More specifically, I examine the possibilities and limitations of this commentary to function as forms of sociality, learning, self-expression, and self-promotion.

Digital modes of audience evaluation—commenting, retweeting, liking, and sharing—are by no means exclusive to the realm of fashion blogging. Rather, they are both a product and an expression of emergent forms of consumer feedback in a new media economy. To some, these practices represent a revolutionary form of interactivity that is symptomatic of a democratized era of information and communication. Blogs, consumer evaluation sites, and user-generated content forums are publicly hailed as online spaces that give "regular people the chance to talk back" (Meyers, 2012, p. 1022). Yet critical analyses of interactive sites like Television Without Pity (Andrejevic, 2008), Facebook (Fuchs, 2012), and Yelp (Kuehn, 2013), among others, suggest that they remain firmly embedded in traditional capitalist structures and relations. The activities of participants in consumer/audience feedback loops have thus been conceptualized as sources of free labor (Andrejevic, 2008) and forms of communication that reduce democratic participation to capitalist exchanges (Kuehn, 2013). The affective dimensions of audience practices have also received attention from critical cultural studies scholars. Alison Hearn (2010), for example, charts how new forms of evaluation in the aptly named digital reputation economy "direct human meaning-making and self-identity in highly motivated and profitable ways" (p. 423; see also Arvidsson & Colleoni, 2012; van Dijck, 2009).

In addition to critical interventions into the political economies of new modes of audience feedback, other scholars have focused on the ways in which these channels may impact the content creation processes within traditional media organizations. Studies of online news production, for instance, have revealed how audience commentary and more quantified metrics (i.e., "traffic") are shaping the routines and orientations of professional journalists (Anderson, 2011; MacGregor, 2007). Magazine editors, too, increasingly rely on polls and other forms of audience feedback to generate ideas for articles and cross-platform media content (Duffy, 2013). Although such findings are useful for understanding the nature and consequences of digital feedback within traditional industrial settings, scholars have yet to devote significant attention to the import of evaluation within more individualized creative contexts.

The fashion blogging community is an apt site to examine the role of digitally enabled feedback on creative producers given that it is commonly understood to be more independent, authentic, and creative than traditional forms of fashion journalism and commentary (see the study by Rocamora [2012] for a productive discussion of the limits of this argument). In this chapter, I examine systems of feedback and critique within the fashion blogosphere with a particular emphasis on the norms, cultures, and politics of commenting. Given the centrality of "community" to blogger practices (Schmidt, 2007; Wei, 2004), I conducted a case study of the IFB, the largest community of fashion bloggers and the self-proclaimed "ultimate resource for fashion blogger[s] to learn about blogging, media kits, fashion, photography and marketing" (Independent Fashion Bloggers, 2013).

Drawing on a discourse analysis of more than 200 articles and 1,000 comments published on the site over a 6-year period, I show how bloggers proselytize a culture of commenting that involves active participation, positive criticism, and forms of self-promotion cloaked in appeals to "genuineness" and "sincerity." I argue that these norms effectively valorize reader participation while reproducing traditional structures of capitalist cultural production that emphasize brand-building labor and the quantification of affective relations. Despite the obvious political economies of commenting, I contend that there are spaces where bloggers may negotiate these codes in ways that afford them sociality, creative expression, and learning.

FASHION BLOGGING IN CONTEXT: PARTICIPATORY CULTURE, AUTHENTICITY, AND COMMUNITY

With the rise of Web 2.0 in the early 2000s, media scholars seemed auspicious about the political possibilities bound up with user-generated content, citizen journalism, and collaborative, wiki-style online communities (e.g., Jenkins, 2006; Rheingold, 1993; Rosen, 2006). Proponents of this techno-utopian perspective saw the potential for digital technologies to be a panacea for systematic inequalities in media, politics, and other social institutions. Others focused on the trappings of influence, expertise, and creativity that were enabled by bottom-up flows of communication and, more broadly, the reconfigured relationship between media producers and consumers (e.g., Bruns, 2008; Quiggan, 2006). In more recent years, the euphoria about the democratizing potential of "new media" has been tempered by more nuanced conceptualizations of the communication-technology-power nexus. Critical media theorists like Andrejevic (2008) and Fuchs (2012), for instance, have argued that narratives of consumer empowerment are deployed to rationalize the data-mining processes and/or exploit the value-generating labor of digital media participants.

These polarizing perspectives have been applied, complicated, and/or enhanced within a wide array of mediated contexts, including blogging (see, for instance, Lovink, 2008; Monaghan & Tunney, 2010; Rettberg, 2008). Since the term blog ("we*b logs*") was coined in 1997, it has been used to describe a diary style of online content creation that is uniquely individualistic and subjective, imbued "with a strong sense of the author's personality, passions, and point of view" (Nardi, Schiano, Gumbrecht, & Swartz, 2004, p. 42). An upshot of this designation is that blogs seemingly "[stand] in ideological opposition to the pressures of commerciality" (Chia, 2012, p. 424). The topics and styles subsumed under the category of "blog" are kaleidoscopic; yet political and hard news blogs have received the lion's share of academic attention to date. In the field of journalism studies, scholars have sought to examine the ways in which blogging departs from traditional journalistic contexts through appeals to subjectivity, authenticity, and autonomy (Carlson, 2007; Lowrey, 2006). Others have examined the extent to which blogs may foster political interest and knowledge with the hopes of creating a more vibrant Habermasian public sphere (Rosen, 2006). Although less attention has been devoted to non-news blogs, particularly those that exist in the margins of what Lopez (2009) refers to as the "masculine construction of the blogosphere," there is an important body of research dedicated to the role of blogs in performing and challenging gender/sexual subjectivities (i.e., Connell, 2013; Herring, Kouper, Scheidt, & Wright, 2004; Lopez, 2009; Van Doorn, Van Zoonen, & Wyatt, 2007).

It is in this context that I turn to the case of fashion blogs, a predominantly feminine genre that has witnessed explosive growth since the first style-related weblogs emerged on the scene in 2002.[1] Scholars of digital media and identity have conceptualized fashion blogs as public forums for performance, self-expression, and even resistance to mainstream fashion and beauty aesthetics (Chittenden, 2010; Connell, 2013; Marwick, 2013; Pham, 2011). Popular narratives about fashion blogs tend to contrast them with traditional sources of fashion news and commentary, particularly women's glossies. Although Rocamora (2012) convincingly challenges the tension between fashion magazines and the blogosphere by describing their relationship as one of "remediation," references to this proverbial "war" continue to circulate in popular culture. An example is the extensive coverage of those fashion bloggers who have been granted access to Fashion Week and other haute couture events; their participation is often framed as an encroachment on territory once exclusively reserved for magazine editors and A-list celebrities.

This rhetorical tension provides the necessary backstory for understanding why fashion blogs are thought to represent a democratization of taste. In contrast to Bourdieu's (1984) understanding of aesthetic judgments as tied to social position, fashion blogs ostensibly break down the binary between the "high culture" world of couture fashion and the accessible styles of the masses. To this end, McQuarrie, Miller, and Phillips (2013) productively explain how the fashion blogger "acts as a connoisseur with a megaphone"; the megaphone metaphor signals the ability of ordinary individuals to acquire a mass audience by "publicly consuming: choosing, evaluating, and engaging with clothing" (p. 146). Central to this definition is the notion of *ordinariness;* bloggers have neither professional experience nor a special institutional or family affiliation that grants them access to various publics (p. 137).

Fashion bloggers themselves have deployed similar narratives to signal the collapse of the expert/amateur boundary. For instance, the description of *The Sartorialist* author Scott Shuman's first book read, "His now famous and much loved blog, the sartorialist.com, is his showcase for the wonderful and varied sartorial tastes of *real people across the globe*" (italics added for emphasis). The notion of "real people" is particularly salient to the rhetoric of fashion blogs and is bound up with a larger ethos of "authenticity," a term which is co-constructed through notions of accessibility, editorial independence/legitimacy, and visual codes that lie outside the conventional fashion magazine aesthetic (Connell, 2013; Duffy, 2013; Rocamora, 2012). Drawing on interviews with fashion bloggers, Marwick (2013) showed how the authenticity ideal is an "organizing principle" that bloggers use to signify their self-expressions, their "honest engagement with commodity goods and brands," and their responsiveness to readers (n.p.). For bloggers, the unique closeness to and engagement with audiences offers a marked point of departure from the closed system of women's magazines (Duffy, 2013; Marwick, 2013). As vintage fashion blogger Sammy Davis reflected, "More and more women are turning to personal blogs for their fashion information, and turning away from the big dot-coms of the magazines" because of the latter's "nebulous voice." Fashion bloggers, by contrast, are "100% authentic" and provide uniquely personal advice to audiences (quoted in Duffy, 2013).

This rhetoric of audience interactivity dovetails with discourses underpinning emergent forms of audience feedback: online ratings, reviews, clicks, links, likes, and so forth. To media and marketing companies, these metrics provide greatly enhanced measures of knowing, evaluating, and tracking audiences (Turow, 2011). Yet these modes of audience evaluation are not just in the province of executives and market researchers; they are increasingly guiding decisions about news content (Anderson, 2011; MacGregor, 2007) and entertainment programming (e.g., Andrejevic, 2008). Other researchers have turned their attention to sources of evaluation that have emerged more recently: consumer review sites, social networks, and online ranking platforms. Challenging narratives of consumer empowerment in the context of review websites like Yelp, Kuehn (2013) argues that the site structures forms of participation that support the project of communicative capitalism. Other political economists note how digitally enabled evaluative sites draw on—or perhaps exploit—consumers' affective relations and investments as part of the "digital reputation economy" (Arvidsson & Colleoni, 2012; Hearn, 2010). Gerlitz and Helmond (2010) similarly describe the development of a "like economy"—a nod toward the Facebook popular social button—which they suggest "allow[s] for transforming intensive social and affective dynamics into comparable metrics and thus add[s] a social and personal qualification to the hit economy" (pp. 3, 25).

As participants in a highly gendered online community, fashion bloggers also rely on these types of "social and affective dynamics" and, more broadly, feedback in the form of reader comments and critique.[2] Yet theories that focus on industry- or organizational-level responses to evaluation might not capture the nature and consequences of feedback within more individualist, independent, or self-expressive digital environments. The fashion blogging community is an apt discursive site to examine the ways in which digital evaluation may structure the relationship between content creators and readers through themes of reciprocity, authenticity, learning, and self-promotion.

CASE STUDY: INDEPENDENT FASHION BLOGGERS

Founded by style blogger Jennine Jacob in 2007, the IFB website is an online resource for fashion bloggers striving to "build a better blog" as they traverse such topics as content creation, design/aesthetics, technology, marketing/monetization, and more. To date, there are more than 54,000 registered IFB members, earning it the designation of "the world's largest fashion blogging community." This rhetoric of community is firmly inscribed into the architecture of the site in the form of member profiles, forums, comment spaces, and links to bloggers' Twitter, Facebook, Pinterest, and Instagram pages.

Promoted as a "resource" and a forum for bloggers to "learn about blogging, media kits, fashion, photography and marketing," the IFB can be productively conceptualized as a participatory learning environment whereby individuals "both enable and elaborate each other's learning input, practices, and products" (Jenkins, Clinton, Purushotma, Robinson, & Weigel, 2006). Members frequently share their experiences, advice, and recommendations in a manner that mirrors other peer-to-peer or collaborative learning environments. And while the site solicits articles from both paid and nonpaid contributors, much of the dialogue between members takes place in the comment sections. These reflexive spaces offer a window into the various practices associated with fashion blogging—including the acts of blog production (creating and maintaining the blog) and consumption (the reciprocal act of reading other blogs). Or, similar to what digital media scholar Chia (2012) writes of blogger manuals, the IFB provides "a glimpse into the socialization of the prosumer [producer/consumer hybrid] subject" (p. 427).

In order to explore the norms surrounding digital feedback and evaluation, I conducted a textual discourse analysis of more than 200 articles and 1,000 comments published on the IFB website over a 6-year period. Particular attention was paid to the function, norms, and politics of commentary, which emerged as the primary means of feedback. I organized the data into two main categories—the provision and the reception of feedback—given that discourses and practices of fashion blogging can be located on a circuit of cultural production.

PROVIDING FEEDBACK: PERFORMING COMMUNITY, ADHERING TO NORMS

While blogging is typically framed as an individual expression of the self, the project of the fashion blogger also involves interacting with other members of the fashion blogosphere (Gaudeul & Peroni, 2010; Marwick, 2013).

And, indeed, IFB members regularly drew upon themes of sociality and collaboration to describe their experiences and social roles as participants in an imagined fashion blogging community. One central way in which community is performed and enacted is through the provision of feedback, and more specifically, by publicly posting comments on others' blogs. However, discourses of feedback were overlaid with clearly articulated norms prescribing the nature and extent of commentary. Three particular norms governed the codes of feedback for members of the IFB; this includes active participation and reciprocity; critique offered in the form of positive feedback; and forms of self-promotion that were thinly veiled as expressions of "sincerity" or "authenticity."

"Reciprocal Behavior, Click Through, and Link Love!"

Norms of reciprocity are considered increasingly salient in the Web 2.0 attention economy, bound up as they are with mutually beneficial systems of social relations (Chia, 2012; Gaudeul & Peroni, 2010). It is against this backdrop that fashion bloggers were urged to "give back to the blogging world" and "support" other members of the community by actively commenting on others' blog posts. Though commenting was superficially framed as an act of goodwill, the structure of exchanges was incentivized with offers of friendship, collaborative knowledge, or the potential for economic gain. For instance, in an article on the "Joys of Blogging," IFB member Lauren identified "community" as the "undisputed king of blogging reasons." After describing how novice bloggers are often "shock[ed]" by the feedback and friendships provided by the community, she added, "It is a delightful world even following commercialisation, all based on reciprocal behaviour, click through [clicking on a given link to land on a new page], and link love [posting a link to another blog one admires]!" In this case, the social experiences and affective pleasures of being involved in a "community" are constructed as reward systems that go beyond—or perhaps supplant—traditional markers of blogger success ("even following commercialisation").

The notion of karma was also invoked to encourage and justify the provision of feedback. In an IFB post titled "Crash Course in Blogger Etiquette," Leia of HiFashion advised:

> If someone comments on your blog, make time to visit their blog. It's nice to get to know your readers. If you have time, leave them a comment, too (you know that warm fuzzy feeling you get inside when someone leaves you a comment? Rack up some good karma by doing the same for someone else!).

By suggesting bloggers can "rack up some good karma" from their commenting activities, Leia conflates the emotional experiences of receiving feedback with the potential for future benefits from the blogosphere—namely reciprocal commentary. The idea that bloggers will eventually be repaid for their engagement with the blogging community was even more explicit in an excerpt from Yuli Ziv's blogging manual, *Fashion 2.0: Blogging Your Way to the Front Row,* which was published on the IFB. Ziv prompted bloggers to "build your relationships with other bloggers based on the principles of partnership, as if you worked together for one big corporation called the Blogosphere." She added, "Positive relationships only help all of us grow in power and profitability, and there's more than enough wealth and prosperity to go around." Directives like this bring the self-promotional aspect of active commenting into stark relief (i.e., references to "power and profitability") while suggesting that "relationships" may also be a performance of community. This is not to deny the significance of blogger relationships and the potential for collaborative learning, but rather to highlight the ways in which these discourses of community may be rationalized.

To this end, other bloggers were quite candid about their aspirations to instrumentalize feedback, providing comments with the explicit expectation that they would be returned. One of the most visible examples of this desire for commentary was a dialogue that took place following the publication of "The Comment Challenge," an article which chronicled blogger Amy's personal task of leaving 500 comments on other individuals' blogs in a single month. When asked to describe her motivation for this "challenge," Amy replied that she hoped to "bring more conversation to the blog community, gain new visitors to my own blog and hopefully make a few people smile in the process." In response to the article, many IFB members publicly stated that they would set similar challenges, ensuring that their numeric goals would include "substantive" or "meaningful" comments (ideals which I discuss in a later section).

The construction of commenting as a "personal challenge" that would spark conversation should not obscure the labor involved in the practices of creating and submitting feedback. Bloggers acknowledged "the work" of creating a community of "value," or "the hours on the computer connecting with other bloggers." In a series outlining how bloggers could promote their personal style posts, IFB writer Taylor Davies suggested that *post promotion* was more laborious than *post creation.* "Back when I was starting out," she explained, "it seemed like it would take me an hour to do a look post and two hours promoting it." Presumably, then, narratives of reciprocity help to justify the considerable investments in time and energy required of effective members of the fashion blogosphere. Of course, not all inflections of feedback were equally valued among bloggers, and IFB members established guidelines for policing the content of comments.

"If You Have Nothing Nice to Say . . ."

Sociocultural theories of aesthetic evaluation have articulated taste hierarchies in the fashion sector as emulations of cultural elitism, as evidence of social positionalities related to class distinction and power, and as judgments of intermediaries working within the cultural circuit (e.g., Blumer, 1969; Bourdieu, 1984; Veblen, 1899). However, "critique" assumes quite a peculiar function and format within the fashion blogosphere, both challenging and reaffirming the latter's construction as a democratic social space. Such discourses of blogger critique were centrally located within norms about the *content* and *valance* of feedback.

Members of the IFB vociferously discouraged negative comments, disparaging the purveyors of these comments as "trolls," "vandals," or "haters." In the earlier mentioned article on blogger etiquette, Leia persuaded bloggers to follow the age-old advice: "If you have nothing nice to say, don't say anything at all." Tying this into notions of individual taste distinction, she continued:

> No one expects you to like or agree with everything you read in the blogosphere. We all have different tastes and styles; it is completely normal to dislike someone else's outfit or post. That doesn't mean you have to be hurtful. Constructive criticism and differing opinions are welcome, but there is a nice way to say something and a rude way to say something. If you can't figure out how to say it nicely, don't say anything at all.

Leia's reference to "constructive criticism" suggests that there is room for systems of critique in the blogosphere; however, widely voiced contempt for negative commenting seemed to dispel this myth. Instead, bloggers were encouraged to provide positive feedback that would ensure that the blogworld continued to be what blogger Reckless Daughter described as "a positive, self-esteem building place." She went on to frame negative comments as "judgment," which seemed antagonistic to the supportive and self-expressive element of the community. As she explained of her fellow members of the blogosphere:

> I feel like I am less likely to judge them and more likely to appreciate what they are doing, their own style no matter what shape, size, style, color scheme, etc. It's such a warm community when it comes to complements [*sic*] and egging each other on with our posts and personal style. Of course, there are people who lean towards more negative comments but I find on the best blogs everyone sort of ignores the pointless negativity and quickly moves on [to] the next.

In these instances, hierarchies of expertise are undermined by a central concern with the nature of content (positive or negative), essentializing larger narratives about the democratization of feedback in the digital age.

Although norms about positive comments were linked to notions of community support and the democratization of taste, the significance of positivity to self-branding practices should not be cast aside. Indeed, this emphasis on favorable comments has been documented in other studies of digital evaluation and reputation management systems. Kuehn (2013), for instance, argues that the architecture of the consumer evaluation site Yelp *standardizes positivity*, as "users are cued to assume tasteful self-presentation and dissuaded from asking questions or critically engaging reviews" (p. 8). Reagle's analysis of the Photo.net community (see Chapter 2 of this volume), too, reveals mechanisms of "manipulation" deployed among existing social networks wherein users "'mate' rated friends, 'revenge' rated enemies, and inflated their own standing" (p. 36). Similarly, while bloggers' emphasis on positive feedback can be read as psychological or ideological, it may also be understood as a calculated effort to build affective relations—an enactment of the neoliberal project of self-branding (e.g., Hearn, 2008). As I discuss in the following section, self-promotional efforts had to be carefully cloaked in seemingly "authentic" sentiments.

"Promote Yourself [by] Not Promoting Yourself"

Negative commentary was not the only type of evaluation eschewed by members of the IFB; overt acts of self-promotion were also critiqued and policed by both informal and formal mechanisms. Bloggers defined self-promotional comments as those created with the explicit aim of drawing attention and traffic back to the commenter's blog; the archetypical self-promotional post was along the lines of: "Nice post. Follow my blog at XYZ." Comments such as this were framed as "insincere," "meaning[less]," and "inauthentic" expressions of feedback, as they seemed to violate the norms of reciprocity and community. As Veronica shared:

> When I was a new member to IFB, I got spam after spam of "follow me and i'll follow you" [messages]. I was naive and even wrote them back and followed them to be nice. . . . I want people to genuinely enjoy my blog/writing, not because it is a numbers game.

Similarly, Marusya V complained about the many bloggers who post: "'Follow me, I'll follow you back,'" because "most of them never will come back to you. Annoying!" Labeling these acts as "annoying" and "spam" served to reaffirm the community's negative perception of self-promotional posts, particularly those that were deemed disingenuous.

Fashion bloggers relied upon various means to discourage and/or deflect attention away from self-aggrandizing behaviors. Perhaps the most common method advocated was to simply ignore the posts; as Judy noted to this end, "If a blogger comments on a post or forum . . . [and] appears insincere/pushy or flat out says something irrelevant/ignores the content—I am more disinclined to check their blog out." Others, meanwhile, saw this violation of community norms as an opportunity to teach neophyte bloggers about the codes of blogger etiquette. Yet the most concentrated effort to regulate the string of self-promotional posts came directly from the IFB editorial team. In November 2010, the editors launched a set of official rules to counteract the "swarm of 'follow me' self-promotional threads" drowning out the "real content." As they explained to bloggers, "Without a real message, self-promotion is just noise."

The discouragement of promotional messages within the context of a digital media space that steadily relies upon participants' self-branding practices may seem contradictory. To elide this tension, bloggers were encouraged to engage in forms of promotion through the provision of "authentic" feedback. Describing this strategy as "usefulness" promotion, the author of a post aptly titled "Self Promotion 101: It's Not All About You" explained: "The best way to effectively promote yourself is not by promoting yourself, create value by doing something to help another person. . . . If you bring them an experience to help them, they'll be more apt to share with others." Similarly, Amy, the blogger chronicled in the earlier mentioned article on "The Comment Challenge," explained her motivation for commenting in a way that enabled her to circumvent glaring contradictions.

> In a way, it definitely IS self-promotion: I'm not denying that in any way. I do think, however, that it is self-promotion in quite a quiet and subtle way and that I'm giving something back to the people who spend a great deal of time on their blogs.

Calculated acts of commenting and other forms of self-promotion thus become acceptable provided they are cloaked in "genuine" expressions.

RECEIVING FEEDBACK: KNOWING READERS, MEASURING SUCCESS, AND RESISTING QUANTIFICATION

Not only did fashion bloggers establish and reinforce guidelines for *providing* feedback, they were also self-reflexive about the *reception* of audience feedback. Indeed, members of the IFB frequently reflected on the significance of comments, likes, shares, and other digitally enabled forms of evaluation in shaping the direction of their creative projects. Such modes of evaluation were frequently positioned as ways to "know your readers," in hopes of providing them with an improved audience experience. However, this emphasis on the qualitative dimensions of blog readers should not obscure the logic of quantifying readership, comments, and other publicly enacted modes of engagement. Bloggers' systematic attempts to solicit feedback from and measure audiences can be directly mapped onto the activities of traditional media producers, thus reproducing long-standing social relations between the producers and the consumers of creative products.

"Know Your Readers"

Offering IFB members suggestions on productive activities to pursue during the holiday season (when blog readership predictably dwindles), Julia of Fashion Pulse Daily encouraged bloggers to "get to know your readers, demographically, even better so that you can cater content to them more succinctly in the future." Deflating the image of blogging as an unfettered expression of the self, Julia's comment reveals how essential constructions of the audience are to the production of blogs. Other IFB members made similar pronouncements for bloggers hoping to buoy their readership. Signaling the potential for blogs to be learning resources, IFB founder Jennine Jacob explained, "Blogging needs to be useful to your reader. They should enjoy and walk away from your blog feeling like they learned something." Johnathan, meanwhile, saw his initial disregard of his audience as a critical stumbling block on the path to success. As he recalled:

> I think the problem was I started out with one point of view (my own) and failed to take into account how others would perceive what I was offering. I think virtually everything [about the blog] has changed in order to make others' experience of visiting my blog more enjoyable.

Packaging this as a "transformation" narrative, Johnathan indicates that his success hinges on the experience of his readers—even if this overshadows his personal perspective.

Other bloggers turned to measures of traffic, engagement, click-through, and other forms of quantitative data that are increasingly valuable within a digital economy. For instance, IFB writer Ashley "Ashe" Robison explained the particular utility of reader surveys in guiding content-related decisions. Describing herself as a blogger who writes across subject categories, she explained, "I may have a passing interest in making something a series—and if my readers have no interest in it, it helps me know where NOT to focus my time." Other bloggers advocated monitoring traffic to gauge the success of different types of content. An IFB post titled "Seven Tips for Setting Blogging Goals in the New Year" compelled bloggers to

> [r]eview the posts that had the most traffic and the most comments. Think of ways you can riff off those posts [with] fresh content and photos, minimize posts that you found to have low traffic. Pay attention to what days have higher traffic and save your best posts for those days, etc. Study, study, study—I promise it's worth it.

In this capacity, creativity and insight are fundamentally guided by the logic of data flow rather than internal standards of creativity or quality.

However, not all bloggers shared the same sentiments about the pursuit of external markers of approval. Several IFB members acknowledged how the concern with growing audiences could lead to a winnowing of creative expression. For instance, in response to an article on blogger ethics, IFB member Maegan was quite explicit about how she had to negotiate internal motivations with external constraints. "It's true that as my readership on my blog grew, my opinionated posts took a backseat. It's just the way it goes. . . . I'm trying to inspire creativity and the two don't go hand in hand." Another blogger focused specifically on the adverse effects of metrics, noting: "Watching those lines jerk up and down, meticulously agonizing over why one post did better than another—it can drive a girl nuts and totally drain my creative energy." This tension is emblematic of the larger duality between creativity and constraint that has long characterized work in the media and culture industries. As Hesmondhalgh and Baker (2011) argue, "When creative workers care very greatly about the size of their audiences and try to anticipate what audiences might think, there might be a danger of workers losing contact with their own sense of excellence" (p. 201). Although Hesmondhalgh and Baker's finding stems from research on paid media professionals, evidence from the blogosphere suggests that amateur cultural producers face similar struggles when thinking about their audiences—including notions of their "size."

"Comments as Currency"

For fashion bloggers who construct the public reception of their creative products as essential to the blogging experience, readership metrics may validate their investments of time and energy. Or as IFB member Lou Jones succinctly stated, "What's the point in blogging if no-one is coming to your blog?" Accordingly, bloggers who received little or no feedback on their blog were disheartened about their lack of recognition among members of the community. As Tracey complained, "My blog is fairly new and just getting people to comment is frustrating. I know they're reading it, people will email me or tell me about it, but they just won't comment." Her frustration was not directed at the number of readers *per se* but, rather, the failure of these readers to provide *public* feedback. Another fledgling fashion blogger, Ruth, confessed to knowing "how crushing it is when no-one comments at all (was it really that bad!?!)." For Ruth, the number of comments a post receives is directly tied to its quality. This invokes a critical comment made about blogging culture that inspired the title of Lovink's (2008) book, *Zero Comments,* which is an "unambiguous statistic that means absolutely nobody cares."

A predictable outcome of this conflation of commentary with recognition was an emphasis on quantification, whereby the number of comments a post received was used to benchmark blogger achievement and status. The earlier mentioned article "The Comment Challenge" foregrounded the importance of metrics in the politics of the blogosphere. As the article began, "Commenting is a building block of blogging. One way to gauge the success of our posts [is] by the number of comments it receives (along with whether it's been stumbled or tweeted)." In response to the provocation, many responded with accounts of how blogging comments were used to signal success both personally and professionally. To IFB member Grace, "Comments are like currency. . . . It makes us feel like people are actually paying attention to what we put out there." The notion of reputation as currency invokes post-Fordist directives to brand and market the self (Hearn, 2008, 2010), whereby the self-brand has the potential to translate into real economic values.

McQuarrie and colleagues (2013) point out that among fashion bloggers, the discursive shift from interacting with "readers" to creating content for "audiences" is a significant one that is bound up with the ascension of advertising/marketing opportunities for seemingly "ordinary" individuals. This underscores the emergent political economies of blogging, wherein bloggers hoping to achieve even a modicum of success from advertising partnerships must have a baseline level of followers or commenters. Usually, affiliate marketers provide specific guidelines on the number of readers/comments a blogger needs to monetize her site. For instance, individuals remarked on how Style Coalition (a marketing platform for "influencers") requires at least 10,000 viewers; another expressed concern that you need at least 3,000 unique daily page views "in order to monetize it at the right price." This translates into a system of value hierarchies that privileges those that seem best able to deploy their affective relations.

Moreover, IFB members were encouraged to use various tools and technologies to efficiently track their audiences, such as Google Analytics or another third-party traffic counter. This directive applied not only to one's personal blog, but to all vestiges of their personal brand across the growing bevy of social networking sites. When using Facebook, for instance, bloggers were prompted to "take note of what days you got the most 'likes' or the most visits, and see what you posted that day—it will give you clues for how best to use your page." Drawing on her former experience as a brand manager, blogger Grace advised fellow bloggers:

> Know your stats. At any time, I'd need to know my sales figures, marketing budget and how much I had left to spend, the works. I kept a cheat sheet. This has carried through to blogging. I track my stats each month and could rattle off my Klout Score, Twitter + Facebook following, Bloglovin' followers, Alexa Score, and their respective percentage increases each month.

These are many of the very same technologies and platforms that strategists in traditional media and cultural industries are relying on to measure their impact in digital spaces.

Despite the fashion blogosphere's outward obsession with traffic, comments, and other quantitative dimensions of "recognition" and "success," some bloggers criticized the valuation of affective relationships. Individuals nodded toward the importance of "genuine expressions" of friendships and environments in which bloggers' worth is not tied to their "traffic." Other bloggers rejected the need for quantified social approval by praising the personal growth and learning made possible by their participation in blogging circuits. While the blogger behind Yellowgoat described "learning new things everyday and getting to know people around the globe" as the best aspect of blogging, another, What Sadie Did, explicitly dismissed the profit-making aims of readership by stating, "I blog for enjoyment, not for commercial activity." Meanwhile, IFB member Lauren constructed her social media experience as therapeutic, noting:

> Whilst blogging can be fun and frivolous, for many it is a chance for therapy, psychological redemption or counselling [*sic*]. Whether writing posts to get supportive and impartial advice, or as a form of expressive therapy on a public level, this unique platform for self-expression has brought hope into a lot of people's lives. We should never forget this as one of the true brilliant things about blogging.

This is not to suggest that bloggers were fully resistant to the dominant norms and codes of the blogosphere; rather, they were able to draw meaning from feedback beyond more instrumental functions.

DISCUSSION AND CONCLUSION

Like so many other social media subcultures, the fashion blogosphere is affectionately known as a "community," which is co-constructed through the practices of participants located within a vast network of technological, social, and economic infrastructures (Schmidt, 2007; Wei, 2004). Yet some important elements of this term "community" need to be teased out in order to draw attention to the norms, politics, and hierarchies that may undermine—or at least complicate—more collaborative constructions of online communities. By this, I refer to the underlying political economies of "communities," which as van Dijck (2009) productively argues, "overwhelming[ly] . . . coincide with consumer groups or entertainment platforms" (p. 45). In particular, discourses of community enacted through the provision and reception of feedback are shot through with nuance and contradiction. Engaging with other fashion bloggers through comments, for instance, is superficially articulated as an act of goodwill that privileges the collective over the individual. Yet the commentary norms that are created and reinforced suggest that evaluation is used in part to *stage community.*

As part of this staging, bloggers are encouraged to provide feedback according to the prescribed norms of reciprocity, positivity, and sincerity. Adherence to these norms is guided by blogger politics and more formally sanctioned codes that govern behavior on the site (i.e., formal policies and technical features). Of course, some of these norms are inherently paradoxical, such as the directives to "be sincere" while simultaneously offering only "positive feedback" (after all, couldn't someone provide a *genuinely* negative or critical comment?). To traverse these inconsistent ideals, bloggers are instructed to practice "useful self-promotion," by cloaking self-aggrandizing hype in "authentic" expressions and behaviors. Such performances of the self are invocations of what Pooley (2010) describes as calculated authenticity, which is manifest in "carefully curated identities" and the strategic management and promotion of the self (pp. 72, 83).

Overlaid on this self-branding ethos are considerations of and prescriptions for social and affective relations, which may be deployed to "garner attention, reputation, and potentially, profit" (Hearn, 2010, p. 427). As Hearn (2008, 2010) and others productively point out, the structuring of affect and similar self-branding initiatives are symptomatic of the larger capitalist project of *working* on the self. And, indeed, some bloggers acknowledged that their participation in the blogger evaluation circuit required considerable investments of time and energy—the labor of feedback. The imperative to devote time to commenting is amplified by the insistence on quantification—counting comments and other forms of feedback, measuring traffic, and evaluating the "popularity" of certain features and posts. After all, these metrics are financially incentivized within contemporary attention/reputation economies, wherein advertisers reward those with the most "connections" in the form of paid ads, sponsored posts, and affiliate links. In this respect, the fashion blogosphere is organized according to a hierarchy of social relations wherein the number of followers/comments gets coded as success—or, perhaps more accurately, as the potential for profitability. However, as Chia (2012) usefully points out in a study of blogger politics *writ large*, a digital divide structures the blogosphere by separating

> the expressive agency of subjects from the sociotechnical prescriptions of UGC [user-generated content], the creative class of probloggers from their plebeian hopefuls, and the mass of unwaged professional-amateurs from the social media goliaths that profit from their aggregated microcontributions.
>
> (pp. 430–31)

Put simply, few bloggers financially profit from their promotional efforts in a substantial way.

Against the backdrop of these discourses and practical realities, fashion blogging emerges as a field that appears strikingly similar to the traditional sites of creative production to which it is often set in opposition. Creative and promotional labor, efforts to "know" audiences, and a preoccupation with metrics—these are all tasks intimately familiar to producers in traditional media industries. Additionally, bloggers' inflections on the tradeoff between individual self-expression and external social approval can be contextualized within a larger tension between creativity and constraint that has long been characteristic of work in the culture industries (see, for example, du Gay, 1997; Hesmondhalgh & Baker, 2011). Does this suggest that the only difference between fashion bloggers and professional media creators is the issue of compensation? Are social media participants cultural dupes blindly doing the work of paid content creators as part of a larger capitalist project that aims to eke out as much free, exploited labor as possible?

Despite the political economies of commenting that I have outlined in this chapter, I would argue against these totalizing assumptions. The benefits accrued by participants in these systems—social relationships, creative expressions of the self, learning, and possibilities for real profitability (even if only for a few)—are much more than shallow returns that effectively feed into the capitalist ideology. These are real exchanges that convey important social, psychological, and material rewards to bloggers and other social media participants. In particular, the constructions of the blogosphere as a "therap[eutic]" and "self-esteem building" digital space that provides opportunities for "learning new things" reveal important gradations regarding constructions of community and evaluation. These issues should not be swept aside by critical theorists seeking to map out the reconfigured relationships between producers and consumers in Web 2.0; rather they must be understood from the perspectives of those who are living in and through digital creative environments. I thus close with a call for future researchers to understand emergent cultures of social media production by talking to—and learning from—the very participants in these systems.

NOTES

1. Although there may be earlier cases, mainstream media coverage tends to treat "fashion blogs" as a monolithic category; however, they vary tremendously in content, format, and tone—ranging from couture runway recaps to "street style" photography to niche blogs on plus-size looks, vintage finds, and hijab fashion, among others.
2. In fact, a series of articles circulating in the fashion blog community in 2013 engaged with the question of whether a blog would still be considered "a blog" if there weren't any comments. They did not think so, noting that comments make blogs, encouraging bloggers to "produce content that resonates with your readers" (Independent Fashion Bloggers, April 29, 2013).

REFERENCES

Anderson, C.W. (2011). Between creative and quantified audiences: Web metrics and changing patterns of newswork in local US newsrooms. *Journalism, 12*(5), 550–566.

Andrejevic, M. (2008). Watching television without pity: The productivity of online fans. *Television & New Media, 9*(1), 24–46.

Arvidsson, A., & Colleoni, E. (2012). Value in informational capitalism and on the Internet. *The Information Society, 28*(3), 135–150.

Blumer, H. (1969). Fashion: From class differentiation to collective selection. *Sociological Quarterly, 10,* 275–291.

Bourdieu, P. (1984). *Distinction* (Richard Nice, Trans.). Cambridge, MA: Harvard University Press.

Brown, C. (2011, March 25) Viewpoint: Amateur fashionistas blog their way to the top. *Centretown News Online.* Retrieved from centretownnewsonline.ca

Bruns, A. (2008). *Blogs, Wikipedia, Second Life, and beyond: From production to produsage* (Vol. 45). New York: Peter Lang.

Carlson, M. (2007). Blogs and journalistic authority: The role of blogs in US election day 2004 coverage. *Journalism Studies, 8*(2), 264–279.

Chia, A. (2012). Welcome to me-mart: The politics of user-generated content in personal blogs. *American Behavioral Scientist, 56*(4), 421–438.

Chittenden, T. (2010). Digital dressing up: Modelling female teen identity in the discursive spaces of the fashion blogosphere. *Journal of Youth Studies, 13*(4), 505–520.

Connell, C. (2013). Fashionable resistance: Queer "fa (t) shion" blogging as counterdiscourse. *WSQ: Women's Studies Quarterly, 41*(1), 209–224.

du Gay, P. (Ed.). (1997). *Production of culture/cultures of production* (Vol. 4). London: Sage.

Duffy, B.E. (2013). *Remake, remodel: Women's magazines in the digital age.* Urbana, IL: University of Illinois Press.

Fuchs, C. (2012). With or without Marx? With or without capitalism? A rejoinder to Adam Arvidsson and Eleanor Colleoni. *tripleC: Cognition, Communication, Co-operation, 10*(2), 633–645.

Gaudeul, A., & Peroni, C. (2010). Reciprocal attention and norm of reciprocity in blogging networks. *Jena Economic Research Papers, 20,* 1–19.

Gerlitz, C., & Helmond, A. (2013). The like economy: Social buttons and the data-intensive web. *New Media & Society.* doi: 10.1177/1461444812472322.

Givhan, R. (2007). Everyone's a fashion critic. *Harper's Bazaar.* Retrieved from www.harpersbazaar.com/fashion/fashion-articles/fashion-critic-givhan-0907

Hearn, A. (2008). Meat, mask, burden: Probing the contours of the branded self. *Journal of Consumer Culture, 8*(2), 197–217.

Hearn, A. (2010). Structuring feeling: Web 2.0, online ranking and rating, and the digital 'reputation' economy. *Ephemera: Theory & Politics in Organization, 10,* 421–438.

Herring, S.C., Kouper, I., Scheidt, L.A., & Wright, E. (2004). Women and children last: The discursive construction of weblogs. In L. Gurak, S. Antonijevic, L. Johnson, C. Ratliff, & J. Reyman (Eds.), *Into the blogosphere: Rhetoric, community, and culture of weblogs.* Minneapolis: University of Minnesota Press.

Hesmondhalgh, D., & Baker, S. (2011). *Creative labour: Media work in three cultural industries.* London: Routledge.

Independent Fashion Bloggers. (2013). Retrieved from http://heartifb.com/

Jenkins, H. (2006). *Convergence culture: Where old and new media collide.* New York: NYU Press.

Jenkins, H., Clinton K., Purushotma, R., Robinson, A. J., & Weigel, M. (2006). *Confronting the challenges of participatory culture: Media education for the 21st century.* Chicago, IL: The MacArthur Foundation. Retrieved from www.digitallearning.macfound.org/site/c.enJLKQNlFiG/b.2108773/apps/nl/content2.asp?content_id=%7B CD911571-0240-4714-A93B-1D0C07C7B6C1%7D

Kuehn, K.M. (2013). There's got to be a review democracy: Communicative capitalism, neoliberal citizenship and the politics of participation on the consumer valuation website Yelp.com. *International Journal of Communication, 7,* 607–625.

Lopez, L. K. (2009). The radical act of mommy blogging: Redefining motherhood through the blogosphere. *New Media & Society, 11*(5), 729–747.

Lovink, G. (2007). *Zero comments: Blogging and critical Internet culture.* New York: Routledge.

Lowrey, W. (2006). Mapping the journalism-blogging relationship. *Journalism, 7*(4), 477–500.

MacGregor, P. (2007). Tracking the online audience: Metric data start a subtle revolution. *Journalism Studies, 8*(2), 280–298.

Marwick, A. (2013, July). "They're really profound women, they're entrepreneurs": Conceptions of authenticity in fashion blogging. Paper presented at the 7th International AIII Conference on Weblogs and Social Media, Cambridge, MA.

McQuarrie, E. F., Miller, J., & Phillips, B. J. (2013). The megaphone effect: Taste and audience in fashion blogging. *Journal of Consumer Research, 40*(1), 136–158.

Meyers, E. A. (2012). 'Blogs give regular people the chance to talk back': Rethinking professional media hierarchies in new media. *New Media & Society, 14*(6), 1022–1038.

Monaghan, G., & Tunney, S. (2010). *Web journalism: A new form of citizenship?* Sussex: Sussex Academic Press.

Nardi, B. A., Schiano, D. J., Gumbrecht, M., & Swartz, L. (2004). Why we blog. *Communications of the ACM, 47*(12), 41–46. Retrieved from http://citeseerx.ist.psu.edu/viewdoc/download?doi=10.1.1.105.1286&rep=rep1&type=pdf

Pham, M. H. T. (2011). Blog ambition: Fashion, feelings, and the political economy of the digital raced body. *Camera Obscura, 26*(1 76), 1–37.

Pooley, J. (2010). The authenticity bind: From flappers to Facebook. In M. Aronczyk & D. Powers (Eds.), *Blowing up the brand: Critical perspectives on promotional culture* (pp. 71–92). New York: Peter Lang.

Quiggin, J. (2006). Blogs, wikis and creative innovation. *International Journal of Cultural Studies, 9*(4), 481–496.

Rettberg, J. W. (2008). *Blogging.* Cambridge, UK: Polity Press.

Rheingold, H. (1993). *The virtual community: Homesteading on the electronic frontier.* Reading, MA: Addison-Wesley.

Rocamora, A. (2012) Hypertextuality and remediation in the fashion media: The case of fashion blogs. *Journalism Practice, 6*(1), 92–106.

Rosen, J. (2006). The people formerly known as the audience. *Pressthink.* Retrieved from http://journalism.nyu.edu/pubzone/weblogs/pressthink/2006/06/27/ppl_frmr.html

Schmidt, J. (2011). Blogging practices: An analytical framework. *Journal of Computer-Mediated Communication, 12*(4), 1409–1427.

Turow, J. (2012). *The daily you: How the new advertising industry is defining your identity and your worth.* New Haven, CT: Yale University Press.

van Dijck, J. (2009). Users like you? Theorizing agency in user-generated content. *Media, Culture, and Society, 31*(1), 41–59.

Van Doorn, N., Van Zoonen, L., & Wyatt, S. (2007). Writing from experience: Presentations of gender identity on weblogs. *European Journal of Women's Studies, 14*(2), 143–158.

Veblen, T. (1899). *The theory of the leisure class: An economic study in the evolution of institutions.* Macmillan & Company Ltd.

Wei, C. (2004). Formation of norms in a blog community. In L. Gurak, S. Antonijevic, L. Johnson, & C. Ratliff (Eds.), *Into the blogosphere: Rhetoric, community, and culture in weblogs.* Minneapolis: University of Minnesota Press. Retrieved from http://blog.lib.umn.edu/blogosphere/formation_of_norms.html

4 Who Judges the Judges?

Evaluating Competition as a Technique of Evaluation in Online Game Design Forums

Aaron Trammell

Let's begin this essay with a brief hypothetical. After playing hundreds of games, a player decides to become a board game designer. She decides to start by entering a contest hosted in a popular design forum and designs a game that satisfies all of the criteria of good design that she has picked up through her experience playing games. This means that she deliberately tries not to incorporate mechanics that exclude other players early on in the game, she makes smart statistical tables to govern all of the game's chance mechanisms (decks of cards and dice), she considers the design with a clear theme in mind (let us say the Wild West), and she makes choices which reinforce this theme. The game is called *Westworld,* and after it is designed, our friend, the player, submits it to a jury of her peers for playtesting and evaluation. This jury is very much like the player; they also occasionally design games based on the hundreds they have played themselves. After playing *Westworld,* the jury evaluates the game on a number of criteria, including graphic design, clarity of rules, fun, and overall experience. These criteria are evaluated numerically on a five-point scale; the numbers are added together and then divided by the amount of total reviewers. Finally these averages are all added together, and the total value is used as an index of comparison with the other submissions to the contest. The designer scores well, but not perfectly. There are many other designers who receive better scores. They wait 3 months for another contest to come around, lick their wounds, and decide to try again, this time having had a little more experience.

This scenario, although fictional, is modeled after the competitive evaluative frameworks that proliferate in the game design community today. And while in this example a jury of the designer's peers completed the evaluation, there are also many instances where publication companies hire experienced testers to critique and evaluate the game itself. Importantly, there is a good deal of recursivity baked into this model. Not only is it common knowledge among game designers that playtesting is fundamental to good game design, the crowdsourced review process presupposes a sensibility which demands that reviewers be familiar with the operation of several familiar game mechanics and how they balance and work with one another. Good game design evaluation comes from an intuition about play that can only be gained from the experience of playtesting one's own games and from playing many of the other games available on the market.

This hypothetical was posed in this context as a way to begin a critical discussion around the ways that competition is used to evaluate good game design. Ideally, game design contests operate like a filter that separates the wheat from the chaff. Competition works as a cultural technique which is used to regulate the production of games. As a therapeutic technique, this prompts designers to create with an eye to the types of decisions that fit snugly within a general aesthetic of the cultures within which these games will be played and consumed. This therapy does not exist, however, without a poisonous potential as well. The market, as it exists today, also presupposes a framework that is fundamentally competitive. It is this paper's argument that this sense of market competition, however similar to the aesthetics of evaluation (which can be therapeutic), is a mirage that condemns the aesthetics of game design to the ceaseless repetition of the status quo.

The key question in this chapter is whether grassroots design communities manage practices of competition in a way that is notably different from the hierarchical and market-driven techniques that have historically been the wheelhouse of game publishers. The Internet has allowed for the efficient and effective organization of discussion forums and game design collectives, which, due to their ability to organize and regulate themselves somewhat autonomously, have the potential to evaluate and design for an aesthetic that is somewhat independent of the market. By looking at grassroots design communities, we can better understand how informal learning practices are shared and evaluated. At the same time, these grassroots communities allow for a point of comparison through which competition can be seen as functioning independently from the market.

How do game design communities use competition as a technique of evaluation, and what are its therapeutic and poisonous tendencies? Websites like BoardGameGeek (boardgamegeek.com) and Board Game Designers Forum (bgdf.com) encourage a grassroots game design community by hosting forums where users can discuss game design. Often these work-in-progress threads are stimulated by game design competitions where designers are offered a pot of virtual or real currency for the "best-designed" game. Competition produces an order of taste within these grassroots communities. However, while in its best instances, this order of taste has the potential to produce creatively engaging and unique designs, it simultaneously produces an order of stale and repetitive designs. This dichotomy prompts a comparative analysis between the values of agonistic (competitive) play with other, more process-based practices of creative engagement. What are the strengths of a competition when implemented as an evaluative practice? How does competition sit as a technique of gamification? What sensibilities does competition cultivate within the "players" of the design game? And, most importantly, are there instances of successful design that have been generated without the agonistic and consumerist tendencies which competition fosters within digital learning environments?

COMPETITION AS CULTURAL TECHNIQUE

Competition, as a specific mode of play, should be primarily understood as a cultural technique. And while, in a historical context, competition is most closely associated with the rational assessment of difference (chance, on the other hand, has been historically associated with the divine assessment of difference), there is a particular isomorphism at play today between competition in the sense of play and competition in the sense of capitalism. This is notably problematic, as competition, if it is to function properly as a rational technique of assessment, must uphold a set of principles regarding equality, which have been shown to be problematic in the context of the market.

A key feature of all cultural techniques, as defined by the cultural philosopher Thomas Macho (2003), is that the labels which we use to categorize them necessarily predate the practice of the technique itself. For instance, our bodies developed a practice of writing long before it was described as such. For this reason, media theorist Bernhard Siegert (2008) has argued that this sense of technique holds a promise to make sense of dichotomous ontologies, which seek to reinstitute a Cartesian ethos that juxtaposes idea and practice against one another (p. 30). And although the example called upon in Siegert's essay is writing (being specifically a bodily technique which is socially cultivated), the very same framework can easily be applied to competition, which historically has been a technique through which bodies have honed a particular skill-set through a set of socially specific virtues of excellence.

Competition has, in fact, long preexisted its formal intonation as a technique, and because of this, it can be productively approached in the sense that Macho and Siegert approach other techniques, such as music, writing, reading, counting, and painting. One advantage of this theoretical lens is that it allows for a reading that concerns itself, namely, with the accumulation of psychic energy, what Bernard Stiegler would refer to as psycho-power (Crogan, 2010, pp. 159–60). And where traditional readings of competition, such as those famously made by Johan Huizinga (1980) and Roger Caillois (2001), take for granted an assumption that competition fills a particular, yet useful, niche in the progress narratives of modernity, through Stiegler's reading of cultural techniques this potential must be bracketed off. In other words, competition works as a driving force in these progress narratives because it allows for the emergence and evaluation of difference, but in doing so, this evaluation must consider the ways that competition, as a technique of innovation, may yield stale results if it is evaluated only by the standards and whims of the market.

Stiegler's concept of psycho-power implies, namely, the extension of Foucault's concept of biopower to new spaces of psychic labor. Arguing that the main project of late capitalism has been more concerned with the construction and cultivation of human behavior, not matter, Stiegler advocates for a construct of psycho-power which keeps all techniques which help to focus collective matters of psychic labor under its umbrella. Competition, then, when applied as a contest of innovation, is both a cultural and a psychic technique, insofar as it invokes the cultivation of ideas. Furthermore, when applied to game design, this lens makes clear the importance of immaterial creative work to these projects. There has been a shift in what we valorize as a culture since the earliest instantiation of competition as a technique.

This point is not belabored in the least by Caillois (2001), who notes a plethora of bloody historical contests in his taxonomy of competition. Duels, tournaments, courtly wars, and more have all functioned as ways to dither out the more powerful through equal social contest (p. 15). But there is a twist in his assessment as he delves deeper into the parallels between society and play. In particular, Caillois notes, games of competition find their opposition in the practices of everyday life. He writes, "Above all, play is a parallel, independent activity, opposed to the acts and decisions of ordinary life by special characteristics appropriate to play" (p. 62). By this, Caillois builds on Huizinga's idea of the magic circle that can be crudely defined as a safe ritual space of play wherein the practices of everyday life are replicated, yet separated from the activities of play. What occurs in this magic circle varies, and it is indeed influenced by the social and cultural conditions of the time. In this sense, the duels and tournaments, which may have functioned as contests of machismo and military strength in feudal society, hold a different significance in today's culture, because we prioritize a different set of values.

For Caillois, competition in a game that simulates the market and competition within the market itself necessitate two separate schemes of interpretation. Most importantly, competition within a game may hold some egalitarian pretense, as its virtue is to provide an equivalent ground for the judgment of virtue. Such pretense vanishes, however, within the auspices of the market, where "there is no limit on manipulation except the fear of scandal or prison" (p. 62). The market, in this sense, makes an appeal to the egalitarian virtues of competition while simultaneously masking an anything-goes economic terrain with few key regulations.

The philosopher Mihai Spariosu (1989) charts discourse around the topic of play through a polemic that notes a dichotomy around the topic of rationality. For Spariosu, these different timbres of play are constantly in dialogue and juxtaposition with one another. Rationality is always set up as an imposition within a primordial mode of play that is at once creative and pre-rational (p. 6). The market, in this sense, is regulated along the axis of law, and therefore, there is a sense wherein a set of economic laws, such as those put forth by Adam Smith (1982) relating to the "invisible hand" of capitalism, are trusted to maintain a smooth flow in the market. But, as pointed out earlier, the market is not an ideal space of play; instead, several interested parties already manipulate it.

These manipulations are concrete, as pointed out by legal theorists Lawrence Lessig (2008) and Aram Sinnreich (2010); the market strangles creativity with the draconic legislation that is erected around intellectual property. These laws alone transform the market into a play space that is far from ideal. Thematic motifs (such as characters and brands) in games may be the subject of copyright, while game mechanics (like dice rolling and set collection) cannot be. This is the reason that Monopoly can be released under several different titles: Cat-opoly, Rutgers-opoly, Ghettopoly, and more. The core mechanics of the game—rolling dice, buying property, and trading property—cannot be restricted under intellectual property law, while the Monopoly Man can. And, within this one simple example, it is also clear the ways in which the uneven playing field of the market serves only to provoke the unending duplication of the status quo through design.

For this reason, competition should be seen as a cultural technique. In particular, it is a cultural technique that is fundamentally embedded within the logic of the market. Although competition certainly holds the potential to produce designs that do not instantiate the ceaseless repetition of the market, there are scant few spaces where these radical aesthetics are possible. Unfortunately, as Stiegler (2009) points out, the hypnosis of sophistry, or the difference and disagreement necessary for democracy to function, is the very remedy that poisons the form itself. He writes that the mimetic gregariousness of crowds, in fact, poisons the city (p. 36). In a very similar sense, the isomorphism between the market and competition invariably results in an evaluative technique that ultimately stifles most potential for true innovation, since competition is aligned directly with the needs of the market, and evaluation is subject to the whims of a crowdsourced public.

THE CULTURE OF GAME DESIGN

Different Components, Different Industries

Game design, as a cultural phenomenon, has been read by cultural critics like Nick Dyer-Witheford and Greig de Peuter (2009) as a phenomenon that, in its mass-market form, replicates the fundamentals of consumer capitalism within its design mechanics. To this point, they note the ways that players are often encouraged to amass capital through the accumulation of money and guns, in the service of a particular sense of neoliberal culture. The games they analyze, *Grand Theft Auto*, *America's Army*, and *World of Warcraft*, are all market staples, and at least two of the three (*America's Army* and *World of Warcraft*) are linked to distinct secondary markets (the United States military and the black market for MMORPGs [massively multiplayer online role-playing games]). In this sense, these examples specifically address the ways in which the market valorizes game design principles, which support the very fundamentals of the market. This is not to argue that there are not games which resist this overly dogmatic reading of the market. Anne Anthropy (2012) has, in fact, advocated for several strong facets of a grassroots game design ethic, but the examples of Dyer-Witheford and de Peuter do, at the least, reflect a problematic set of design elements which overdetermine games released on the market.

While the video game design market has been plagued by the themes noted above (violence, neoliberal economics, the military-industrial complex, and more), there exists a sense in which analog games, or board, card, and role-playing games, highlight some alternate potentials of resistance. First and foremost, the analog game design industry is not nearly as profitable as the video game industry. Many analog game publishers still identify the trade as primarily a hobby occupation. Second, there is a lower barrier to entry in the analog game design sector. While a video game requires a considerable amount of labor (coding labor, public relations and marketing, art and sound design, storyboarding, and direction), analog games are often produced by one or two notably kinetic individuals with materials which can be as basic as a set of index cards and a marker. Finally, the two types of games have notably different marketing industries. Where video games are often evaluated by individuals in a far-reaching marketing loop which spans media and solicits a number of boutique industry magazines (*Game Informer, Electronic Gaming Monthly, Gamespot,* and *IGN,* to name a few), the analog game sector hosts a small handful of industry publications and promotes its products mainly through user-driven sites, such as BoardGameGeek.

The key difference between these video game publications and sites like BoardGameGeek is that because there is less money flowing through the board game industry, their evaluation and review base is funded primarily through user donations. The reviewers on BoardGameGeek work for free, as they are not payrolled through the for-profit game journalism industry. But, although pay scales are notably different, these amateur reviewers take their practice very seriously, writing genuine reviews, seeking to contribute to this burgeoning community but also perhaps hoping to gain enough notoriety that free games for review might be sent their way from the publishing community.

The Production of Taste

The board game industry is an interesting site of analysis precisely because less money flows through it. Because of this, it is easier to see where the market's influence is recognized by participants in the design scene and where it is decidedly untethered. In the video game industry, tastes are largely dictated by a set of narratives constructed by the market and the review industry.

Consalvo (2009) in her research on cheating has gestured to the close-knit relationship between review publications and the cultures of taste therein. She observed that publications like *Nintendo Power* would publish hint and cheat guides to explain to their user bases how to hack the game in ways that would allow them to see more of what had been programmed. If a game were too hard, these codebooks would allow players to skip ahead to see more of the game and, thus, allow them a different perspective on the experience. In this way Nintendo, which owned *Nintendo Power,* was able to cultivate a consumer base that was able to explore games on a deeper level and, therefore, was interested in exploring them for the evaluative aspects the reviewers would highlight in their reviews: for example, story, graphics, sound, and gameplay.

On BoardGameGeek, reviewers often graft similar categories onto their reviews. There is, however, more variation than there is in the video game industry. Story, graphics, sound, and gameplay are generally replaced with more platform-specific categories like fun, components, clarity of rules, and complexity. Many of these criteria appear also in the rubric identified in the section below. Even though there is more flexibility and agency in this grassroots review context, there are still many reviewers who tend toward categorical and numerical metrics.

Additionally, there is a culture of collaboration at work within board game design forums. When games are reviewed and critiqued, there is a sense of co-construction and building, as in the collaborative spaces of open source software (Kelty, 2009), recognized by the community members. Designers are interested in the craft of design, and this is supported through a mesh of collaborative peer learning practices that operate through the sharing of documents, wisdom, thoughts, and reviews. Even though this paper critiques the sense of competition at stake in design, there is an important sense of collaborative mirroring which is instantiated in these communities. Designers learn by sharing information and mentoring one another, and these moments of mentoring are often moments of sharing and informal learning.

For the above reasons, analog game design forums are important sites of analysis, as they are far more removed from the trappings of the market than are video game design forums. And while there is a strong sense that a community of practice forms through the modes of evaluation used by these designers, it is also important to critique the tendencies of the games these communities produce. For this reason, it is especially concerning when the techniques of the market, such as competition, can be seen filling a primary role in analog game design forums. And therefore, it is by analyzing analog game design forums that this paper seeks to situate the degree to which competition serves as a carrier of the poisons of the market as it is used as a fundamental mode of evaluation in analog game design. Conversely, this begs the question as to whether competition ever produces a set of remedies to the market poisons through virtue of its use as an evaluative technique.

BOARD GAME DESIGN FORUMS

Anatomy of the Forum

The forums hosted at BoardGameGeek and Board Game Design Forums are spaces that invite a true diaspora of ideas. As far as web-based utopias go, these two spaces come as close to supporting a legitimate grassroots development community as is possible. To this point, the key barrier to entry into either community has been the construction of usernames and passwords.[1] This, of course, necessitates a computer and enough know-how to use it. And although the BoardGameGeek community is not a specialist design community, its user base is extremely broad, and because of this, the "Board Game Design" subset of forums is notably active, often cycling through 30 to 50 threads of conversation on any given day. Board Game Design Forums[2] is notably more insular, but it hosts a specialized user base that relies solely on the forums for board game design tips.

Both forums are essentially lists of topics or threads. The original poster generally moderates each thread, even though a set of global moderators also exists to help resolve debates and flag users who may be posting off-topic or inappropriate content. In both forums, there are about five different types of threads that are frequently posted by users: reference, work in progress, general questions, critique, and design contests.

Reference threads are definitive insofar as they are user-produced directories of information that seek to satisfy some concrete need of the community. Examples include threads listing board game design contests, companies where raw materials can be purchased for the production of games, or even blogs that discuss game design. Reference threads are often well appreciated by the user base and are modified as time passes, as this collective pool of knowledge is of keen interest and use to the communities hosted on the sites.

Work-in-progress threads are collaborative spaces that may or may not be maintained in conjunction with a design contest. In a work-in-progress thread, designers often post the assets that compose their game and solicit feedback from the community about their design decisions and process. Images of the playtesting process are posted here as well. Assets are distributed through pdf docs for community developers to print and test in their own homes. Here, the print and play culture often functions as a closed playtesting community that helps the designer complete an important but difficult part of the evaluation process. And even though many developers post copies of their games in these spaces without copyright protection, it is commonly understood (and reiterated) by members of the community that their intellectual property will not be jeopardized, as very little money is earned from the development of board games. The lack of financial bounty encourages a culture of trust within the community.

Threads which focus on general questions normally involve an original poster who would like to solicit feedback from the forum about some aspect of his or her game design. Questions are sometimes posed about how to navigate the site, because the search box and layout are not very intuitive. Other questions pertain specifically to design. Sometimes users ask whether key game mechanics have had any precedents or whether the community has any recommendations for games that might serve as a point of creative comparison. The community is often very receptive to the threads set up as questions, but sometimes members will troll others if a question is offered that has been dealt with in some prior thread. It is good etiquette to search whether a question has been previously posted before it is brought to the community.

Just as some threads allow for the community to solicit and react to questions, other threads focus specifically on the critique of design elements in either one's own or some other game. Critique threads are a good space to find conversations that deal with the aesthetics of design. As the practice of critique involves the articulation of a particular set of design aesthetics, themes regarding the philosophy of design emerge in these threads and repeat themselves as players who review and critique games learn from the other reviews and critiques. The aesthetics of the market are reified in these threads. Good critique requires a point of comparison, and therefore, threads which focus on critique often use preexisting games as an example and benchmark against which the homebrew games discussed in the forum can be compared.

Finally, companies and individual users of the site sporadically hold design contests where grassroots game submissions are evaluated against one another. These design contests are often themed: one-player game design contest, compact game design contests, iron game design challenges (design must be completed within a short period, perhaps one month), and more. Publishers have been known to observe (or even more, to host) these design contests, occasionally moving a game to publication if it is refined enough. But if the contest is user driven, the reward of good game design is often a combination of notoriety and some form of forum-specific online currency. While there is a mode of professional scaffolding at play in these design contests, more often than not they are a way for players to collaborate with one another and geek out over their shared hobby.

Reading the Rubric: Poisonous Evaluation

One example of a competitive technique that has poisonous tendencies is the evaluation rubric. Moving forward from the assumption that games should be designed according to a static set of criteria, rubrics funnel the psychic power of creativity toward an end that is already predetermined. In other words, rubrics are a tautological technique insofar as they presuppose a progress narrative with clear design criteria. In the example given, Carl Mickton[3] a successful Utah-based game designer,[4] has circulated a rubric of evaluation on the Board Game Designers Guild of Utah website, a niche site which sustains its own local game design community. Within this rubric, not only does Mickton suggest a method for reviewing games quickly, he also suggests (and qualifies) six criteria for excellence in design: clarity, flow, balance, length, integration, and fun. These criteria serve as a perfectly typical example of the ways that games are evaluated. They accurately reflect the virtues of good design often echoed by participants in the forums of BoardGameGeek and the Board Game Design Forum, but when considered as a part of a design ethos that is fundamentally connected to the drives of the market, these criteria become more problematic.

In order to consider the ways that these criteria lead to a practice of evaluation which is problematic insofar as it is directional, it is important to consider each criterion from a variety of perspectives and to consider the degrees to which each is indebted to the market. It is only by dithering out these potentialities that the therapy of evaluation can be seen as holding a separate nature than the poison.

The virtues of clarity, according to Mickton, are: "Very streamlined layout / The players can easily see what is going on in all areas of the game / Rules are very clear and easy to understand (no areas of ambiguity)." His rubric advocates for a strong sense of spatially distinct design and a lack of ambiguity in the rules. The point here is that cluttered cards and boards may serve to frustrate players more than instigate involvement in the game. Some of the symptoms of this problem can be seen in design forums among players debating the interpretation of rules, and it is true that ambiguous rule sets can relate to fundamentally unplayable games. However, there is another way to view ambiguity, as Matthew Fuller and Andrew Goffey (2012) argue. Ambiguity can function as a strategic practice in today's world because it deliberately evokes a plethora of interpretations around an object or practice (p. 31). From this vantage, "clarity" indicates design decisions that favor the interpretation of the author over those of the audience. House rules and regional variants were the traditional offspring of the ambiguous rule set. Clarity is not necessarily problematic, but ambiguity has resulted in many fantastic interpretations of games as well.

When describing what good flow is in game design, Mickton writes: "No unnecessary procedures / Minimal to no fiddliness / Very few if any exceptions to the rules / Very streamlined." Here again, there is a mutually agreed-upon pact of minimalism inherent in the design of games. This assumes, however, a historical directionality in which progress can be seen as an offshoot of streamlined design features. In the political game experiments held by the RAND Corporation in the 1950s and 1960s, rule sets were deliberately cluttered because the designers sought to find ways to simulate a phenomenon through mathematical techniques in the most accurate fashion possible (Ghamari-Tabrizi, 2005). This technique of design has been critiqued by military strategist and game designer Jerry Pournelle; he notes that the complex rule sets of political games often do not result in the same kind of fun that the streamlined commercial rules of commercial games do (Pournelle, 1971a, 1971b).

Another commonly accepted technique of evaluation regards game balance. It is widely understood that better games have more balance. "Very balanced game that is fair for all players," Mickton explains. "No strategic loopholes / Any and all elements of luck in the game are appropriate in their significance." The issue of balance, as a matter of fact, is so important that it has even produced departments of funded playtesters in the game design industry (Dyer-Witheford & de Peuter, 2009). Extensive testing must be done before a game is taken to market, because poor balancing completely undermines the sense of perfect and fair competition that can be had within the game itself. However, while balance is a virtue in immersive and engaging game design, many games, such as those in the emergent Nordic live-action role-playing genre, operate within the assumption that in order to convey a transformative narrative, players should play to lose (Stark, 2012). This means forfeiting the assumption that players should see goals as an end. Instead, they should work primarily to contextualize goals within the auspices of the game's overall narrative.

Just as balance is important to a game's performance on the market, so too is length. Mickton explains, "The game's length is appropriate for what it offers." The point here is that games often overstay their welcome, and savvy designers will avoid this pitfall and adjust the game length accordingly. Nonetheless, as Mary Flanagan (2009) has pointed out, games that have been singled out for their artistic merit often offer things which demand inappropriate lengths. Examples include simulations that explore battles on a realistic scale or ambiguous games (like Yoko Ono's piece "Play It by Trust," a chess set where all the pieces are white, and victory is ambiguous). The market demands that length produce dramatic tension, and therefore it demands lengths between 30 minutes and 2 hours. Art, on the other hand, allows this category to be amorphous and accommodates any length as long as it challenges players to think critically about their actions.

Integration is another virtue expressed in Mickton's rubric. "The mechanics and the theme strongly complement each other," he writes. "The various elements strongly integrate to create a unified game." The point here is that the game's narrative should be coherent and supported by a set of mechanics, rather than pasted onto a set of mechanics somewhat haphazardly. And while this is an important decision to make in matters of structured storytelling, it is a decidedly seductive point that winnows out matters of experimentation in game design. Different combinations of mechanics and themes create different tones and moods; in short, they have different chemistries together. Though it may be enticing to design a game with mechanics which rigidly support a single thematic motif, the serendipitous expression that comes only from improvisation and experimentation is given no chance to enter the design picture. Integration is another common motif that serves primarily to wedge the game designer into the position of interactive storyteller, as opposed to composer or artist.

Mickton's final criterion of evaluation is fun. Emotion, in this case, is the primary means of understanding fun. He writes, "Consistent emotional connection or tension throughout the game / Very interesting theme that strongly engages the imagination of the players / The game was very fun to play." These are the traditional metrics of fun that accompany practices of game design. The affective bonds we form with games have been transformed into a science of hypnosis and engagement by game consulting firms, such as Xeodesign, which offer consulting services structured around psychological approaches to play. Specifically, the focus is on how to produce audiences through the affects of fun. This uses-and-gratifications style of approach to games and play is not problematic in and of itself, but it does posit a view of audiences that is particular to the structure of market production through which games are produced. For instance, if a game works well as a social game but perhaps misses an audience of hardcore gamers, Xeodesign recommends to "add points and more strategies." And in this way, the evaluation of fun can be seen primarily as a way to produce audiences in games in order to best serve market niches and needs.

Having gone through the many ways that Mickton recommends that games be evaluated, some questions still remain unanswered. Given that the techniques listed are indeed representative of the standard practices in the game design communities, the question still remains as to whether or not these techniques are therapeutic or poisonous. And, while I have tried to explain that these techniques, at the very least, all somehow showcase a philosophy of game design which favors decisions in line with the market and although the market is not poisonous in and of itself, it is this paper's argument that designing for the aesthetics of the market is itself a poisonous practice, as it leads designers to reproduce a status quo order of tastes within these communities.

THE ORDER OF TASTE

Elsewhere in this volume, Suhr asks, "Although ranking implies having an order, does this order shape itself in digital environments or are there calculated efforts in which this order is pronounced?" To answer this question, this study considers digital environments to be amplifiers of the order of tastes already pronounced by the market. The board game design forums explored in this study work as echo chambers (Karpf, 2012), where a set of ideas bounce around and are lauded for their virtues by the opinion leaders in that space. Even though much work in serious game design is being taken up by labs, like Tiltfactor, where games are developed with socially transformative ends in mind, many of the hobbyists in the design forums studied here truly believe that the design philosophy outlined in the rubric above leads to better games—"better" being a largely personal judgment.

Such judgments do not take the overdeterministic way that the market influences our standards of taste particularly seriously, and when they do, it is largely bracketed off as a decision reflecting a participant's desire to publish his or her game, not to defy the capture of capital. So, while there is a sense of agency around the production of tastes, which are then quantified and metered, in digital environments, there is a second sense which becomes apparent in design competitions. These contests reveal that taste production is almost completely assimilated by the logic and trappings of the market. Design competitions always feature a concrete set of criteria that serve primarily as the key means of evaluation. These criteria, as outlined in the prior section, help to produce games with the aesthetics of the market as a focus, not necessarily transformative play. Finally, the goals of game design competitions are a microcosm of the goals produced through market ends. Games are made under the auspices of a general design philosophy which holds a generic (and uncritical) progress narrative about good design as its fundamental tenet, and designers are offered economic rewards for good design within these parameters. Competition is anathema to creativity when it is put to the service of an aesthetic which has been built through the contrivances of taste constructed by the market.

AN ALTERNATIVE TO CONTEST

Although this paper has explored game design competitions as a particularly problematic mode of evaluation, it is important to note that there is also a strong community in these forums oriented around a more process-driven approach within work-in-progress threads. These threads typically include a sense of collective mentoring that is more reflective of the design process on the whole. This is not to say that work-in-progress threads do not also find themselves mirroring the discourses brought about by the echo chamber of the market, but it is to imply that there is no sense of competition within these threads making matters worse. Work-in-progress threads accomplish three key things for designers using BoardGameGeek and Board Game Design Forum to help produce their games. First, they create a space for prototypes of the game to be distributed and for the design process to be recorded by the designer and then critiqued by the community. Second, work-in-progress threads allow for a space of qualitative critique that resists the easy design criteria provided by rubrics. Finally, these threads create an affective space of community support so that designers feel like they are engaging with an actual audience instead of designing only for themselves and therefore engaging in navel gazing.

The qualitative aspects of work-in-progress threads help to refine design in a supportive way that does not fall into the simple logic of market competition. Nonetheless, even though there is the potential for a constructive space of feedback that does not cater to the needs of the market, many of the criteria described above have been internalized by the community and are integral to the qualitative feedback process as well. The market's logic is still immanent in these contexts, and even though qualitative feedback can help to make the sense of competition here less explicit, evaluation necessitates competition to function, and for this reason, it often colludes with the market even in seemingly mundane circumstances.

CONCLUSION

The goal of this paper was to describe the ways in which competition is used as a tool of evaluation in game design communities. This paper has highlighted that although competition is itself a technique with the potential to produce creative and interesting ideas and designs, it necessitates a set of standards to work. Standards are, more often than not, the implements and inventions of a market that seeks to appeal to the most people possible. This is the paradox of competition. While on the one hand, it offers a method for the evaluation and judgment of difference, when put to the whim of the market, contests do not necessarily result in improvement but instead lead to the replication of the status quo. In the case of game design, where contests are often judged by players who have a strong faith in the ability of competition to showcase the strongest ideas, the idea of the edgy or the avant garde is even harder to realize for those reasons.

It is important to note, additionally, that communities of practice also form around these forms of competition and that these communities are particularly important to those who participate in them. While competition propels the market toward a set of ends that are not necessarily in the best interests of a plural design aesthetic, there is a definite sense of craft and reciprocity within the technique as well. Designers are supported by their communities by virtue of the fact that they have a place where they can discuss their work and find support for their hobbies. These communities of practice are supported by informal learning practices, and as such, they produce design art which pushes at the market standards and has, in rare cases, the potential to disrupt the sensibilities of the market as well. And, because even qualitative moments of feedback still rely on the same standards of judgment and competition, it seems that the best spaces to search for new potentials of creation and development may rely less on balance and more on disruption. Anthropy (2012) has described the ways that she developed small artistic games for the commercial site Shockwave and has been able to earn enough money to continue production through advertising proceeds. Even though there is a sense that this is, in fact, more tethered to the market itself than many board game design projects, it is interesting that mini-games have been able to grapple with issues of identity, queerness, and alienation as well. Evaluation, balance, and competition all rely on deliberate action and time. On the other hand, small games of disruption require a sensibility to trends and aesthetics. While competition may produce a more balanced game, designers have more agency in the design process when competition is not a consideration and when designs are sussed out blindly with only personal taste in mind.

NOTES

1. A username and password are not required on BoardGameGeek when browsing posts, but they are required when users attempt to post things themselves.
2. This is a site distinct from the "Board Game Design Forums" on BoardGameGeek.
3. Carl Mickton is the fictional alias of a known board game designer.
4. Carl has published one game with Rio Grande Games, a major board game publisher.

REFERENCES

Anthropy, A. (2012). *Rise of the videogame zinesters: How freaks, normals, amateurs, artists, dreamers, drop-outs, queers, housewives, and people like you are taking back an art form.* New York: Seven Stories Press.

Caillois, R. (2001). *Man, play, and games.* Urbana: University of Illinois Press.

Consalvo, M. (2009). *Cheating: Gaining advantage in videogames.* Cambridge, MA: MIT Press.

Crogan, P. (2010). Knowledge, care, and transindividuation: An interview with Bernard Stiegler. *Cultural Politics, 6*(2), 157–179.

Dyer-Witheford, N., & de Peuter, G. (2009). *Games of empire: Global capitalism and video games.* Minneapolis: University of Minnesota Press.

Fuller, M., & Goffey, A. (2012). *Evil media.* Cambridge, MA: MIT Press.

Flanagan, M. (2009). *Critical play: Radical game design.* Cambridge, MA: MIT Press.

Ghamari-Tabrizi, S. (2005). *The worlds of Herman Kahn: The intuitive science of thermonuclear war.* Cambridge, MA: Harvard University Press.

Huizinga, J. (1980). *Homo ludens: A study of the play-element in culture.* Boston: Beacon Press.

Karpf, D. (2012). *The MoveOn effect: The unexpected transformation of American political advocacy.* New York: Oxford University Press.

Kelty, C. (2009). *Two bits: The cultural significance of free software.* Durham, NC: Duke University Press.

Lessig, L. (2008). *Remix: Making art and commerce thrive in the hybrid economy.* New York: Penguin Press.

Macho, T. (2003). Zeit und zahl: Kalender- und zeitrechnung als kulturetechniken [Time and number: Calendar and time as technoculture]. In Sybille Krämer & Horst Bredekamp (Eds.), *Bild-Schrift-Zahl* [Image-font-number] (pp. 179–92). Munich: Wilhelm Fink Verlag.

Pournelle, J. (1971a, January-February). Simulating the art of war. *The Avalon Hill General,* 8–9.

Pournelle, J. (1971b, March-April). Simulating the art of war—part II. *The Avalon Hill General,* 8–9.

Siegert, B. (2008). Cacography or communication? Cultural techniques in German media studies. *Grey Room, 28*, 26–47.
Sinnreich, A. (2010). *Mashed up: Music, technology, and the rise of configurable culture*. Amherst: University of Massachusetts Press.
Smith, A. (1982). *The wealth of nations*. New York: Penguin Classics.
Spariosu, M. (1989). *Dionysus reborn: Play and the aesthetic dimension in modern philosophical and scientific discourse*. Ithaca, NY: Cornell University Press.
Stark, L. (2012). *Leaving mundania? Inside the transformative world of live action role-playing games*. Chicago, IL: Chicago Review Press.
Stiegler, B. (2009). Teleologics of the snail: The errant self wired to a WiMax network. *Theory, Culture & Society, 26*(2–3), 33–45.

5 Constructing Learning through the Creative Evaluation of Visual Arts Production

Linda Vigdor

The crit, as the art studio critique is popularly known, is a core element of an arts education. It prepares artists for what is essentially a lifelong evaluation practice that sustains an artist's creative practice and production over a career. During a crit, an artist presents her/his work to peers and/or instructors, collectors, gallery owners, etc. (though rarely to the public) and receives feedback on the work presented. The crit may be formal or informal in structure, but it will have a structure, whether explicit or implicit. One of the key rules, as Steve DeFrank, a sculpture and drawing teacher at the School of Visual Arts[1] (SVA) in New York City, shares (crit observation, February 5, 2013) is that "saying I like it" is forbidden. Why? Because a simple *like* is viewed as a cop-out, an inability or refusal to engage with the work itself, and as contributing no value to the artists' or viewers' creative, technical, affective, or cognitive development. In short, a mere like offers little to foster learning or creative outputs. Yet, liking has become social capital on social media networks—being *liked* is often the endgame. As social networks become platforms for the evaluation of visual artworks, a new digital divide emerges. Digitally mediated commenting/liking practices may mirror the structure and goals of the studio crit in intent, but as currently practiced, they rarely reach the rigor, creativity, intent, or learning value of the traditional crit.

To argue this point, I examine two crit sessions at SVA and compare the discourse and structures with commenting and liking on two online visual arts communities: DeviantArt (DA; www.deviantart.com) and WetCanvas (WC; www.wetcanvas.com). Member artists post their work and may receive feedback from other members of the community. Both sites claim large, diverse memberships—in media and styles represented, geographic location, arts training, and purpose for being on the site. Artists upload images of their work for a range of reasons: marketing, having a presence within the community, creating an online portfolio, and receiving or giving feedback. I selected the DA and WC communities for their popularity, because members of both sites have posted positions on how to critique art, and because each community's commenting practice interprets the notion of critique in different ways. To maintain some parallels with the SVA crits, I focused on fine art paintings in my study of DA and WC.

The art studio crit has traditionally occupied a closed space, with high costs of admission. In contrast, the Internet has made it possible to move critiquing into digitally mediated contexts, creating seemingly more democratic, broadly accessible opportunities for artists to benefit from peer feedback. Artists post their images to wholly web-based artist communities, which may function simultaneously as online galleries, sales sites, and social networks. Artist peers may or may not come with similar ideas around art making, what constitutes "good" art, or even what constitutes useful feedback. Anyone registered as a member of DA or WC may post comments or likes or say nothing at all. Rules or conventions for giving feedback are both more open and more restrictive than in the traditional art studio crit. DeviantArt and WetCanvas communities are open in who can participate and how, but there are rules that dictate whether real or fictitious names are to be used; that artists must post only their own work; how often one may post a work for critique; and sometimes, how to get and give feedback. Website interfaces present a different kind of structure than in the art studio crit, which adheres to a long tradition that is customized by instructors and students.

Critiques on online portfolio sites are framed by what are now familiar and ubiquitous conventions for commenting and liking on the Internet (Erard, 2013), and there is a notion that comment spaces represent a cultural turn toward a new democratic discourse. Erard points out that the structure of commenting is bound to what was technically possible in the 1970s, on bulletin board discussion forums. Noncustomizable by users, comment spaces are a nonnegotiable structure. However, the quality of discourse within commenting communities may vary widely. Across SVA, DA, and WC, an important component is whether and how crits are moderated or monitored. Much of the difference locates in a community's position—and commenting *practices*—on *liking* artworks presented for feedback. The fact that liking remains the dominant critical stance on web-based artists' sites, in comments such as "awesome" and "beautiful," should be of concern.

Liking transforms the relationship of critique to creative production—from supporting artistic development to providing affirmation. It is a radical departure from evaluation in the traditional studio crit, where artists are actively mentored in how to connect process–practice, content–intents, and media–technique in ways that actively foster skills of reflexive and critical-evaluative thinking. Internet critique spaces may give the appearance of providing enhanced opportunities to receive critical feedback, but as the learning focus of the crit is superseded by an affirmation culture in social networks, these spaces manifest another digital/cultural divide (for an analysis of the digital divide, see Jaworski, 2014). Critique morphs into feedback as affirmation, comments such as "good job, well detailed and shaded" and "stunning!!! what a great concept too!!" (DA, December 12, 2012) become the norm, replacing the evaluative thinking that goes on in the studio crit. In comments such as "I keep seeing a negative symbol disarmed" (SVA student, February 2, 2012), we see the student building critical and generative thinking skills. Because online communities seem inclusive and invite open commenting, it is easy to assume that the democratic aura of social media networks supports equally democratic opportunities for learning through creative evaluation. Conceptions of what constitutes critique or feedback change as affirmation replaces the evaluative thinking that is so critical to creativity. In contrast, the traditional art studio crit is cognitively intense in how it develops critical and evaluative thinking but is largely only available within a closed community. The artist must be admitted to the program, pay tuition, adhere to an instructor's course format, submit required work, and regularly participate in crits. Although studio crits may appear to be organic and unruly, they enact a long-standing tradition and structure that varies only slightly, even when customized in practice. Online artists' communities are generally free, and there are no grades or instructors dictating rules for commenting. However, the ubiquitous commenting interface (Erard, 2013) becomes the mediator of social discourse. Technical structure replaces discursive rules or conventions and changes the practice and intents of critiquing.

Evaluations of creative production of artworks on DA and WC are mediated by a digital interface organized around linear discourse through which a community learns to conform to norms. There is an essential role that the crit has played in artists' cognitive and creative development. Within the new online commenting spaces, a new digital divide is emergent in how learning is positioned in relation to feedback. In this digital divide, there is a codependency between creative production and affirmation. The critical feedback observed on DA and WC relies on affirmation or judgments made about technical skills. Absent is the sort of critical discourse that grounds the reflexive and generative thinking so central to the traditional crit.

The questions I am concerned with are: What happens in the discursive interactions of a crit? What is said, how is it said, and how does a peer-critic know (or learn) what to say, or artists what to ask for from their peer-critics? How and when does the crit function as both a learning event and an evaluation instrument? Similarly, what is the commenting discourse on artists' online portfolio sites? *Likes* are counted, but to what end? In this anytime-anywhere-anyone evaluation environment, what kinds of evaluations—crits—are offered, when, and by whom? And, most importantly, what are the implications for learning in these different crit formats and spaces?

EVALUATION, ASSESSMENT, AND EVALUATIVE THINKING

Evaluation conjures up different things across perspectives, practices, and disciplines. For example, in education, evaluation is often studied as a science, refers to a practice that measures learning outcomes, and is explicitly differentiated from assessment. Evaluative thinking, however, describes a capacity, albeit one that can be developed. Stanford University's definition provides a reference point for how I interpret evaluation in the context of this paper:

> Evaluation is the systematic process of gathering, analyzing, and using information from multiple sources to judge the merit or worth of a program, project or entity. . . . Evaluation also includes value judgments concerning the desirability of results.
>
> (Stanford University, n.d.)

I interpret *creative* evaluation to include the systematic processes of making, and learning to make, *rigorous* value judgments regarding an artist's processes, development, use of materials, and skills as well as judgments expressed of the work itself. Critical feedback itself may also be evaluated on similar criteria. I am concerned with evaluation as a critique practice that is focused on learning and development—related to, but not the same as—evaluating an artwork on its aesthetic value (e.g., as characterized by Dickie [1988]). Learning to evaluate, via the crit (and to receive critique), is the foundational learning that connects creative intents, practices, and production. Hetland, Winner, Veenema, and Sheridan (2007) describe *eight studio habits of mind* (p. 7) that they observed in a number of K-12 art classes, where making art and participating in the creative culture of the class helped students develop the following capacities: craft skills, engagement and persistence, envisioning, expressing, observing, reflecting, stretching and exploring, and understanding the art world. One of the insights of Hetland and colleagues' 2007 study is that making art is about much more than producing a creative work. Creative production involves a number of capacities, and it is through working and participating in the evaluative culture of the classroom community that student artists develop.

Sir Ken Robinson is one of the most prominent advocates for making room for creativity in education and is noted for his piercing critiques of the banality of current educational structures. For Robinson and his colleagues (NACCCE, 1999), creativity may begin with active engagement in making something in a deliberate way (p. 31), but it also "involves a second and reciprocal mode of thought: an *evaluative* mode. . . . The outcome of an imaginative activity can only be called creative if it is of value in relation to the task at hand" (p. 33). That is, deliberative intent is linked to creative output; and thus, learning to question or judge intents, outputs, and their intersection must be recognized as an essential component of the creative process. As Robinson et al. put it,

> In any creative process there are likely to be dead-ends: ideas and designs that do not work. There may be many failures. . . . Evaluating which ideas do work, which do not requires judgment and criticism. . . . [C]reative thinking always involves some critical thinking.
>
> (NACCCE, 1999, p. 33)

Robinson et al. passionately promote the idea that the core focus of education should be on building capacities for generative and evaluative thinking. Robinson argues for education broadly, not just art education. Still, in an arts context, creative production is inseparable from creative evaluation, and both are inseparable from learning, both formal and informal.

CREATIVE EVALUATION AND THE DEVELOPMENT OF VISUAL ARTISTS

The traditional art studio crit is an example of how creative, generative, and evaluative thinking skills and dispositions are taught and learned. Looking at creative production and its evaluation from this perspective highlights the fundamental role of learning as it is intertwined with critique. My study of critique practices and discourses on the DA and WC social network sites and in traditional art studio crit sessions at SVA suggests an emergent digital divide that is different from the already well-documented digital divide in access to computers and technological literacies. This divide manifests as a gap in generative and evaluative thinking skills and dispositions, as the liking culture of social media replaces other forms of evaluative thinking. This shift may be observed in comment spaces on the DeviantArt site, where phrases not unlike the following dominate the discourse: "This is beautiful. I can tell that you were really just letting your heart guide the brush with this one. It shows in every line, every curve, and all the subliminal colours. . . . I'm incredibly impressed. I'd pay money for a painting like this" (DA, December 12, 2012). However, this divide is not a fait accompli. Although not easy to find, a DA archive contains members' posts that take varying positions on how to critique art but that express a desire for more substance (I discuss these later in the chapter). Comments posted on WC are substantively different. Rather than statements such as "sooo sweet" (DA, December 12, 2012), comments will be something like:

> Remember when doing children, to always use very gentle colors, and not a lot of them! Keep your palette very soft and very very simple. . . . Absolutely lose the umber colors around the eyes and anywhere you have used it for shadow.
>
> (WetCanvas, December 31, 2012)

The affirmation culture persists, but value is judged based on seemingly formulaic notions of technique and aesthetics.

Drawing from the NACCCE (1999) and Hetland et al.'s (2007) ideas that intersect creativity and learning, it is useful to think about creative evaluation through the lens of Bloom's taxonomy (Armstrong, 2013). A stage theory of the development of thinking skills, the taxonomy describes levels that we move through, as learners, 1 being the lowest level.

For my purposes, I have tweaked the taxonomy as follows.

1. Concrete—content/subject and fact focused
2. Procedural—"how to," focused on methods, tools, and materials
3. Sensual—material, affective, or physical engagements with a work
4. Conceptual—analytic, abstract, focused on ideas
5. Evaluative—constructive critique and judgments based on steps 1–4
6. Reflexive—self-examining, metacognitive, empathetic
7. Generative—inquiry driven, aimed at supporting the creation of new work/knowledge

The crit is indispensable because feedback is crucial to an artist's development; illuminates a community's creative, intellectual, aesthetic, and political sensibilities; and is the process wherein a community's commitments and values are *constructed.* Critiques are not the sole domain of the arts. Soep (2006) conducted an ethnographic study of learning through critique, looking at students engaged in collaborative projects in informal, out-of-school environments (creating radio stories for broadcast). For her, "critique is a form of assessment through which young people jointly judge their own work and that of their peers" (p. 748):

> Critique manifests itself as an episode of learning by engaging young people in joint assessment events that are improvisational, reciprocal, and oriented toward the future of the work under review. . . . [C]ritique is likely to arise within specific conditions: when stakes are intense, metastandards are subjected to review, accountability is mutual and interactively sustained, and interdisciplinary practice is mandatory.
>
> (p. 748)

Building from Soep's research, the crit is highlighted as an evaluative practice that supports learning and development—by individuals and communities. And learning is production rather than product. Key is that learning, as in the crit, happens through dialogues that are derived from a practice that provokes thinking about the connections among intents, processes, and production. Engaging in critical evaluation, thinking develops along a spectrum, from concrete to generative. In crits at SVA, this mentoring unfolds through discursive interactions. A student offers that "it reminds me of a scab" and DeFrank interjects with: "Same thing like I said to Sallie, make that into a comment that Kimberly can take home. . . . So Kim, notice what people are saying" (SVA, February 5, 2013). A crucial point is that a student will give critical feedback, but that feedback is also critiqued. Both the artwork and the feedback are put under a critical lens.

Comments on DA serve a culture where affirmation, rather than learning, is prized. Here, posts rely on phrases such as "I want to jump in! Beautiful effect!" (DA, December 12, 2012). And the like button is exclusively a popularity measure. Opinion substitutes for evaluation, and critique happens on the most basic level. Liking provides, in a single word or action, a summative judgment. The criteria for liking tends to be opaque and rarely moves higher than level 2 or 3 of Bloom's taxonomy (procedural or sensual).

WetCanvas, as a community, seems to be more invested in substantive feedback; comments are more focused and detailed. For example:

> In general, I think your colors are too intense. . . . Look at any group of beach paintings by masters and you'll see far more subtle hues. Also, nature must be randomized to look good. . . . [Y]ou want to stay away from repetition in your composition.
>
> (WC, December 31, 2012)

On close examination, the feedback is issuing a kind of manifesto of how a painting should be constructed. This type of critique suggests thinking that largely hovers between the concrete (the accuracy of the representation), the procedural (focused on technique and materials), and the sensual (describes emotions generated in the viewer). Only rarely will a comment engage with the art or artist on a conceptual or evaluative level.

Communities learn together in that a culture of critique and commenting both informs the learning and is impacted by the crit process. But differences in the type and quality of critiques are wide. That is, learning, whether in the studio crit or in a virtual critique space, happens through a "collaborative construction of knowledge through social negotiation, a key feature of a constructivist learning environment" (Gunawardena, Lowe, & Anderson, 1997, p. 399). Ian Hacking (1999) argues that social construction describes knowledge that grounds the interpretation or construction of subjects, objects, and their intersection. In essence, critique communities are an "intellectual locus for the creation and use of knowledge . . . cultural and political sites in a productive and legitimizing enterprise, setting the parameters of knowledge building and inquiry" (Vigdor, 2010, p. 33). What constitutes critique is constructed and learned within a community.

The rise of social media and networks has generated enthusiasm for their participatory cultures, and yet there has been little critical attention paid to how these might better promote the development of higher-order thinking and creativity. Artists (for example) have a new ease of access to a global community where they may share their creative work and both give and receive feedback. Because these spaces serve as social learning sites, it is important to understand (and perhaps help to shape) how they are coming to define what constitutes critique. To the degree that we value the ways that art making and critiquing develop important thinking skills, the commenting discourses on DA and WC suggest some points of concern.

METHODOLOGY

I compared in-studio art crit sessions at SVA with comment threads on DA and WC. At SVA, I observed two crit sessions in undergraduate sculpture and drawing classes (selected because I know the instructor, graduated from the school, and was likely to get access). On DA and WC, I selected comment threads if they met two criteria: the work was posted as a fine art painting media and it received at least eight comments. To analyze the data, I employed an interaction-discourse analysis (Gunawardena et al., 1997), where segments of face-to-face dialogue at SVA and asynchronous comments posted on DA and WC were my units of analysis. Through interpretive reading (pragmatic hermeneutics), I developed a set of themes and subthemes: (a) level of thinking (based around Bloom's taxonomy), (b) social construction (scaffolding, community affirmation, normalization), (c) structure (rules, interface, constraints), and (d) use of language/rhetoric (opinion, swear words, phrasing complexity).

CREATIVE EVALUATION AS PRACTICED IN THREE CRITIQUE ENVIRONMENTS

In both traditional face-to-face studio crits and digitally mediated comment spaces, knowledges are constructed through formal and informal interactions around (a) knowledge of how to receive and use critical feedback, (b) community understandings of what constitutes feedback, and (c) technical, discursive, and conceptual factors. Evaluative cultures, regardless of their differences, engage in "collaborative construction of knowledge through social negotiation" (Gunawardena et al., 1997, p. 402), but key is that being able to critique or evaluate is dependent on both the evaluator's cognitive development and engagement and the environment or culture within which evaluations are performed. Vygotsky's (1978) work on learning as socially mediated and constructed provides a useful lens for characterizing crit and commenting practices. One of his major contributions was his *zone of proximal development* (ZPD); a person may have limited knowledge of how to do something, and a teacher, mentor, or more advanced peer guides the learner to a higher level of skill or knowledge. This space, between what is known and what could be known with assistance, is the ZPD. Vygotsky's focus was the individual learner. Smith (cited in Gunawardena et al., 1997) found the same type of learning through mentoring, described as group-mediated cognition where "the situation itself exerts a strong mediating effect on individuals' cognitive and conceptual processes" (p. 409).

Similar to most digitally mediated networks, the basic structure for commenting and liking on DA or WC conforms to what is now a dominant convention on the Internet (e.g., Facebook, Amazon, the Huffington Post), where commenters respond to someone else's posted object, behavior, politics, and so on. Two types of rules frame how studio crits and commenting unfold. Formalized rules define appropriate language and behaviors, such as turn taking. Informal rules evolve as conventions for giving feedback play out within a community. Hitting the like button has become a way of crowdsourcing a positive, yet passive, response to most anything—the technology frames *how* to like, and the community, its significance. DeviantArt is essentially a liking culture, whereas on WetCanvas there is no like button. At SVA, liking is explicitly "banned" from the discourse; moreover, there is a set of teacher-defined rules—a structure—even as the behaviors and language are casual (laughing, storytelling, and colorful language pervade DeFrank's crit sessions). At SVA the teaching artist functions as a mentor, and students as "knowledgeable peers." Crits are moderated or curated to help student artists develop their evaluative-thinking "wings." The art school crit takes place within what we understand as formal learning, whereas the interactions on DA and WC fit an informal learning model. These intersect, however: at SVA, classroom crits have a distinctly informal quality, and students' formal art making ("homework") often blurs any boundary between formal and informal or school versus life. Through the studio crit, each of the seven levels of thinking identified in Bloom's taxonomy becomes an integral part of the artists' skill-set.

Exhibit 1: The School of Visual Arts

The SVA is a prominent, private art and design school in New York City. It offers undergraduate and master's degrees, has an international student body, and the faculty is largely composed of renowned creative professionals. Tuition is currently $16,135 per semester for full-time study. In DeFrank's classes, the crit is embedded into the fabric of the course and is integral to students' development of creative and evaluative habits of mind that, as Hefland argues, are crucial components of art making. His students are required to submit written project proposals using his standard form. Students are asked to develop and put into writing the following information (with the understanding that everything may change as the artist produces the work):

1. Goofy title
2. Project description that includes a statement of a problem to solve
3. The student's self-defined proposed "boundaries" that set a time limit and the materials the artist will work with, as well as any other limits the artist wants to work within
4. Research. What articles were found? What books were looked at? What informed the artist and the project?
5. An expected critique date, which cannot exceed 4 weeks

Crits are scheduled into regular class meetings, and in that sense are formal; despite the informal banter and students who wander in and out of class, there is an underlying structure and set of ground rules that frame how the crit will proceed and what is allowed/expected of the presenting artist, DeFrank, and knowledgeable peers (students giving feedback).

Ground rules of the crits are: students must not say "I like it," and the artist whose work is being critiqued is not allowed to talk until after his or her peers have given their feedback. Before the artist is allowed to speak, DeFrank reads the artist's original proposal. In producing the artwork, students are allowed, and encouraged, to veer from their initial statement; this respects and frames the problem-focused creative working process. The process is both organic and intentional and encompasses both informal and formal learning because making the art so often interweaves with the artists' "non-school" lives. Students are given 4 weeks to complete their projects. During crits, DeFrank actively mentors, guiding students to hone in on multiple aspects of the presented work as well as reflexively examine the content or quality of their criticisms. A sample exchange:

Jimmy: It looks like someone just filled in the red . . . but, I can't say "like," right?

DeFrank: What?

Jimmy: I can't say really "like," right?

DeFrank: You cannot say—well everybody has. I've been a little lax on that, but no, I would prefer you not to; every time you say "like," I say "mother fucker"

Jimmy: I am ***amazed*** by the marks on the inside of the animals.

DeFrank: Like this stuff in here?

Jimmy: It's exceptional to me, the detail that I also ~~like~~, that I admire [SD laughs appreciatively], because I don't even know how you did it. It's a tiny detail, it's so minimal, which makes it beautiful even though it's an extremely gruesome topic. So there's beauty in the gross.

DeFrank: Is it—OK, are we finding a theme tonight? Is this the theme of tonight's critiques? How funny is that? Maybe it's a groupthink, it's the gestalt of the room? But wow. I love that.

(SVA, February 5, 2013)

The atmosphere of the crit is quite casual and familiar; both students and teacher tell personal stories, often using "fuck" for emphasis. DeFrank maintains control over the crit with a gentle and humorous presence, even as some students wander away and come back on seemingly their own frames of reference. Most of the students talk during the crits, yet a few do not or do so rarely. DeFrank sets the tone and teaches the students how to critique, in part through modeling (Bandura, 1971). His primary mode of teaching is mentoring—viewed as an exemplar of Vygotsky's (1978) scaffolding and ZPD. DeFrank encourages students to explore and experiment in their art making but within self-imposed boundaries. These limits provide "hooks" during the crits. DeFrank is supportive but also asks probing questions and pushes students to critically think outside of their comfort zones. The intensity and depth of the crits also help to reframe the experience and value of *failure*. This was particularly evident during the drawing class crits of projects where the assignment was to intentionally make a work that the student thought would fail. An excerpt of the crit illuminates the depth of the dialogue:

DeFrank: You said something—If I didn't know the assignment was to go down in flames of failure. I wouldn't know, right? And I think that's one of the big points of this project. With that said, what do you think, if we get into the head of Vivian, what do you think she—I mean I agree with you, I think these are beautiful drawings.

Stephie: It's not failure in the sense of not . . . it's just going and not worrying. It's like accepting *if* you fail rather than trying *to* fail.

DeFrank: Accepting when or if?

Stephie: IF.

DeFrank [laughs]: You know, Stephie, I don't think you know how important that sounds when you are talking about working in one's studio. The process—if I could live like that! So it's like, to recap, it's sort of like letting go. Say it again?

Stephie: Like you were talking about before—to paraphrase—like a sense of abandon. Like if you fail, then it happens. But let's just work. It's kind of what I feel—just keep working, you know, and not care too much.

The above passage highlights another core feature of the crit: the intimate interplay of informal and formal, of play and work. The assignment and crit session provoked students to dig deeply into the question "How do you know something is a failure?" In explicitly exploring the idea of critiquing a failure as if it is not, helped students become metacognitively aware of how play and failure are integral to their creative production. As one student put it, the failure project gave students "permission and the freedom to make bad choices," and during the crit, to cultivate a disposition to play, with a purpose. Playful choices, subsequently examined, become a point of departure for new ideas or help to clarify earlier ones. Critiquing the failure projects highlighted an essential interplay among play, creation, critique, reflection, and learning.

The crit is an opportunity to teach and learn the skills of close observation; critical thinking; and discursive, peer-to-peer evaluation. Simply expressing an opinion would be to miss the point. Crit conversations provide scaffolds to higher levels of thinking; what is construed as good feedback is developed in and through social discourse—both formal and informal. Language is harnessed to express and wrestle with complex ideas, where the crit itself is about both providing crucial feedback to the artist and mentoring students in how to critique effectively and appropriately within a social group. It is an exemplar of Vygotsky's ZPD in action and of the social construction of learning and meaning. Key is that the notion of what it means to critique or evaluate creative production is built within the community.

Exhibit 2: DeviantArt.com

The DeviantArt community constructs a different notion of critique. DA's mission is to "**entertain, inspire,** and **empower** the artist in all of us" (*About Us* page, bold in original). The community was founded in August 2000 and claims over 27 million registered members, 65 million unique visitors per month, and to be the largest online social network for artists and art enthusiasts. Self-described as a "community destination" and "exhibition, promotion, and sharing platform," members post "over 160,000 daily uploads of original art works ranging from traditional media, such as painting and sculpture, to digital art, pixel art, films and anime."

Members post their artwork under a specific category, and unless they indicate otherwise, the work is available to the community for commenting. Feedback skews heavily to the genre of "I like it" or "It's beautiful." Notably, artworks that get comments are a minority. The following is a representative example of the language and content of comments observed on DA (December 12, 2012):

Atti:	AWESOME!
cat000:	this looks really cool!
dr04:	OMG
XSeuzz:	likEE!!
Nindza:	Wow, awesome work.
MustoX:	nicee!!!!!! i like it
Kairu000:	This is amazing

Language use is simple—the aim seems to be to come up with colorful ways to indicate approval. This community construes feedback as *affirmation*, if the work warrants. Members have the means to solicit or deflect critiques of their work by posting stamps to their pages such as "Advanced Critique Desired," "Critique Me—I Don't Sue," and "Read Before You Write." These seem to be rarely used. Notably, deep within the DA website is an archive of members' posts that indicate at least a subset of the community that desires serious, critical feedback. An excerpt from Grekkikay's (2009) post on how to critique art:

> While I myself have no problems as far as favoriting instead of commenting is concerned, since a lot of deviants are like this, I thought it

> was right to tell people how to comment *correctly*. . . . These are simply guidelines for posting a comment that can *really* help in the long run as far as becoming a better critiquer and a better commenter in general. . . . *Short comments, such as "lol" or "that's awesome!" are generally not well-liked by the community.*

A few of the rules he elaborates are that commenters should back up their opinions and that these opinions should take a strong position. One should also keep in mind that the artist has feelings, "but don't let them get in the way of expressing your opinion." If the artist takes offense, but you have been nice, it's not your fault. "Artists need to learn that they won't always get their butts patted." Also, give some compliments, but be consistent in your comments.

Grekkikay (2009) also differentiates the worthiness of types of work to receive specific genres of comments, which he categorizes as true, serious, funny, or role-play commentary. In his view, the type of comment should be tied to the degree of seriousness of the artist in making the work. Artwork that is "drawn just plainly out of boredom or [that] has no significant meaning" should expect commentary that mirrors "what you truly think—you may act as silly or as serious as you want." If an artwork seems to want to be taken seriously (based on its subject matter or "deep, symbolic meaning"), it should get a serious commentary—no joking allowed. Serious commentary "is usually structured by using long, elaborate sentences, with near perfect grammar." Funny comments are to be given to joke artwork, and these comments "usually disregard grammar" because, "trust me, it's easy to tell whether or not this commentary has as much effort put into it as serious commentary."

Other posters on how to critique offer their own interpretations. Netnessie, for example, contributed "Critique Is Dead" (September 21, 2006) to argue that critique itself is dead on DA because of the quality or lack of constructive feedback. She explains, in extensive detail, why this will be the demise of the community. The post itself received 541 comments, the most recent in October 2013. Within the DA community there appears to be at least two different concepts of giving feedback: (a) affirmation and exclaiming one's opinion in simple, often colorful, phrases is the norm and (b) it is a community with an unconsummated desire for substantive critique.

Exhibit 3: WetCanvas.com

WetCanvas is a smaller community, founded in 1998, "in an effort to better leverage technology to assist visual artists in sharing information and making new contacts and friends." The community hosts over 3 million web pages per month, with over 500,000 unique visitors. Comments on WC tend to give more substantive feedback than is offered on DeviantArt. The community's conventions for how artists post their work may inspire more serious commenting. Artists are expected to post, with the artwork, a short statement of information and to pose one or more questions that they hope commenters will address. Also, critique is given a dedicated channel or forum on WC that is easy to find via a dropdown menu on the home page (under "Content Areas"). The Critique Center clearly has a learning focus; it features an archive of past critiques in what is called the Learning Gallery. Here artists can learn from past professional critiques of anonymously posted artwork. There is a separate forum for User Critiques, where artists may post their work to either the public or structured critique subforums. Both forums prominently display links to their rules for participating. One set of directions states, "Please think about your comments carefully prior to posting and please try to be analytical in your critique." Critiques should address the following:

- How can this piece be improved upon?
- What could others learn from the piece?
- What was done well?
- What needs more work?
- Could even more be done?
- What could be done about it?
- Before hitting that "submit" button . . . reflect on what the submitting artist and others will *learn* from your post.

WC also provides "positive and negative critique" checklists. Positive feedback would address elements such as focus or impact area, mood, creativity, composition, counterpoint, and flow. Negative feedback would focus on problems such as technical inaccuracy, lack of imagination, content discrepancy, style discrepancy, and lack of interpretation. The general advice is to "try to think of yourself as being hired by the artist as a mentor or teacher, or perhaps a defense attorney, whose job is to make your client's work look its best in court (even if it is hideous)." These directives and the site's organization appear to minimize the popularity focus that pervades commenting on DeviantArt.

The following is an example critique thread posted on WetCanvas. Along with a brief description, the artist posed two specific questions for the group to address:

1. There is not much color in the painting. Did I keep it too simple?
2. What do you think of the shadow of the pole (on the street)? I painted this to give the street an extra accent. The same applies for the small box in the right side wall at the left side.

The first comment focused on composition issues:

> I am not sure about the pole shadow, the dark against the light of the road tends to be seen as a drop or chasm. There needs to be an additional reference to ground the road. The shadow is quite odd.

The second commenter also focused on composition details and color:

> In my opinion, I definitely think it could use more detail and colour. . . . I would definitely add the lanterns on the gate doorway and the tiles on the roof as well as some detail hint of the iron detail on top of the wall. . . . I guess you are trying for an abstract of the scene . . . but if you ask about colour and shadow etc, then I think there could definitely be a little more of both to give the work some perspective and solidity. . . . Thank you for sharing your work, the scene is an interesting mixture and not an easy one!!!

The following two commenters merely agreed with the second:

> Arthur, I concur with Debz. She is right on in everything that she said. Good luck to you and hope you work on this one"
>
> ----------
>
> What Debz said.

The next person suggested a rethinking of the painting's conceptual approach and offered ideas on how to go about it:

> If you were to leave the painting in this stage, would you be interested in turning it into an abstract piece? I saw a video on youtube yesterday about how to melt crayon (that's been fixed to a drawing) with a blow dryer. . . . Shoot, you could even go over this drawing with impressionistic stabs with the brush.

Although the above comments provide detailed feedback, the thinking does not go above levels 1 and 2 of Bloom's taxonomy. The focus on technique and representational content reflects a community primarily dedicated to sharing "how to" information and offering suggestions to improve the aesthetics of a specific artwork. What is not evident are complex phrasings or conversations that take on conceptual issues or that encourage playful exploration.

CRITIQUE PRACTICES AND CULTURES OF LEARNING

DeviantArt and WetCanvas are not formal learning sites—there is no teacher or grades. Yet, the number of posts on how to critique or comment on art suggests a desire to learn and develop, even as this desire may be unfulfilled. Critiques on WC tend to offer constructive feedback based on the viewer's personal opinions about whether the artist has captured the facts and displays sufficient technical or aesthetic skill. Comments posted to artists on DeviantArt rely on adjectives to express appreciation of the work. Crits at

SVA encompass much of the above but forefront conceptual and reflexive feedback.

The SVA, DA, and WC communities engage with critique in different ways and thus support different types of learning, evident in their levels of complexity of discourse or thinking. As practiced, commenting on DA is constrained only by the commenting interface. The community largely ignores members' posts on how to critique. This may in part be due to the fact that the "how to critique" posts are buried deep in the site (I found them using the search function; DeviantArt, 2013). The dominant commenting culture is affirmation, expressed in simple, if emotive, language. WetCanvas runs within a similar commenting interface but is more attentive to enforcing its parameters for critique. It does this in part by directing artists to state up front what they would like addressed in comments. The WC community has coalesced around a shared interest in sharing knowledge around technique, media, and accuracy of representation. There is no mentor pushing the artists to higher levels of thinking. Critique in DeFrank's classes is more complex in terms of the thinking expected and the mentoring that pushes students to continually think more deeply and creatively, developing students' capacities to think evaluatively, reflexively, and generatively. In a crit at SVA, artists are pushed beyond what they currently know and believe, whereas feedback on DA and WC, to different degrees, reflects to what is already known and believed.

Cultural, rather than technological, differences are reflected in community differences regarding how critique is understood and practiced. Crits on both DA and WC are, on the one hand, free form and, on the other hand, organized and mediated within the boundaries of social media commenting and liking conventions but as well by the culture of each community. Although both communities house "instructions" for how to comment, actual commenting practices are socially constructed in the everyday comments on each site.

Crit sessions in the art studio are substantively different from DA and WC, in their dialogic character, critical depth, and mentoring relationships. We evaluate, and learn to evaluate, within a community and culture, in a coevolution of culture and cognition. Creativity, as a form of cognition, is therefore also shaped within a culture (James, 1996; Ruff, 2010; Sawyer & DeZutter, 2009). Creative production is intertwined with higher-order thinking skills and failure is viewed necessary and as an opportunity to venture into the unknown through a mix of playful engagement and reflexive evaluation of the experience and its outcomes.

Evaluation of creative production within social media networks is fueled by a culture of participatory commenting and liking. On the surface, this portends new opportunities for sharing and learning. Yet there are significant constraints in opportunities for learning and developing higher-level thinking skills. While the art studio crit builds on a long tradition of rigorous evaluation and learning, digital evaluations made possible by new comment/like technologies have yet to reach a similar level of rigor. The traditional art studio class and an online artists' portfolio site may share a commitment to fostering creative production and critique, but while digital media have expanded opportunities for sharing work and giving or receiving comments, there is a large gap in opportunities for building the thinking skills essential to creative practice. Exponentially expanding the possibilities of both whom and how many people can weigh in on an artwork via digitally mediated social networks has spawned a watered-down notion of critique. Given the unconsummated desire of artists for more rigorous commenting, the traditional art studio crit is a good model of how structured yet flexible and dialogic evaluation supports and grows creative production and thinking.

Social media allows 24/7 learning, collaboration, and interaction, with no geographic or temporal boundaries. It has given us "any time any place learning" and "anytime-anywhere-anyone" commenting in the context of what Jenkins (2006) calls convergence or participatory culture. In this participatory culture,

> [p]articipants . . . are expected to interact with each other according to a new set of rules which none of us fully understands. Convergence does not occur through media appliances—however sophisticated they may become. Convergence occurs within the brains of individual consumers. Yet, each of us constructs our own personal mythology from bits and fragments of information we have extracted from the ongoing flow of media around us and transformed into resources through which we make sense of our everyday lives.
>
> (para. 3)

The ramification of a critique/commenting culture that settles for affirmation or opinions on technique is a digital divide that is not simply about access to technology, but instead, builds from popular sites that sideline opportunities to support creative, critical, evaluative, and generative thinking. The convergence culture both opens up and constrains opportunities for learning. As important as access to creative technologies and knowing how to use them effectively are scaffolds that promote learning the habits of mind that are essential to creative thinking. Robinson and colleagues on the NACCCE (1999) identify key thinking skills as being able to:

- observe and question and reimagine what is seen and "known" about the world
- approach failure as integral to process
- critically evaluate [and] mentor . . . and
- communicate ideas and concepts in multiple formats.

The studio art crit is a model that mentors participants in all four skills and both structural constraints and social interaction. The crit is a vehicle for learning and development and is rarely focused on consumption per se. Liking and commenting, as practiced on DeviantArt, requires no commitment, asks little of the commenter, and remains aloof from substantive content or meanings of the artwork; it reflects a consumption orientation to creative production that is well served by affirmations and popularity contests. WetCanvas comments are less driven by an affirmation culture, but the community has coalesced around feedback that develops technique rather than higher-order evaluative thinking skills. In contrast, the studio crit asks a lot of everyone: it is a participatory culture of creative and rigorous evaluation, where learning to think evaluatively is perhaps more important than what is produced. A creative production is the means to engage in critical, creative evaluative thinking.

Netnessie's (2007) deconstruction of the commenting culture on DA highlights perceived problems: "the system, not its members, has began [*sic*] dictating what its society deems as acceptable." Netnessie recognizes that the DA system itself does not dictate the social commenting trends on DA but instead, "the system is limiting the user, and this limitation is the cause of its problems." Specific structural limitations are the "favorite" function that allows the viewer to either favorite a piece or not, which sets in motion a popularity scale that has little to do with the quality of the work. What Netnessie calls the "bandwagon effect" has become significant in validating an artwork, more than any significant artistic knowledge in the community. In essence, a crowdsourced popularity simply produces more popularity, independent of any "expert" critique. Netnessie sums up the problems with critiques on DA as follows: (a) a lack of knowledge of "what art actually is," (b) "people do not write constructive criticisms," (c) "people are unable to write criticism and suggestions due to fear of backlash," and (d) "people do not provide feedback on feedback, and therefore prevent discussion and further understanding."

Netnessie's critique suggests that within these social media artist communities, gaining or constructing the popularity of an artist has taken precedence over giving serious, constructive feedback. But there is frustration and discontent because the community does not deliver on its promise as a space where artists come together to help each other develop. The desire, at least among the more serious artists, is for an informal learning community.

It is evident that artists themselves are struggling to create effective critical creative evaluation communities in online social networks. For both artists and people interested in higher-level learning, it is an open question as to whether the online crit might evolve to better serve the artists and become a model for supporting the building of generative and evaluative—as well as creative—thinking. This paper does not solve the problem, but I do hope it inspires a rationale to take up the challenge.

NOTE

1. Names of all School of Visual Arts students have been changed, as have screen names of WetCanvas and DeviantArt commenters.

REFERENCES

Armstrong, P. (2013). Bloom's taxonomy. Retrieved from http://cft.vanderbilt.edu/teaching-guides/pedagogical/blooms-taxonomy/

Bandura, A. (1971). *Social learning theory.* New York: General Learning Press.

DeviantArt. (2013). Search: how to critique. Retrieved from www.deviantart.com/?q=How+to+critique

Dickie, G. (1988). *Evaluating art.* Philadelphia: Temple University Press.

Erard, M. (2013, September 22). No comments. *New York Times.* Retrieved from www.nytimes.com/2013/09/22/magazine/no-comments.html

Grekkikay. (2009). Commenting on art correctly. Retrieved from grekkikay.deviantart.com/journal/Commenting-on-Art-Correctly-214210921

Gunawardena, C.N., Lowe, C.A., & Anderson, T. (1997). Analysis of a global online debate and the development of an interaction analysis model for examining social construction of knowledge in computer conferencing. *Journal Educational Computing Research, 17*(4), 397–431.

Hacking, I. (1999). *The social construction of what.* Cambridge, MA: Harvard University Press.

Hetland, L., Winner, E., Veenema, S., & Sheridan, K.M. (2007). *Studio thinking: The real benefits of visual arts education.* New York: Teachers College Press.

James, P. (1996). The construction of learning and teaching in a sculpture studio class. *Studies in Art Education: A Journal of Issues and Research, 37*(3), 145–159.

Jaworski, K. (2014). New research shows digital divide still persists in the U.S. *Nonprofit Quarterly.* Retrieved from https://nonprofitquarterly.org/index.php?option=com_content&view=article&id=17531:new-research-shows-digital-divide-still-persists-in-the-us&catid=155:nonprofit-newswire&Itemid=986

Jenkins, H. (2006). Welcome to convergence culture. Retrieved from http://henryjenkins.org/2006/06/welcome_to_convergence_culture.html

NACCCE [National Advisory Committee on Creative and Cultural Education]. (1999). *All our futures: Creativity, culture and education.* Retrieved from http://sirkenrobinson.com/pdf/allourfutures.pdf

Netnessie. (2007). Critique is dead. Retrieved from www.deviantart.com/art/CRITIQUE-IS-DEAD-40196363

Ruff, J. (2010). Collaboration, critique and classroom culture. *UnBoxed*, issue 6. Retrieved from www.hightechhigh.org/unboxed/issue6/collaboration

Sawyer, R.K., & DeZutter, S. (2009). Distributed creativity: How collective creations emerge from collaboration. *Psychology of Aesthetics, Creativity, and the Arts, 3*(2), 81–92.

Soep, E. (2006). Critique: Assessment and the production of learning. *Teachers College Record, 108*(4), 748–777.

Stanford University. (n.d.). Assessment: FAQ. *Institutional Research & Decision Support (IR & DS).* Retrieved from www.stanford.edu/dept/pres-provost/irds/assessment/faq.html#FAQ6

Vigdor, L. (2010). *An intersectional reading of Gender & Technology* (Doctoral Dissertation). University of Illinois. Retrieved from www.ideals.illinois.edu/handle/2142/17049

Vygotsky, L.S. (1978). *Mind in society: The development of the higher psychological processes.* Cambridge, MA: Harvard University Press.

6 Evaluation and Self-evaluation on YouTube

Designing the Self in Makeup Tutorials

Ramon Reichert

INTRODUCTION

In liberal democratic societies, inspection procedures constitute a dominant form and practice of knowledge (Agamben, 1993; Andrejevic, 2011, pp. 278–87). Inspection procedures are widely recognized and usually referred to by the collective term "evaluation." Evaluation is believed to be the predominant vehicle to measure the impact of emancipation, democratization, and social equity. Vast areas of everyday and popular culture are surrounded by a variety of evaluation practices. In this context, not only has a new control instrument emerged, but new forms of managing oneself and others have arisen as well (Strathern, 2003). The term "evaluation" is on everyone's lips because it is aptly malleable and expansible, and it is colloquially used to mean something between "assessing" and "grading." The social media of Web 2.0 play an important role in the current boom of evaluation. In other words, the Internet has given birth to a communication culture of mutual and permanent evaluation, which takes hold of the entire social and cultural space and often adopts the form of entrepreneurial practices.

Everyday and popular culture is flooded, to a large extent, by a multitude of performance determination methods, verification procedures, diagnostic methods, and personality tests (Christensen, 2011, pp. 233–53). Evaluations, testing procedures, questionnaires, and statistics have become the norm on the Internet as well, where they influence how we think, perceive, work, remember, and communicate. Feedback systems, performance comparisons, quality rankings, monitoring, matching, benchmarking, statistical controls, flexible process control, self-awareness catalysts, satisfaction surveys—all of these systemic-cybernetic control functions and observatory connections of mutual assessment and judgment are functional elements of media technology in Web 2.0. Applications of postdisciplinary Web 2.0 technologies are based on a cybernetic model which presupposes the individual as a system that processes information and adapts as flexibly as possible to existing standards set by its environment as long as it continues to be "informed" by responses (feedback). The "informational control" of vast parts of society by means of search and analysis engines is a power mode of its own, which is based on the logic of self-organization, interconnectedness, and feedback, and it results in media-specific forms of subjectification. Instead of regulating individuals directly, which would bring about vast amounts of overhead, feedback loops are installed to signal to the individual when aberrations of the norm occur. In the field of online media, the "conduct of conduct," as identified by Michel Foucault (1991, p. 100) as the key formula for the exercise of power, takes the shape of control via feedback-driven self-control.

When an individual observes him/herself or others, continuous feedback creates a cycle of mutual observation on the basis of which adaptations are possible and interventions can be planned (cf. Causey, 2006). In this context, the individual is supposed to be able to perceive specific effects and, at the same time, the causes of these effects. This indicates a characteristic understanding of causality, i.e., a systemic-cybernetic observatory connection constituted by creating control cycles in the form of feedback loops, which can be used to regulate either oneself or others, depending on the direction the observation takes. Expanding systemic-cybernetic control functions in Web 2.0 raises issues concerning systems and models, regulation, circular causality, feedback, equilibrium, adaptation, and control. The required adaptations do not suggest to those controlled that they must achieve a certain ideal value. The control technology of "gentle adaptation" attempts to set an interminable dynamic of self-optimization in motion, which is supposed to be produced by the subject within the boundaries of his or her own individual initiative and self-responsibility.

Accordingly, a new kind of informationization dynamic related to self-practices begins to emerge against the backdrop of the global distribution of web-based applications and of administrative institutions strategically opening up to systems of open knowledge. Not unlike scientific evaluation, everyday evaluation presupposes the option of changing and controlling the behavior of the subjects involved. Response systems and feedback loops suggest that the subjects be shaped to a certain extent in order to become socially effective. Their technological scheme aims to assert knowledge on the level of everyday practices. Response systems will turn "general everyday perception" into "structural monitoring" used to systematically observe, score, judge, and successfully change a certain kind of behavior. Feedback systems can substantially help activate practices of evaluative self-observation. However, manifold codes of observatory knowledge based on "objectifying" and "neutralizing" knowledge technologies cannot belie the fact that every kind of knowledge has inherent social and normative concepts and is fundamentally dependent on political and economic contexts.

Individuals on the web are therefore subject to permanent mutual observation and grading. Social network sites involve a set of cybernetic practices, such as assessment, evaluation, supervision, coaching, monitoring, feedback systems, and matching or efficiency/effectiveness measuring. Control, regulation, and governance of the self have always formed a key approach in educational practice. With the rise of cybernetic processes of symbolic control and the bottom-up methods of evaluative feedbacks, complex, nonlinear processes are becoming central, which combine the contingency, openness, and interconnectedness of Web 2.0 media culture into powerful communities and variable systems. Against this backdrop, the "lifelong learning" of individuals and organizations, people and governments, enterprises and administrations, represents a kind of continuous feedback itself (Brockmeier, 2000, pp. 51–73; 2001, pp. 247–80).

Response systems place the learning subjects in flexibilized test situations, where they have to prove themselves as versatile, adaptable users. Referring to the makeup videos examined in this paper, this means that the producers of YouTube makeup videos understand themselves primarily as interconnected subjects who do not act autonomously and independently but who derive their social impact and the attention they receive via the medium from their own willingness to participate in social networking within online feedback systems.

The online feedback systems implemented on the web pick up on elements of *group dynamics* from psychotherapy, of *opinion polling,* and of *human resource management.* In the context of *group dynamics,* feedback acts as a response to a person concerning his or her behavior, serving to optimize his or her internal and external perception. The group-dynamic field consists of how people perceive themselves and how others perceive them, with these images being considered noncongruent. In order to make these processes clear and to practice them, and in order to improve internal and external perceptions, feedback is expressly used as an exercise in group-dynamic training. *Opinion polls* collect data and information at the behest of enterprises, political parties, and public institutions. Said data serve as a basis for marketing strategies, election platforms, and administrative as well as executive measures. In *human resource management,* feedback is also intended as a means of synchronizing the current condition with the desired condition when it comes to setting and achieving goals, or as a response measure following job interviews or tasks done on the job. Cases of application in human resource management include 360-degree feedbacks or 180-degree feedbacks for executives, as well as team feedbacks. Cases of application in quality management include customer feedbacks, but also seminar evaluations. In human resource management, feedback exclusively refers to oral or written response, while in industrial and organizational psychology, it covers more generally the nonverbal and unconscious aspects of communication, such as gestures and facial expressions.

Response systems and feedback loops also play an important role in the context of social generalization of control technologies, which legitimize informational practices in large parts of society. In this social framework, feedback generates widely branched social knowledge and is capable of normalizing even decentralized practices. Against this applicational backdrop, evaluative knowledge through observation has emerged as an essential means of control in information- and knowledge-based societies. Along these lines, self-reflection and creativity are considered crucial for achievement, and personal development has become an obligation for each and everybody. Extending control to one's own self, however, does not necessarily entail a gain in autonomy, because the subjects themselves are supposed to be controlled; this includes, for example, documenting one's own creative abilities and potentials via electronic portfolios and electronic diaries.

The entanglement of evaluation, power practices, and subjectification adds a historical angle to the genealogy of evaluation as a modern, scientifically systematized observation technology, because only through it does it become evident how extensively evaluation has always been included in more comprehensive scientific paradigms and general discursive formations and which transmogrifications evaluation knowledge has undergone. Accordingly, the historical approach clearly shows how evaluation has emerged as a comprehensive political technology. Against the backdrop of a discussion about human capital and educational economics, concepts which were developed during the 18th century, evaluative observatory knowledge has been increasingly refined and differentiated. Evaluation is not only some kind of scientific method for grading processes, but, being a historical form of knowledge, it involves a certain level of rationalization and disciplining. On the other hand, evaluation also plays a role in the context of the social generalization of control technologies, which allows control over large parts of society. The knowledge technique of evaluation in its institutionalized form can be traced back to the sociopolitical reform programs of the 1950s and 1960s in the United States. Reform programs underwent assessment in various fields, including education, health, food, and infrastructure. Evaluation is a form of intervening research initiated by governments, aimed at specifically controlling social change and thereby increasing the rationality of public administration. As neoliberal practices (e.g., New Public Management) emerged in society during the early 1990s, evaluation became an instrument of measuring performance and enhancing efficiency. In the 1920s and 1930s, scientific evaluative knowledge created important discursive threads in the milieu of Taylorism, i.e., Scientific Management, organizational theory, group research, test psychology, and Fordism. Evaluation has developed from being a political means used in its context of origin for assessing social programs in the field of educational practice into a mere tool of economization and standardization. It has penetrated deep into subjects' social practices, where it creates manifold impulses subjects can use to permanently evaluate themselves and to put themselves under self-observation. The discourse of evaluation has sparked reflective, observation-based knowledge about minuting, systematizing, and grading observations, reaching deep into the micro-levels of self-practices. The effects of evaluation as a technology of systematic, institutionalized, permanent (self-)observation include that through them, individuals initiate self-observation and self-monitoring practices and that the pressure is increased on individuals to act efficiently all the time. The label "evaluation" has now become synonymous with a systematic, data-based description and assessment of certain objects, persons, or actions. However, gathering "useful" knowledge on behalf of clients, participants, and relevant persons through the detailed and systematized collection of information does not result in profound insights, but it is mainly intended to suggest unambiguous knowledge and certainty in making decisions. Unfortunately, this evaluative knowledge is always infiltrated by normative concepts about efficient or inefficient categories, which, although they substantially influence the generation of said evaluative knowledge, are hardly addressed by the discourse on evaluation. Discussions on the status of evaluation-like procedures typically ignore the argument that the validity of standardized documentation tools is extremely low and that the objectivity of a majority of external evaluations is highly dubious. In this context, it would seem appropriate to assume that the hegemonic enforcement of evaluation as everyday control knowledge based on observation depends on its mergence into institutionalized forms of practice. Society increasingly views technocratic and bureaucratic planning rationality as normal and commonplace, which becomes apparent in various fields: self-evaluation techniques, individual curricula vitae, and employment and education biographies are not excluded from the overall evaluation wave. Furthermore, e-commerce business operates with "mass feedback technologies" (Beniger, 1986, p. 20), which establish their own data and information networks, including opinion polls, consumer research, and testing methods from the field of advertising psychology. In collaborative networks, evaluation presents itself as complex social knowledge based on observation of everyday practices.

User-generated content is increasingly expected to adapt to entrepreneurial practices in both technical and organizational terms. Feedback systems, like "ranking," simulate market transparency for open competition, as the videos on YouTube are globally and constantly ranked and statistically rated by means of informational graphics. The permanent feedback created by evaluation produces a cycle of control, turning general everyday perceptions into structural monitoring; computer-based inspection procedures provide offers of simplification as they present complex relationships employing knowledge techniques used in financial accounting (diagrams, tables, counters, etc.). This specific form of observation-based social knowledge suggests that the subjects' abilities invariably require improvement concerning their performance. In that sense, subjective observation-based knowledge is enhanced by being systematized in theoretical, media-related, and institutional terms, and it thereby becomes an important medium of rationalization. The term "medium" has a double meaning in this context, referring to a means of observation as well as a medium of knowledge—as is the case when knowledge appears in an electronic form as a formula, table, statistic, text, etc.

A scientific paradigm like evaluation knowledge implies a certain subjectification on the level of institutional or everyday practices in order to become historically effective. In New Public Management, speculations are already thriving that the economization of lifestyles has a rewarding and promotional effect on the development of human capital. At this interface of subject constitution, the internalization of the *managerial government* creates a normative framework, which places *self-evaluation,* the *feedback system, quality control,* and *performance comparison* in a mutual relationship. When programs and goals of performance and efficiency enhancement are designed, normative concepts are always included in order to stabilize hegemonic orders. Altogether, the normative order aims for its own naturalization, thereby ultimately suggesting a mundane normality of economic rationality, where values like "performance," "effectiveness," and "efficiency" appear to be "self-evident" and "casual" expressions of "normal" behavior. In this context, orders of knowledge and procedures of normalization find themselves in an interrelationship, not just empirically but also categorically. Knowledge is a prerequisite for the normalization of knowledge, which is in turn a prerequisite for the generation and development of knowledge. These interrelations of knowledge and evaluation clearly show that evaluative techniques are as such proactively involved in the construction of success, which is the sole basis for conclusions concerning performance. In their interminable dynamics, data processes are characteristic of the processes of subject constitution on the web. The events that are relevant for self-practices occur only in the aftermath of corresponding processing procedures, which make knowledge virtual by cultivating networks, lists, mean values, rankings, etc. Eventually, data-based knowledge processing makes the fields of practice of "amateurs" and "professionals" assimilate. In that sense, a new kind of job application culture seems to have emerged along with the socially powerful networking culture: one that generates new media forms of self-thematization and often adopts the shape of self-entrepreneurial behavior. In the following, we discuss three central processes of evaluation and self-evaluation on the online video platform YouTube in connection with the following social technologies of networking:

(1) The discussion of moving images on YouTube will center on what performative role the initiators of video uploads play. Social network sites, currently booming on the web, have produced a new regime of subjectification, with proactive self-optimizers as the ruling characters. They are expected to master the art of smart self-governance and to hold their ground even when facing the forces of flexibilization. They have to prove their permanent state of mobilization by their digital showcase portfolio (in our exemplary case, the YouTube channel for makeup tutorials), which they are expected to update regularly and maintain open for feedback. Against this background, what status do collective framing processes on online portals have when it comes to production of meaning, negotiation, and distribution of moving images?

(2) The tendency to resignify and reiterate existing content (mash-up, remix) points to an aspect of the performative closely connected to collective

and collaborative framing processes. Again, performative practice is mainly shown as something that creates an excess, which can no longer be attributed to any intersubjectively controllable field of discourse. In that sense, the productive power of the performative presents itself not simply by creating something but by dealing with what we have not created ourselves. Looked at that way, the performance can be understood as an excess of meaning that not only implements a new performative framing but, in retrospect, modifies existing content.

(3) Performative processes on the Internet are the result of technological enablement. Specifically, it is computer-assisted information and communication technologies that regulate the modes, the validity, and the distribution of content generated by users. As a consequence, web media and the technologically completed actions therein are essential parts of the production of meaning and significance and need to be included in the methodology of examining performative processes. This issue, in addition to having a heuristic meaning within the theoretical discursive practice, opens up critical questions beyond the dichotomy of technological determinism versus technological euphoria—questions concerning the scope of action of performative enablement in technological environments.

MAKEUP TUTORIALS ON YOUTUBE

The rise of the social media in Web 2.0 has thoroughly changed the status of moving images in the web. They have become a venue of open production of meaning and of permanent discussion. Moderated comment functions, hypertext, ranking, and voting systems via collective and collaborative framing processes map audiovisual content to multimedia and discursive environments (cf. van Dijck, 2007). With putting on makeup being a critical component of visual self-staging in the new subject-centered media, the genre of makeup tutorials has emerged as an exceptionally popular online video format that exerts substantial influence on its users' identity formation and participatory culture.

Makeup tutorials are designed for practical use and can therefore be considered "practical films." They are predominantly produced by female adolescents, feature themselves, and mainly impart knowledge based on personal experience in the fields of lifestyle and body skill, which provides show-how information in peer-to-peer networks as opposed to a manual or an encyclopedia. The core assertion is that makeup videos, rather than aiming to be perceived as a "creative work," operate as a means of "facilitation" of cultural and social negotiation processes based on tactically "weak" authorship. When makeup videos are thus understood to be "ensembles of discursive events" (Foucault, 1982, p. 231), this observation is oriented along the performativity of the medium, allowing a view that seeks to think of makeup videos as contributions to negotiation processes in two different respects. First, they appear as improvised knowledge, which explicitly demands rearrangement[1]: "This is my very first makeup video, so I hope you are not too harsh with me. Useful criticism and advice are most welcome" (Carpediem1201, October 29, 2009). Second, the different kinds of character registers in makeup videos make a point of stimulating the interactive potential of social network sites. A significant pattern of makeup tutorials is the creation of communicative proximity through the medium. This proximity, however, is complex and cannot always be found in the video image itself. Apart from the mise-en-scène, it is often a written comment that makes a crucial gesture by declaring the video as a work in progress made without any intention of being perfect: "This is all to say that this is more like a 'work in progress' kind of look" (Temptalia ad YouTube-Video Makeup Tutorial and Tips: Stream of Consciousness: www.youtube.com/watch?v=dhGSSbecXbQ). As far as the history of media discourses is concerned, the references to further reading that creators often attach to their makeup tutorials may well be understood as a continuation of the discussion on a paradigm shift of interactivity (intermedia, happening, fluxus) and on the "open work" (Eco, 1989), which has been intensely going on since the 1960s. In this context, structural homologies can be made between the efforts to question the subject of the author as a constitutive agent, the work as a completed entity, and the call for interaction and collaboration voiced in the social media of Web 2.0. Along these lines, when makeup tutorials become venues of cultural circulation and aesthetic conflicts, we are provided with the possibility not only to isolate them as a genre within the field of film and media studies, but also to address them as cultural and media-based practice employing a more capacious view (cf. Reichert, 2013).

ONLINE EVALUATION IN THE CLOSED CIRCUIT

While private space used to be defined as an actual space separated from the external world, in which individuals prepared for their public presentation of self (Goffman, 1959), makeup tutorials shift the conventional limits between private and public space. They turn the domestic sphere traditionally attributed to the female into a medialized venue of public contemplation and collective production of meaning. Although makeup tutorials have been associated with the female realm, both due to their protagonists and based on other discursive procedures, they have contributed to a shift in visual strategies of female representation. Female adolescents have adopted the means of production used in media recording, storage, and distribution in their makeup videos, thus decentering the privileges of male-dominated relations of production. The media frenzy over makeup videos on YouTube, therefore, represents a new practice of media usage and exploitation of media and self-images. YouTube makeup videos are a format that is integrated into a web culture of circulating representations, technologies, and practices. The media specifics of such online video formats demonstrate that the boundaries between production and reception are constantly shifted and that, as a consequence, deterministic subject positions are resolved. Makeup culture on YouTube is altogether aimed at eliminating the difference between production and reception, and it creates sentience toward an aesthetic that breaks with the conventions of perception established in cinema and television, where only low significance is granted to audience participation.

Moreover, expansion of subject positions begins no later than at the film set, which points to the specific media aesthetic of makeup tutorials. For example, recording makeup videos requires the assembly of a particular experimental setup and self-observation arrangement. As the adolescents, mostly girls, put on makeup by themselves while being "on camera," and as "uncut" material is perceived as particularly true-to-life and authentic within the community, the set design at the shooting location needs to be prepared and planned accordingly. The community has been displaying great demand for videos which operate with the codes of dialogue immediacy and live atmosphere: "People don't want editing and text inserts. They want me to be live and to talk," says CaroLaPrincesse on her YouTube channel (CaroLaPrincesse, September 21, 2012). The technical setup usually consists of a webcam attached to a desktop computer or a laptop. Often the protagonists will place their computer with its webcam in front of or next to a mirror in order to create an additional perspective of their own face. The women applying makeup multiply themselves in their role as observers. This unusual observatory arrangement is then discussed in the platforms as know-how: "It was mighty hard to put the makeup on in front of the webcam because it is back-to-front and I kept being overly confused!" (PODxLadyAga, July 30, 2010). Along with their videos, many makeup artists post comments that contain instructions, recommendations, and confessions, as well as self-doubts, insecurities, and questions. The purpose of placing questions is to establish a participatory platform and a fan community. Along these lines, participatory contextualization of the videos can be understood as an attempt to secure audience appreciation for an extended period of time. Next to the makeup mirror, the protagonists usually see their own image on the computer screen as simultaneously relayed by the webcam, allowing them to monitor and optionally change, pause, or terminate the video recording. Instant availability of images has always been a special characteristic of video. Makeup tutorials take advantage of this technology by creating situational settings in which the spectators involve themselves in the representative situation. The most basic observatory arrangement in makeup videos thus follows the principle of the closed circuit.

The closed-circuit arrangement describes a recording method in which the "recording medium" is directly connected to the "displaying medium." In the closed-circuit observatory arrangement, spectators experience the synchronicity of their actions, and they align them with the digital image—not unlike in the mirror, but not back-to-front as before. The spectators find themselves inside a reality expanded by the medium. This expansion allows for these made-up girls and women to experience themselves no longer within a temporary situation they perceive as the present but in a time-lagged rendition that has more of a retrospective or documentary nature. In this context, the video image is used in the role of a mirror as well as in that of a monitoring device. However, as opposed to the image in the makeup mirror, the video image is dependent on the position of the recording camera, not on its own position in relation to what it depicts. Many producers of makeup videos use the video image transmitted from the webcam to the monitor to simulate the direct gaze into the camera, thereby maintaining immediate communication with the audience. While the observatory arrangement of the closed circuit is used for self-perception mediated by the camera, it also fulfills the film-aesthetic purpose of addressing the community directly. All makeup accessories need to be prepared at the film set before the actual recording. Hence there has to be some kind of screenplay that defines which objects will be used in which sequence and in what order the various procedures will take place. The set design at the makeup table can be simple, but it can also be a very complex installation, and it includes a multivariant repertory which may comprise attaching eyelashes, dying hair, applying nail polish, or creating entire looks for one's face. The medialization of the self during the application of makeup follows specific patterns of staging and is based on different techniques and routines. It requires an interplay of circumstances (such as the availability of consumer hardware), options (such as the combinatorics of styles), and coincidences (such as slips of the tongue during recording). In this sense, makeup videos do not need the prerequisite of a genuinely "constitutive subject" to confer deeper meaning to what is shown, as this is always also determined by the historical and social limitations of the medium. Accordingly, the proximity evoked in the makeup videos is no longer the underlying construct but one created by the medium that emerges from certain conventions of perception without being ultimately determined itself.

AESTHETICS OF AUTHENTICITY

The makeup videos of Lauren Luke, a 27-year-old single mother from Newcastle, England, have been watched by more than one hundred million viewers all over the world. On July 22, 2007, she uploaded her first recordings on YouTube, filmed in her pink-colored bedroom. One of her three dogs can be seen in the background; she used her bedside lamp as an illumination device. Before long, thousands of users clicked on her tutorials, leaving enthusiastic comments. Luke owes her popularity to the low-tech aesthetic that is typical of the online video portal YouTube: her videos represent improvisation, spontaneity, and absence of perfection. Most of the videos are uncut, coarse-grained, and without any intentional dramatic composition. Luke incarnates the bottom-up role model of uncensored and self-sufficient video production. In her makeup videos, she initially steps in front of the camera without wearing make-up—just like any other woman who would stand in front of her mirror in the morning. This process wins her credibility both on a diegetic and on an extradiegetic level. On a diegetic level, she makes transformation into a desirable woman plausible, while on an extradiegetic level, she neatly places authenticity narratives for her product line. Her makeup tutorials on YouTube have vaulted Luke to fame, and she is now worshipped as a YouTube celebrity. As of today, she sells her own beauty-care line on her personal website, has a regular column in *The Guardian*'s weekend supplement, and has recently published a best-selling book entitled *Lauren Luke Looks: 25 Celebrity and Everyday Makeup Tutorials*.

Despite tendencies toward professionalization, authenticity is still regarded by YouTubers as one of the core features for generating attention. In this context of practical instrumentalization, specific markers of authenticity are used to construct visual self-evidence. "Self-evidence" in this context refers to what appears to be undeniable, what is supposed to be obvious upon immediate conception. Authenticity markers are needed not only to increase the voyeuristic appeal but mainly to spark community building and community branding on self-governed YouTube channels. Various kinds of authenticity markers are employed on YouTube to verify certain contents. They include a low-tech style of documentation, a private recording situation, the absence of a photo studio, and the use of commercial consumer hardware. Altogether, the purpose of these video images is to create a casual visuality aiming at amateuristic immediacy. By returning to aesthetic processes that were used in the period of early cinema around 1900, makeup tutorials attempt to enable the viewer to focus on the aesthetic features of the movement in front of the camera (for the analysis of narrative practices, cf. Elsaesser, 2009, p. 155ff.). In order to make the self-evidence plausible, makeup tutorials are filmed in a single take and do not use editing or montage. They operate with a tripod camera, which produces stationary takes. The takes that show the actual makeup scenes are therefore filmed in a single-shot process that entails a motionless background and rigid framing. Within the stationary frame, the actual process of putting on makeup takes place. In the style of the methods used in early cinema, makeup tutorials use the absence of montage and camera movement for the aestheticization of the female realm of experience, for which the framing adopts the role of a window on the world. At the "time of the stationary camera," Gilles Deleuze (1986) wrote about the "movement image" in his book on cinema, "in the first place, the frame is defined by a unique and frontal point of view which is that of the spectator on an invariable set" (p. 24). By returning to the time of the stationary camera and showing only one angle of the room, the tutorial reinstates characters and things as the moving factor: "Movement is therefore not extracted for itself and remains attached to elements, characters and things which serve as its moving body or vehicle" (p. 24). In eschewing staging techniques of approaching and retracting (zoom) or camera movements (panning, tracking), the protagonist bears the responsibility of embodying all forms of movement and making sure she holds the makeup accessories in the camera frame. This revaluation of the field of view recorded in real time is aesthetically intended and suggests that it is life itself that inscribes itself in the medium.

Rebating movement to the protagonist in front of the camera is an approach to revaluate the camera aesthetic in favor of realistic impression, which pushes the stationary takes closer to the tradition of photography. Other methods of authenticity creation include contextualization in writing: using titles, tags, and comments, the filmmakers try to expose the intention of their makeup tutorials and to steer how their videos are perceived. In tactically diminishing the status of their authorship, they try to direct negotiation processes to the video, thus gaining attention. This tactical maneuver of self-criticism as evidence of proximity has won the video titled *My First Makeup Tutorial* more than 6,000 clicks on YouTube and sparked a culture of conspiratory amateur practices that has a fundamentally positive attitude toward improvised, low-tech formats. In her fashion blog *Kosmetik & Beauty Blog. Alles rund ums Thema Beauty, Make-Up und Kosmetik* [Cosmetics and beauty blog: You will learn everything you need about beauty, make-up and cosmetics], the author explicitly confesses to a low-tech aesthetic:

> We "make-up girls" on YouTube do our best for our videos by contemplating technical issues and providing a pleasant atmosphere and lighting in our videos. Of course, those who have 1000–2000 euros worth of camera equipment and 500 euros worth of software did better jobs. But is that something you should be allowed to expect when it says "Broadcast yourself"? Weren't wiggly webcam images, background noises and time lag once what YouTube was all about? Should you be allowed to bash private channel owners for poor technical equipment?
>
> (Cuddlecow, June 24, 2011)

The lion's share of online self-presentation points to the improvised character of these videos and stages proximity as a collective and collaborative communication process, as user Gabrielbur notes: "I know it's not perfect and I know I'm not a makeup pro but I hope you still have fun watching and if you have any comments or suggestions just post them below" (Gabrielbur, February 21, 2013). Numerous self-descriptions make clear that the recipients of the tutorials are friends and acquaintances from the existing social environment of the video producers. Adding to her tutorial *Schmink Tutorial für Amy xD*, user PODx-LadyAga writes, "I just made this video quickly for Amy to show her how to apply eyeliner or at least how I apply it! I am not doing this professionally & don't plan to. Just wanted to show that we in the POD community really help each other out—with EVERYTHING!" (PODxLadyAga, July 30, 2010). While the makeup video appears as a temporary snapshot of performative and discursive procedures, it always remains integrated in hegemonic cultures of imaging and seeing and in media canon formations. In a genre context, it (1) exhibits a plurality of reference images and (2) draws on conventions of mediation in terms of form and content that cinema and television also use. Although the makeup styles of many tutorials are oriented along the media images of female stars and although attention is drawn to the female in the context of film and television, these videos reveal a great number of processes that undermine the idea of womanhood as an object of visual inspection. Makeup videos form a genre of domestic orientation that shows a realm of experience involving everyday female activities. However, this stereotype image of the woman contained in the domestic realm is disrupted on the level of filming and staging, as the entire field of view is connoted by the female protagonist's frontal gaze into the camera and is used as a realm of experience of female subjectivity by manifold modes of addressing. The strategies of frontally gazing into the camera, of making the camera visible during recording, and of discursively addressing the medium and the setup disrupt the assumptions of the closely filmed woman (particularly in close-ups) being per se captured in the ideological trap of narcissism. As Mary Ann Doane (1982) states in connection with the film image for the female spectator, "There is a certain overpresence of the image—she is the image. Given the closeness of this relationship, the female spectator's desire can be described only in terms of a kind of narcissism—the female look demands a becoming" (p. 76).

In the observatory arrangement of makeup tutorials, this imaginary abundance of self-presence does not exist, as the represented woman incessantly oscillates between "presentation" (personal appearance on camera), "observation" (viewing the image on the monitor), and "self-thematization" (commenting on her own actions). The efficiency of these acts of adjustment allow her to create distance "within the image"; they create an "uncertainty" in the female nature represented. Even the fact that she uses gestures, mimicry, and speech to address the viewer does not grant the protagonist a stable position of power, as these audiovisual strategies are themselves subject to the continuing process of dialogic conflict and negotiations on a level of representation. Accordingly, putting on makeup as a collectively shared and negotiated experience in the social media is never a neutral but always a "situated" practice, which references various kinds of viewpoints and interests.

FROM SELF-ADDRESS TO SUBJECTIFICATION

Prima facie, makeup tutorials transfer nothing but practical knowledge that aids in providing one's physical appearance with more expression. In a broader context, however, makeup tutorials develop a depth effect that generates individual and collective identities and extends to life and the body. In targeting the transformation of behavior and lifestyles, makeup videos can be understood as a power technique by which attention is drawn to vital values, like physical beauty and fitness, as social assets. In that sense, makeup tutorials appear not only as a means of individual instruction but also as a form of media, which aims at the practical manipulation of subjects at the interface of physical practices and media techniques. The predominant share and biggest content-based category of the clips uploaded on YouTube has been termed "ego clips" by Birgit Richard; this type of clip exposes "excessive narcissistic self-representation," in which a "broad range from shy chatting up to visual prostitution is observed" (Richard, 2008, p. 227). This is a mainstream format identified through the characteristic appearance of YouTube. The dominant position of ego clips on the YouTube attention market has resulted from the fact that the social media's personalized communication styles are predominant in Web 2.0. In that sense, makeup tutorials can be attributed to the popular genre of ego clips: the close shot, the protagonist's bust portrait, and her frontal gaze into the camera are typical features of makeup tutorials. These stylistic devices of direct address encapsulate the visual strategies of makeup videos and help them generate identification, empathy, and sympathy. Almost every single makeup tutorial employs the stylistic device of direct address as well as a number of conventions of representation used by the declared self to present herself as highly authentic in discursive rituals of genuine spontaneity and informality. According to Michel Foucault (1978), the confession, i.e., the "institutional incitement to speak" (p. 18), is "one of the West's most highly valued techniques for producing truth" (p. 59). The specific connections among power, truth, and subjectification is, thus, no longer the result of repression or suppression but is, instead, based on an increasingly intense discursive formation. In a piece of "independent" and "self-governed" makeup advice, commitment to one particular makeup style comes across as more "impetuous" and "genuine" the more amateurishly it seems to be confessed by the subjects involved. Self-address in this context refers to self-referentiality communicated by means of language, gesture, or facial expression, which constitutively retroacts on its utterer. While the self-address is obviously addressed at the addressing self, it also opens up a second channel of address targeted to an imaginary audience and enables possibility spaces for future spectators. Conventional forms of self-address include, for example, partial self-criticism or signals of irony, and these serve to diminish the narcissistic gesture of self-representation. This willingness to take criticism and these demonstrative maneuvers aim at establishing conspiratory proximity. In that sense, makeup videos are presented not so much as finished pieces of work but rather as improvised drafts. This strategy of diminution and relativization of one's own position in drafting oneself is highly popular among the various communities because it invites other users to participate. The various forms of explicit self-address thus serve to diminish the subject's own position and, as an approach, to attach participatory commitment to the video. This technique of self-thematization has been found to be a very successful strategy to attract attention within the social media of Web 2.0. On the other hand, tutorials also adopt certain formats and genre categories in order to increase their own distinguishability. The makeup tutorial's proximity to television formats is most aptly demonstrated based on its serialized structures and forms of narration. In order to promote viewers' interest and identification and in order to encourage them to collect serial information that they are able to apply to subsequent episodes, makeup videos are divided into successive episodes that are archived on distinct YouTube channels. Viewers can also subscribe to these channels, which additionally enhances their commitment. The serialized and chronological structure of the videos within the YouTube channels suggests the promise that the female fans can personally participate in the latest makeup tips and provides for a certain continuity in the makeup stories all featuring the same character (who is established as a "friend") within the same spaces of action (the same old bedroom backdrop).

In the meantime, a genealogy of makeup tutorials has emerged in the Web 2.0 blogosphere and in secondary media coverage (print media, television, radio), trying to establish traditional discourses of authorship, originality, and definition as creative works. These personalized discourses characterize the level of representation, as well as the level of perception, and are substantially responsible for the emergence of so-called YouTube celebrities and star icons within the realm of online makeup videos, who are simultaneously attributed business stereotypes, like that of a "business woman" who knows how to successfully sell her videos (for business discourses on YouTube, see Burgess & Green, 2009, pp. 89–107). Such hegemonic discourses about so-called YouTube phenomena reveal that the status of the video on the Internet can no longer be explored via its film aesthetics. The central role of the filmic text is replaced by an open and nonlinear heteromediality, which inscribes the video images in volatile and unstable networks of meaning. The status of makeup tutorials in negotiating gender attributes and female capacity to act, therefore, becomes apparent not only on the level of "representation" (which would suggest analysis in the context of film theory) but also in how productions of meaning of womanhood are constructed during the circulation of videos via feedback, explicit recommendation, and hyperlinks. These female productions of meaning are essentially responsible for the status a particular video has within these contexts of reception. Through their online format, makeup tutorials are subject to a permanent, nonlinear, and heterogenic culture of perception. In that sense, the perceptive context of the videos is constantly changing and remains open and incomplete. The significance of makeup tutorials for the construction of female subjectivity is made up of a multifaceted mesh of historically specific and culturally heterogenic discourses and practices. Hence, the producers and consumers of makeup videos are basically engaged in the open and incomplete exchange of mutual and reciprocal constitution. Within their mutual relationship, they can be captured, shaped, and controlled by a number of external techniques, but they are also able to evade this institutional access and to invent new forms, emotions, and intensities. The subject constitution engaged in using the makeup videos oscillates between a weak subject position addressing oneself and a relational dynamic of subjectification. Self-address weakens the authoring subject and thus fosters participatory recognition. Even though, in a way, makeup tutorials reinforce existing conventions of representation and perception, which contribute to the cultural and medium-based construction of individual and collective identities (Hilderbrand, 2007, pp. 48–57), they also always allow the involved subjects margins of diverging productions of meaning (a view shared by Hoskins, 2009, pp. 15–17). As a consequence, the presentational character of makeup videos needs to be broadened. Makeup videos are not only a stage for self-presentation, but they are also a place of "productive feedback loops" between production and reception. In that sense, makeup videos, in their state of matter of differing negotiation processes and participatory possibilities, remain ambiguous, ephemeral, and disputed.

NOTE

1. Some of the quotes from comments on YouTube posts have been translated from German.

REFERENCES

Agamben, G. (1993). *The coming community,* Minneapolis: University of Minnesota Press.

Andrejevic, M. (2011). Surveillance and alienation in the online economy. *Surveillance & Society, 8*(3), 278–287.

Beniger, J. R. (1986). *The control revolution.* Cambridge, MA: Harvard University Press.

Brockmeier, J. (2000). Autobiographical time. *Narrative Inquiry, 10*(1), 51–73.

Brockmeier, J. (2001). From the end to the beginning. Retrospective teleology in autobiography. In D. Carbaugh (Ed.), *Narrative and identity. Studies in autobiography, self and culture* (pp. 247–280). Amsterdam /Philadelphia: Benjamins Publishing.

Burgess, J., & Green, J. (2009). The entrepreneurial vlogger: Participatory culture beyond the professional-amateur divide. In P. Snickars & P. Vonderau (Eds.), *The YouTube reader* (pp. 89–107). Stockholm: National Library of Sweden.

Causey, M. (2006). *Theatre and performance in digital culture: From simulation to embeddedness.* London/New York: Routledge.

Christensen, C. (2011). Discourses of technology and liberation: State aid to net activists in an era of 'Twitter revolutions.' *The Communication Review, 14*(1), 233–253.

Deleuze, G. (1986). *Cinema 1: The movement-image,* Minneapolis: University of Minnesota Press.

Doane, M. A. (1982). Film and the masquerade: Theorising the female spectator. *Screen, 23*(3–4), 74–88.
Eco, U. (1989). *The open work*. Cambridge, MA: Harvard University Press.
Elsaesser, T. (2009). Tales of epiphany and entropy: Paranarrative worlds on YouTube. In W. Buckland (Ed.), *Film theory and contemporary Hollywood movies* (pp. 155–166). London: Taylor & Francis.
Foucault, M. (1978). *The history of sexuality. Volume 1: An introduction*. New York: Vintage Books.
Foucault, M. (1982). *The archaeology of knowledge and the discourse on language*. New York: Pantheon.
Foucault, M. (1991). Governmentality. In G. Burchell, C. Gordon, & P. Miller (Eds.), *The Foucault effect: Studies in governmentality* (pp. 87–104). Hemel Hempstead, UK: Harvester Wheatsheaf.
Goffman, E. (1959). *The presentation of self in everyday life*. Garden City, NY: Anchor.
Hilderbrand, L. (2007). Youtube: Where cultural memory and copyright converge. *Film Quarterly*, *61*(1), 48–57.
Hoskins, D. (2009). "Do you YouTube?" Using online video in women's studies courses. *Feminist Collections, 30*(2), 15–17.
Reichert, R. (2013). Social media storytelling. In B. Kracke & M. Ries (Eds.), *Expanded narration* (pp. 341–358). Bielefeld: transcript.
Richard, B. (2008). Art 2.0: Kunst aus der YouTube! Bildguerilla und Medienmeister. In B. Richard & A. Ruhl (Eds.), *Konsumguerilla. Widerstand gegen Massenkultur?* [Hacking consumerism: Resistance against mass culture?] (pp. 225–246). Frankfurt/Main: Campus.
Strathern, M. (2000). *Audit cultures: Anthropological studies in accountability, ethics and the academy*. London: Routledge.
van Dijck, J. (2007). *Mediated memories in the digital age*. Stanford, CA: Stanford University Press.

7 No Learning, No Spec

Spec Work Competitions and the Spec Movement

Helen Kennedy

INTRODUCTION

The amateur cultural production that networked digital environments make possible has been greeted with a spectacular amount of celebratory rhetoric, in both popular and academic writing (Benkler, 2006; Bruns, 2008; Leadbetter, 2008; Shirky, 2008). Despite some criticisms of amateur participation in cultural economies—because it results in inferior quality productions compared with the fruits of professional labor (Keen, 2008), because participatory, amateur cultures are not really participatory (van Dijck, 2009), or because new opportunities for profit-making and control result from the extraction of data from amateur content (Andrejevic, 2011; Hearn, 2010)—optimistic, celebratory discourses of the amateur prevail. This paper counterbalances the dominant celebratory discourse surrounding amateur cultural production by focusing on some of its more negative consequences. Specifically, it concentrates on spec work competitions and the anti-spec movement within the field of design.

Spec work, short for speculative work, involves people producing goods, usually cultural goods, without a guarantee of getting paid. For some designers, the most troublesome manifestation of spec work is the spec work competition, which brings amateur and professional designers together in competition with each other for payment for a design job which all of them undertake. Spec work competitions mobilize a process which is becoming increasingly central to amateur cultural economies, crowdsourcing, or the outsourcing of tasks historically carried out by paid employees to the crowd.

Crowdsourced speculative work competitions are criticized by anti-spec design professionals for a number of reasons. These include: they devalue design; they offer unfair compensation; they can result in problematic lawsuits; they employ minors; and they lead to a host of unethical practices, by clients, competition hosts, and designers. Instead of participating in speculative work competitions, therefore, critics propose pro bono work as a more ethical—and educational—alternative. In this paper, I argue that such responses to spec work are not simply the panicked reactions of a profession under threat of invasion by amateur troops, as is implied in some academic commentary. Rather, critical responses to spec work need to be understood in relation to the professional ethics of designers, which they feel are thrown into question by this particular amateur economy. Concern with what constitutes a good design learning experience forms an integral part of designers' professional ethics, as I highlight below.

The paper, therefore, makes a number of contributions. As well as countering celebrations of amateur cultural production, it highlights the role played by ethics and values in professional creative labor, building on other discussions of ethics and cultural work, by Banks (2006, 2007), Hesmondhalgh and Baker (2010), and Kennedy (2012), among others. At the same time, it exposes the tensions that arise when professionals and amateurs, paid and unpaid workers, are brought together. It also proposes that spec work competitions should be seen not as offering informal learning opportunities, as is proposed by their advocates, but rather as yet another example of the increasingly precarious conditions of creative work, which have been well documented (for example by Ross [2003], McRobbie [2002], and Oakley [2007]). Finally, the paper contributes empirical research with professional media producers about the impact of amateur activity (specifically, spec work) on their work, which to date has been somewhat lacking.

The paper proceeds to map out the rise of amateur cultural production, with particular attention to the networked environments which facilitate crowdsourced activities like spec work competitions. I then go on to describe spec work initiatives, before discussing critical responses to them from within the design professions. I draw on online material from anti-spec campaigns such as NO!SPEC (www.no-spec.com), AntiSpec (http://antispec.com), and SpecWatch (www.specwatch.info), as well as dialogues with people working in the anti-spec movement.

THE RISE OF AMATEUR CULTURAL PRODUCTION

The term "amateur" is used to describe a person who engages in particular pursuits without pay or formal training, but rather because of a passionate interest in, or love of, the pursuit—the word does, after all, derive from the French *amateur*, or "lover of." The recent rise of the culture-producing amateur is generally associated with the birth of Web 2.0 and the possibilities for participation that related technologies opened up. Benkler's *The Wealth of Networks: How Social Production Transforms Markets and Freedom* (2006) and Bruns's *Blogs, Wikipedia, Second Life and Beyond: From Production to Produsage* (2008) are two well-known commentaries on the rise of amateur cultural production in networked, Web 2.0 environments. In his book, Benkler (2006) celebrates the new technical, economic, social, and institutional relations that result from the networked information economy, which lead to radically decentralized nonmarket production and "increased practical individual autonomy" (p. 256) and create a production space for the amateur to occupy. He claims that "in the networked information environment, everyone is free to observe, report, question, and debate, not only in principle, but in actual capability" (p. 272). Benkler presents a detailed and convincing list of examples of amateur production activities which back up his claim, including: content generation systems like Wikipedia; relevance, accreditation, and tagging systems; Project Gutenberg, an archive of free electronic books; projects based on shared processing and storage capacity, like SETI@home; peer-to-peer networks like BitTorrent and Kazaa. This impressive list would seem to testify to the growing value of amateur involvement in cultural production.

Like Benkler, Bruns highlights the ways in which the particular characteristics of Web 2.0, such as its information-pull techniques, widely available tools of production and distribution, and easily shareable and modifiable content, lead to the inevitable emergence of an already-more-active user. Using the web, writes Bruns (2008), implies "active expression and communication of views, values, beliefs, ideas, knowledge and creativity" (p. 15)—produsage rather than usage. Because of this, the production value chain is transformed. There are no longer producers and consumers, or professionals and amateurs, but rather participants, sometimes using, sometimes producing—producers amongst whom all is equal: "Producers and users of media content are both simply nodes in a neutral network and communicate with each other on an equal level" (p. 14). The rise of the producer robs the cultural industries of "their position at the privileged end of the production value chain"; they are reduced "to the level of all other participants in the networks" (p. 30).

For Bruns, crowdsourcing is one positive example of the commercial embrace of produsage and of firms responding well to these challenges. In the few years that have passed since Bruns published his book, the crowdsourcing of different forms of technical, creative, and cultural labor has become well established. Examples include Amazon Mechanical Turk (Amazon, 2012), a service which allows companies to post, known as Human Intelligence Tasks, or HITs, and individuals to complete these tasks for a financial reward determined by the task-setting company. Twitter's bird logo was famously crowdsourced for only $6 through iStockphoto (van Buskirk, 2009), as were translations of aspects of Facebook and LinkedIn. Other forms of labor which have been crowdsourced include the generation of product ideas—computer company Dell, for example, runs IdeaStorm, which allows its users to suggest product ideas, some of which eventually get built and shipped (Hunt, 2009). Spin-offs from crowdsourcing include crowdfunding, such as the online collaborative film community Wreckamovie, which crowdsources not only film production tasks, but also the financing of film making (Hjorth, 2011).

Crowdsourcing ventures like these are welcomed by Bruns because they serve to make the "nodes in the production network" equal. Yet most crowdsourced tasks were historically carried out by paid employees, and crowdsourcing is therefore likely to impact on professional workers in ways that are problematic. To date, little empirical research has been carried out with professional cultural producers to examine their responses to the rise of amateur production practices that are sometimes captured through crowdsourcing. Few exceptions exist. Within journalism scholarship, research has been carried out into the range of ways in which amateur activity impacts on paid professionals, such as: journalists' negotiations of their relationships with users; the challenges of amateur content for newsrooms; and journalists' perceptions of the effects of amateur content on newsroom norms, values, and routines (Rebillard & Touboul, 2010; Singer, 2009; Singer & Ashman, 2009; Thurman, 2010). Such research is needed in a broader range of creative and cultural industries, in order to enhance our understanding of mutating amateur/professional relationships and of the opportunities for informal learning that such mutations might, or might not, offer.

In contrast to the optimistic analyses offered by Benkler and Bruns, critical voices point to some of the problems with amateur cultural production which are not addressed in celebratory discourses. One criticism relates to the issue of quality. Andrew Keen's *The Cult of the Amateur: How Blogs, MySpace, YouTube and the Rest of Today's User-Generated Media Are Killing Our Culture and Economy* (2008) is a polemic against the quality of amateur cultural content, in which YouTube clips are found wanting in comparison with classical cinema. As the subtitle suggests, the banality of amateur content across a range of social media is read as a threat to cultural standards—this is the "threat" of amateur activity read rather differently. In contrast, Benkler (2006) argues that although the quality of amateur production may be debatable, the act of producing culture makes people better "readers, listeners, and viewers of professionally produced culture" (p. 295), because culture is more transparent and malleable and because such practices lead to the emergence of a critical, participatory folk culture. Thus such practices are seen to offer informal opportunities for learning about culture and cultural criticism.

A more significant criticism of amateur cultural production questions whether participatory production is indeed participatory. For example, in his study of iStockphoto, Brabham (2008) found that participants in the iStockphoto community were both homogeneous and elite, not reflecting the diversity of users suggested by Benkler's (2006) notion that "anyone, anywhere, for any reason" (p. 295) can participate in networked social production. Van Dijck highlights the low numbers of active participants in amateur production cultures with reference to the (scientifically unproven) "1% rule": "If you get a group of 100 people online then one will create content, 10 will 'interact' with it (commenting or offering improvements) and the other 89 will just view it" (Arthur, 2006, cited in van Dijck, 2009, p. 44). Furthermore, van Dijck argues that it is important "to distinguish different levels of participation in order to get a more nuanced idea of what participation entails" (p. 44). This is because user production activities take place on "a variable scale of labour relations" (p. 51), she argues, with a range of contractual forms and a diversity of locations on the amateur/professional spectrum. In the case of one particular kind of design, web design, this is certainly the case. People who are active in produsage communities, participating in FLOSS (free/libre open source software) or other amateur/unpaid design activities, and people who earn money designing websites are not necessarily two distinct groups of people, despite the tendency in some literature to imply that this is the case (such as Berry, 2008). Instead, web designers participate in these activities on "a variable scale of labor relations," as van Dijck suggests. In proposing that it is more productive to attend to the specificities of amateur/participatory production practices than to simplistically label all participants as equal nodes in a network, van Dijck points to some of the questions that the anti-spec movement and this paper engage with, especially: which terms of participation in amateur production are acceptable and which are not?

Another criticism of amateur cultural production focuses on the exploitative conditions in which such production takes place. Terranova (2000) was among the first to recognize this in her widely read article "Free Labor: Producing Culture for the Digital Economy." In this paper, Terranova acknowledged that free labor is willfully given and enjoyed in digital, amateur economies. But she also hinted at the arduous conditions experienced by the armies of volunteers working, for example, as chat hosts for AOL, through her evocative terminology of "NetSlaves" working in "24–7 electronic sweatshops" and feeling the "pain of being burned by digital media" (p. 33). More recently, acknowledging the important contribution made by Terranova's article, Hesmondhalgh (2010) asked if free labor is always necessarily exploited, pointing to a range of types of "free" labor which are willfully given and enjoyed (to use Terranova's terms), such as football coaching or playing music, but which, he argues, cannot be deemed to be "exploitative" in the same way that other forms of free labor can be. For Hesmondhalgh, the internship system, rapidly growing across the globe, is a much more troubling example of free labor than, say, online evaluation such as liking and rating creative products, which produces data that have value for commercial companies.

This paper brings together van Dijck's argument that we need to differentiate types and conditions of amateur activity with Hesmondhalgh's suggestion that some forms of free/amateur labor are of greater concern than others. Liking, ranking, commenting, and rating do not all take place under the same conditions, contests and competitions vary greatly too, and designers themselves attend to such differences. Elsewhere (Kennedy, 2012), I have argued that (web) designers respond positively to forms of amateur production which do not undermine professional values, such as user-generated content produced for the websites that they design. Designers' responses to this kind of amateur activity differ from their responses to spec work for the reasons hinted at by Hesmondhalgh and van Dijck: the former is of less concern because it is not seen to undermine professional ethics and because the terms of participation are considered to be acceptable. The ethics and values of designers therefore play a significant role in designers' negotiation of amateur activity, influencing their responses to distinct forms of amateur production, which need to be differentiated in terms of their impact on professional practice, ethics, and values, and opportunities for learning. In making this proposition, I am building on recent scholarship which might be said to represent a "turn to values" within cultural industries studies (such as Banks, 2006, 2007; Hesmondhalgh & Baker, 2010; Kennedy, 2012). This scholarship highlights the role played by the ethics of individual cultural workers in the ways in which they approach their work, as well as pointing to the values that underlie notions of professionalism in cultural work. Following in this tradition, I argue that critical responses to spec work from within the design profession need to be understood in relation to the professional ethics and values of designers, which some feel are thrown into question by this particular form of amateur activity.

SPEC WORK COMPETITIONS AND THE ANTI-SPEC MOVEMENT

Spec work competitions within the design industries usually work like this: clients post design contests, participants submit design ideas, and the winning design receives a prize, a sum of money decided by the client. 99designs (http://99designs.com), a company with offices in the U.S., U.K., Australia, and Canada, is one company which hosts spec work competitions. On its website, it describes itself as "the number 1 marketplace for crowdsourced, creative design." An introductory video explains the process as follows:

> With 99designs, you get dozens of designers to work on your project. We help you host a design contest, where a crowd of designers compete to give you the design you love, or your money back. Here's how it works. Tell us what you need—logo, business card, website, or even product packaging, then tell us how much you'd like to pay. That's right, you decide how much you pay. The more you offer, the more design concepts you'll see. Within hours, designs begin to pour in. After that, tell everybody what you like and what you don't like, so the designers can improve their designs. After seven days, you'll have pages of designs from dozens of designers. Then comes the really fun part. Check out all the designs until you find the perfect match. Rest assured, if you don't get a design you love, we'll give you your money back. 99designs is simply the best way to get graphic design done affordably, and with no risk.[1]

According to the company's US website, more than 100,000 projects had been launched on the site by January 2012; $471,592 was on offer on 1,533 open projects, and an average of 117 designs per project were being produced. Over $1 million had been paid out in the previous month. A couple of years earlier, in February 2010, 99designs claimed to have almost 60,000 participants, had run more than 37,000 contests, received 3,674,262 designs, and awarded $9,404,789 in prize money.

99designs has been subject to particularly vociferous attack by designers taking an anti-spec stance. Criticisms leveled at 99designs and other companies hosting spec work competitions are numerous, and can be summarized as follows: they devalue design; they offer unfair compensation; they can result in problematic lawsuits; they employ minors; and they lead to a host of unethical practices by clients, competition hosts, and designers themselves. As such, they do not offer positive opportunities for design learning. I say more about each of these issues below.

The main criticism leveled at spec work competitions like those hosted by 99designs is that such initiatives fail to acknowledge the value of design. In such contexts, it is unlikely that participants will learn about the value of design. Mocking the "value" that 99designs attaches to design work at the Future of Web Design conference in London in 2008, Australian designer Brett Welch suggested that dividing the total prize money by the total number of designs submitted would give an indication of just how much 99designs (de)values design. Taking the second set of figures presented above, that would mean: $9,404,789 prize money / 3,674,262 designs = just under $2.56 per submitted design. Although this does not reflect actual amounts paid out, it was used to suggest that the company attached very little value to the labor of design.

Anti-spec campaigners argue that spec work competitions devalue design because they do not fully acknowledge the labor involved in the design process. Many designers argue that "design is only partly decoration" (Zeldman, 2007). Design is primarily problem solving, and visual design should start only after extensive communication between client and designer, which, in turn, should clarify precisely which problems need to be solved. As the website of one anti-spec organization, NO!SPEC, stated in 2010, the design process is "more than simply tapping at a keyboard or clicking a mouse. It's about understanding the nature of a communication challenge and then using one's brain to find the appropriate solution." Spec work competitions fail to acknowledge this, leaping into the design process at the "decoration" phase, it is argued. Clients lose out because, according to some critics, in the absence of communication, designers cannot thoroughly research the visual communication challenge being posed, and therefore cannot produce an appropriate design solution for the client. Participants lose out because they do not learn about the full design process. Poor quality results not because of *who* is doing the designing, as Keen (2008) suggests, but because of the process by which it is done. Designer and author David Airey (2007a) points out:

> When designers deal with clients, they build a relationship. This relationship begins from the very first impression one has of the other, and ideally continues for many years.

> As the client, you should know that your designer values your business. They're not providing you with a design based purely on aesthetics, and one that took perhaps 30 minutes to create. They're looking deep into your business plan, your company mission, your background, your way of dealing with people, and many other aspects of your brand.

What is lost in spec work competitions, according to their critics, is design professionalism: critics like Airey point to the value of designers' professional expertise in *communication,* which they argue is at the heart of design, yet which budding designers cannot learn about in the conditions set up within spec work competitions.

A second way in which spec work competitions are seen to devalue design is through their unfair compensation for the work done. Put simply, the pay is low. AIGA, the professional association for designers, stated on its website that

> professional designers should be compensated fairly for the value of their work. . . . AIGA acknowledges that speculative work—that is, work done prior to engagement with a client in anticipation of being paid—occurs among clients and designers. Instead of working speculatively, AIGA strongly encourages designers to enter into projects with full engagement to continue to show the value of their creative endeavor. Designers and clients should be aware of all potential risks before entering into speculative work.
>
> (AIGA, 2010)

Anti-spec initiative NO!SPEC put it like this on its website in 2010: "Any contest that expects a designer to work for free . . . encourages the undervaluing of a designer's labor, which ultimately undermines the quality of any professional workplace."

Spec work competitions therefore devalue design because they pay a small amount of money for only part of the job and so fail to recognize the range of work involved in the design process. They also devalue design because they pay only part of the workforce involved in the job, as only the competition winner receives financial reward, not the other entrants, who number more than one hundred per competition in the case of 99designs. The NO!SPEC website poses this question to clients thinking of starting a design competition: "Would you work for free with the hope of POSSIBLY being properly compensated?" The promotion of this particular kind of "free labor" through spec work competitions is fiercely criticized, described in 2010 by NO!SPEC as "a disreputable practice in and of itself." Critics of spec work further emphasize this point by comparing spec work processes in design industries with the operations of other trades. In response to an article proclaiming the benefits of a logo design contest for a teen suicide prevention organization (Adams, 2007), one commentator asked if the author would pay only 1 of 12 mechanics who fixed his car. Another said, "No doubt Eric [the author] is perfectly willing to post HIS job . . . and see if someone is willing to take a little less money to do what he does?" (Adams, 2007).

As well as devaluing design work and forcing down pay, spec work competitions are criticized because of the potentially damaging legal consequences of engaging in such activities. In a blog post entitled "Don't Design on Spec," leading web designer Jeffrey Zeldman (2007) points out that AIGA, quoted above, has extensive archives detailing legal cases which have resulted from spec work. In many cases, submitted spec work is rejected, only for the "client" to publish disturbingly similar design work, produced by another, cheaper designer at a later date—and lawsuits often follow. Zeldman summarizes such incidents with this fictional account:

> Per Acme Anvil Co.'s request, Joe's agency designs comps on spec in hopes of winning the Acme redesign project.
>
> Acme Anvil Co. informs Joe's agency that someone else got the job.
>
> Six months later, Acme Anvil Co. launches its redesigned website. Joe's VP of new business visits the site and discovers that it looks similar to one of the supposedly rejected designs Joe's agency had submitted.
>
> Joe's agency calls Joe's attorneys. A nasty lawsuit ensues. No matter who wins the suit, it will be costly and annoying—a drag on resources and morale—for all. If Joe's agency wins, word goes out that they are the kind of agency that sues if they don't get a job. If Joe's agency loses, they may have to lay off staff or close their doors. All because they were willing to design on spec.
>
> (Zeldman, 2007)

In this fictional representation of real-world scenarios, legal problems arise because of a lack of clearly defined usage rights. The campaigning body NO!SPEC points out that participants in spec work competitions often have to sign a contract waiving their rights to their own creative work, passing them over to competition hosts. This contrasts sharply with the practice common in professional relationships which involves the client and designer specifying the rights of usage of design work in an initial contract. Thus spec work competitions fail once more to offer the opportunity for participants to learn about professional design practice. In the absence of such clearly specified arrangements, competition hosts or clients can employ cheaper designers to modify submitted designs and pass them off as their own, without much fear of legal retribution. An example of such ill-defined usage rights can be seen in a brochure promoting a student spec work competition in the north of England in 2011, targeted directly at students and therefore constructing itself as related in some way to learning. Called Two Birds One Stone, the competition encouraged clients, or "brand partners," to participate because they would benefit from "more campaign ideas than an infinite amount of monkeys could produce with an infinite amount of brainstorms" (Two Birds One Stone, 2011). With these words, the brochure suggested that brand partners might build on ideas presented by losing students, without the students getting any credit for their work or having any legal recourse. Thus spec work competitions give out confusing messages about the legal as well as financial aspects of design work.

A further criticism of spec work competitions focuses on their engagement of minors. Design blogs Logo Design Love and The Logo Factory have both drawn attention to the age of so-called designers submitting to spec work initiatives like 99designs. Both have pointed out that 99designs promotes itself as a world-leading design marketplace, yet some designers are as young as 11 years old (Douglas, 2010a; Logo Design Love, 2010). As Steve Douglas puts it, writing on The Logo Factory, "Spec work websites pitch the work of 11-year-olds as a viable alternative to hiring professionals" (Douglas, 2010a). Both of these blogs display screengrabs of the profiles of members whose ages range from 11 to 15 as evidence of this. Douglas suggests that many more child participants may lie about their ages, in order to be taken seriously in spec work competitions. A post entitled "The Kiddie Designers of 99designs" on Logo Design Love refers back to 99designs' self-promotion as a world-leading design marketplace with the following assertion: "I don't know what your definition of a leading business is, but I'd hazard a guess it doesn't include said leader collecting its share of payment up-front, then having children provide the service, with each kid merely hoping to get paid" (Logo Design Love, 2010).

So although crowdsourcing is widely understood as a practice which outsources work to the nonprofessional crowd, spec work organizations often attempt to obscure the amateur character of their operations, such as the involvement of children in their competitions. 99designs and similar companies such as CrowdSpring describe their "community members" as designers, as it is clearly not in their interests to highlight the fact that significant numbers of minors and amateurs are included in their numbers. Indeed, many anti-spec commentators point out that the majority of *professional* designers would not participate in spec work competitions, further suggesting that the large numbers of "designers" on spec work sites are nonprofessionals. Spec work competitions could be seen as amateur economies masquerading as professional, with terms of engagement which are considered to be both unethical and potentially illegal.

Spec work competitions are criticized for the unethical practices that result from them on the part of clients, competition hosts, and designers themselves. Some of these practices have already been discussed, such as the use of submitted designs without payment to or recognition of the people who designed them. Such criticisms often come from people who have participated in spec work contests, as witnessed in a post submitted to NO!SPEC about one person's spec work experiences (Stone, 2007). Here, the author argued that contest holders frequently abandon contests, never declaring a winner or awarding a prize, claiming that none of the hundreds of submissions to their $100 contests are good enough. What's more, contest holders either fail to communicate with designers, give misleading feedback, or accept low bids under the table, she claims.

The author of this post also criticizes spec work participants themselves, for plagiarizing, "trash talking" other designers, or underbidding. Pitting designers against each other "like roosters in a ring," said NO!SPEC in 2010, spec work competitions inevitably result in plagiarism, it is suggested, because plagiarism makes it possible to crank out large numbers of designs, which is necessary in order to earn a living when the reward on offer for each design is between $100 and $300. In Douglas' blog post about the age of spec work participants discussed above, he points out that in discussion forums relating to individual competitions on spec work sites, accusations among participants are rife, and often foul-mouthed. As he suggests, this is not an ideal environment for children to learn about the design "profession" (Douglas, 2010a).

Competition hosts are also unethical, suggest critics, pointing out that hosts pay designers only a small fraction of the total fee claimed from clients. NO!SPEC compares spec work competitions to sweatshops, "where the few benefit over the many." In another article on The Logo Factory, Steve Douglas also draws attention to the unethical ways in which the numbers of active, professional designer participants are constructed (Douglas, 2010b). He points out that 99designs' 153,000+ and Crowdspring's 47,000+ members (as listed at his time of writing) actually reflected registered users, not active designers, and included among their numbers competition hosts as well as members interested in submitting designs. Of these total numbers, only about 1/3 had submitted designs. On Crowdspring, of the approximately 15,000 "designers who have participated," less than 2,500 had submitted more than one design. An analysis of "last seen" dates suggested that "the majority of these designers will not be entering a Crowdspring contest again." Like the construction of members as "designers" and therefore professional, these figures gloss over the actual numbers of active participants in a way that critics find problematic and unethical.

Widespread anger at such unethical practices has led to the establishment of a range of anti-spec initiatives. Concerned about the increasing number of legitimate design opportunities being replaced by spec work competitions, NO!SPEC was established to liaise with a number of stakeholders and encourage them to participate by sending protest letters and writing petitions and posts, among whom educators are included, a clear indication that for the anti-spec lobby, it is important to highlight the problems of spec work to those undergoing formal education (www.no-spec.com/about/). AntiSpec aims to mobilize designers to communicate the anti-spec message. SpecWatch takes a different approach: instead of campaigning against spec work, it presents facts and data relating to spec work, linking to publicly available online sources which serve to verify these facts. SpecWatch, like AntiSpec, has close to 3,000 followers on Twitter. This fact, the numerous responses to blog posts debating the subject of speculative work, panels such as "Is spec work evil?" at the prestigious digital designers SXWSi (South By South West Interactive) conference, and support for the anti-spec movement from significant individuals like Debbie Millman, president of AIGA, all serve as evidence of the strength of opposition to spec work from within the design profession.

Instead of participating in spec work initiatives, critics advocate pro bono work as a preferable way to learn about design—that is, donating professional expertise, or undertaking professional work, in the full knowledge that no payment will be received (in contrast to spec work, where participants hope to be paid). A shorter version of the phrase *pro bono publico,* or "for the public good," pro bono work is proposed as a more ethical alternative to spec work. In the case of the logo contest for the teen suicide prevention organization mentioned above, critics suggested that, given the charitable status of the organization that needed the logo, instead of running a spec work competition, the client should have approached a designer and asked him or her to produce a logo pro bono (Adams, 2007). Elsewhere, at the end of a presentation about web design workflow at the AnEventApart conference in Chicago in 2009, web designer and author Andy Clarke suggested that in the time saved by adopting his proposed method, web designers should approach charities and other organizations "for the public good" and offer their services for free. Designer David Airey (2007b) adds his voice to this argument:

> If you're a designer who thinks that design contests are a good way to practice, think about this: you could head out into the local community instead, and approach non-profits who would be delighted with your help. The benefits are much greater than taking part in any contest; you're guaranteed feedback, you improve your communication skills, your hard work is going towards a good cause, and you're networking with local business owners too (vital if you plan on becoming self-employed).

Not all commentators are equally supportive of pro bono work or critical of spec work competitions, however. Some of those engaging in online debate about the topic display incomprehension of the criticisms of spec work outlined above. "Spec is being done—and it will continue to be done—by free people making free choices in the pursuit of opportunity," said one respondent to the debate about the teen suicide prevention organization logo contest (Adams, 2007). In response to criticisms of 99designs on designer blog Positive Space, another commentator posted this vehement message to the blog owner:

> The only reason you have a problem with spec work is because it takes away from YOUR work. In a democratic society, it's up to business

> leaders/owners to develop new ways to crush the competition. I suggest you stop whining, and use this energy to find a better way to fatten your pockets.
>
> (Zinni, 2008)

Steve Douglas acknowledges that arguments such as "we're all adults here" and "it's our adult choice whether to enter competitions or not" are common defenses of spec work, but as he clearly demonstrates, not all competition entrants are adults (Douglas, 2010a). Proponents of such views appear to accept the increasing precariousness of the creative industries, mentioned in the introduction, and these industries' growing dependence both on unpaid labor and on individual designers shouldering the burden of responsibility for dealing with these precarious conditions. A belief in the primacy of the individual is also evident among those commentators who counter criticisms of spec work by arguing that the talent of experienced designers will prevail. One observer on NO!SPEC stated that there is no need for established professional designers to fear competition from inexperienced amateurs in crowdsourced contests, because "talent always wins out" (Stone, 2007). Such commentators betray a belief in the freedom to self-determine and in the possibility of making it in the creative industries "primarily through individual effort and creative talent alone" (Banks, 2007, p. 65). In response to the proposal that individual talent is all that is needed, another commentator responded, "Talent is only one small part of what we as designers do. It is not like we instantly dream up these concepts in a minute of creative expression. Intelligent design solutions take time, research, and lots of hard work" (Stone, 2007). Yet spec work competitions do not offer budding designers the opportunity to learn these design fundamentals.

AGAINST SPEC WORK COMPETITIONS

Without doubt, the rise of amateur economies has led to a range of opportunities for user participation in cultural production, for creativity and for self-expression. But the growth of amateur economies is not without problems, and to counterbalance the celebratory rhetoric that dominates debate, this paper has focused on a problematic manifestation of amateur cultural production, spec work competitions, and how these impact upon designers' sense of their own professionalism. It has shown how outsourcing design to the amateur crowd is deemed to devalue design work by many professional designers. Critics see companies like 99designs, with their $100 pay-outs and exploitation of designers' near voluntary labor, as unethical in various ways: because they reduce the value of labor in the design process, underpaying designers or not paying them at all; they engage children in design work; and they promote unethical practices like underbidding, plagiarizing, and unfair criticism. By doing so, they do not offer the opportunities for learning that their advocates suggest. Instead of designing on spec, some leading designers and anti-spec activists promote the more ethical practice of pro bono work, which has its roots in the idea that professionals should contribute their expertise for the public good, or *pro bono publico*. While some commentators in the design community celebrate the alleged freedom to participate in spec work competitions as an integral part of creative self-realization, critical voices problematize the reification of talent and freedom that can be found in these celebratory positions. It should be noted that none of these commentators suggests that spec work competitions offer good opportunities for learning, and it should be clear from the discussion in this chapter that there is no evidence of constructive evaluation in spec work competitions. In this case, connectivity does not result in interactivity, useful feedback, or learning. The characteristics of spec work competitions to which anti-spec activists object seem to suggest that this is not an ideal environment in which to learn about design professionalism. In contrast, the pro bono model allows budding designers to develop their skills in the communicative and problem-solving elements of the design process.

Designers' responses to crowdsourcing design can be understood in relation to their ethics and values and the extent to which they feel that these are thrown into question by online activities like contests and competitions. The terms of participation in spec work competitions are considered by many designers to be unacceptable and unethical. In this paper, I have suggested that this position does not represent the voices of hysterical workers attempting to protect "their position at the privileged end of the production value chain," as Bruns (2008, p. 30) puts it. Rather, the anti-spec voice is concerned about what designers consider to be intolerable working conditions. If professional web designers are worried, it is not about their loss of privilege, but about the loss of value, the potential loss of professional ethics, and the problematic terms of participation in this particular amateur economy.

Professional designers are usually paid to design and develop products which solve communications problems. They also volunteer sometimes, giving away their labor for free—either through pro bono work, their blogs and tweets, or active membership of online and other communities. But professionals in the cultural and other sectors have always volunteered their skill. For many designers, the specific location of the fruits of their labor between the two poles of volunteerism and professionalism that van Dijck (2009) identifies matters less than their professional ethics and values, whether they are paid for their work or not. These professional ethics and values are clearly undermined when designers are rewarded less than $3 per submitted design in competition with 11 year olds. As Douglas argues, this is not an ideal environment in which to learn about design.

Although the homepage of the AntiSpec website states that the design profession is one of few embroiled in spec work, the problems associated with spec work competitions are mirrored in the wider cultural and creative industries. Precarious working conditions, increased individualization, low pay, and the growing requirement that budding creatives perform what Ross (2003) describes as "sacrificial labor" are characteristics of many contemporary creative professions, not just design. Spec work competitions (like Amazon's Mechanical Turk and other companies crowdsourcing creative labor such as oDesk and Freelancer) play a role in normalizing such troubling working conditions. The discourses which legitimize these practices speak the language of individualization, through their appeal to individual effort, talent, and ambition. As Ross Perlin (2011) suggests in his book about intern cultures, such discourses fit neatly with "the go-go rhetoric of the dotcom bubble" (p. 36). Perlin also points to the complicity of universities in the production of discount labor, through their credit-carrying internship programs. It could be added that university educators who encourage their students to participate in spec work competitions are equally complicit. In place of this complicity, as educators, we could respond to competition hosts who ask us to promote their competitions to our students by asking if they would be willing to rethink their plans, to employ a student on the basis of an interview and portfolio, rather than asking the student to work on spec. At the very least, as educators of the next generation of creative professionals, we need to reflect on our role in this race to the bottom (Weir, 2011), and recognize that there is good reason to line up alongside the anti-spec movement and its limited opportunities for learning of any kind, formal or informal.

NOTE

1. A number of similar companies exist around the globe, such as 12designer (www.12designer.com/de/) in Germany.

REFERENCES

Adams, E. J. (2007). The art of business: Logo lessons. *CreativePro*. Retrieved from www.creativepro.com/article/the-art-of-business-logo-lessons

AIGA. (2010). AIGA position on spec work. Retrieved from www.aiga.org/content.cfm/position-spec-work

Airey, D. (2007a). Logo design contests are bad for business. *David Airey*. Retrieved from www.davidairey.com/logo-design-contests-bad-for-business

Airey, D. (2007b). Creative resources. Retrieved from www.davidairey.com/creative-resources-01-november-2007

Amazon. (2012). *Amazon Mechanical Turk*. Retrieved from www.mturk.com/mturk/welcome?state=UjZNUjYxV2c1L3p5TnhaZlYrNU11QkhlNVg4PTIwMTQwNTE4MTk1Mg--

Andrejevic, M. (2011). The work that affective economics does. *Cultural Studies, 25*(4–5), 604–620.

Arthur, C. (2006, July 20). What is the 1% rule? *The Guardian*. Retrieved from www.theguardian.com/technology/2006/jul/20/guardianweeklytechnologysection2
Banks, M. (2006). Moral economy and cultural work. *Sociology, 40*(3), 455–472.
Banks, M. (2007). *The politics of cultural work*. Basingstoke, UK: Palgrave Macmillan.
Benkler, Y. (2006). *The wealth of networks: How social production transforms markets and freedom*. New Haven, CT: Yale University Press.
Berry, D. (2008). *Copy, rip, burn: The politics of open source*. London: Pluto Press.
Brabham, D. C. (2008). Moving the crowd at iStockphoto: The composition of the crowd and motivations for participation in a crowdsourcing application. *First Monday, 13*(6). Retrieved from www.uic.edu/htbin/cgiwrap/bin/ojs/index.php/fm/article/view/2159
Bruns, A. (2008). *Blogs, Wikipedia, second life and beyond: From production to produsage*. New York: Peter Lang.
Douglas, S. (2010a). Children designers on design contest and crowdsourcing sites. *The Logo Factory*. Retrieved from www.thelogofactory.com/logo_blog/index.php/childre-on-design-contest-crowdsourcing-sites
Douglas, S. (2010b). Numbers—the ever-shifting realities of crowd-sourcing and design contest sites. *The Logo Factory*. Retrieved from www.thelogofactory.com/logo_blog/index.php/design-crowdsourcing-overhyped
Hearn, A. (2010). Structuring feeling: Web 2.0, online ranking and rating, and the digital 'reputation' economy. *Ephemera: Theory & Politics in Organization, 10*(3/4). Retrieved from www.ephemerajournal.org/contribution/structuring-feeling-web-20-online-ranking-and-rating-and-digital-%E2%80%98reputation%2%80%99-economy
Hesmondhalgh, D. (2010). User-generated content, free labour and the cultural industries. *Ephemera: Theory & Politics in Organization, 10*(3/4). Retrieved from www.ephemerajournal.org/contribution/user-generated-content-free-labour-and-cultural-industries
Hesmondhalgh, D., & Baker, S. (2010). *Creative labour: Media work in three cultural industries*. London: Routledge.
Hjorth, I. (2011, November). The emergence of cultural peer-production: Independent film making in the Wreckamovie community. Paper given at ECREA Digital Cultures Workshop, Universitat Oberta de Catalunya, Catalonia, Spain.
Hunt, T. (2009). *The whuffie factor: Using the power of social networks to build your business*. New York: Crown Business.
Keen, A. (2008). *The cult of the amateur: How blogs, MySpace, YouTube and the rest of today's user-generated media are killing our culture and economy*. London: Nicholas Brealey Publishing.
Kennedy, H. (2012). *Net work: Ethics and values in web design*. Basingstoke, UK: Palgrave Macmillan.
Leadbetter, C. (2008). *We think: Mass innovation, not mass production*. London: Profile Books Ltd.
Logo Design Love. (2010). The kiddie designers of 99designs. Retrieved from www.logodesignlove.com/99designs-kiddie-designers
McRobbie, A. (2002). Clubs to companies: Notes on the decline of political culture in speeded up creative worlds. *Cultural Studies, 16*(4), 516–531.
Oakley, K. (2007). *Better than working for a living? Skills and labour in the festivals economy*. London: Celebrating Enterprise.
Perlin, R. (2011). *Intern nation: How to earn nothing and learn little in the brave new economy*. London and New York: Verso.
Rebillard, F., & Touboul, A. (2010). Promises unfulfilled? 'Journalism 2.0', user participation and editorial policy on newspaper websites. *Media, Culture & Society, 32*(2), 323–334.

Ross, A. (2003). *No-collar: The humane workplace and its hidden costs.* Philadelphia: Temple University Press.
Shirky, C. (2008). *Here comes everybody: How change happens when people come together.* London: Penguin Books.
Singer, J. B. (2009, December 2). Quality control: Perceived effects of user-generated content on newsroom norms, values and routines. *Journalism Practice,* 1–16.
Singer, J. B., & Ashman, I. (2009). Comment is free, but facts are sacred: User-generated content and ethical constructs at *The Guardian. Journal of Mass Media Ethics, 24,* 3–21.
Stone, T. (2007). The Spec trap: SitePoint. NO!SPEC. Retrieved from www.no-spec.com/archives/the-spec-trap-sitepoint
Terranova, T. (2000). Free labor: Producing culture for the digital economy. *Social Text, 18*(2), 33–57. Retrieved from www.nettime.org/Lists-Archives/nettime-l-0004/msg00013.html
Thurman, N. (2010). Forums for citizen journalists? Adoption of user generated content initiatives by online news media. *New Media and Society, 10*(1), 139–157.
Two Birds One Stone. (2011). *Two Birds One Stone presents . . .* Promotional brochure. Leeds, UK.
van Buskirk, E. (2009). Twitter paid $6 or less for crowdsourced birdie graphic. *Wired.* Retrieved from www.wired.com/epicenter/2009/03/twitter-designe/
van Dijck, J. (2009). Users like you? Theorising agency in user-generated content. *Media, Culture & Society, 31*(1), 41–58.
Weir, A. (2011, July). *Crowdsourced labour: An individualised race to the bottom.* Paper given at the Moral Economies of Creative Labour conference, University of Leeds, Leeds, UK.
Zeldman, J. (2007). Don't design on spec. Retrieved from www.zeldman.com/category/reprints
Zinni, A. (2008). 99designs stoops to a new low and attempts propaganda. *Positive Space.* Retrieved from www.positivespaceblog.com/archives/99design-stoops-to-new-low-attempts-propaganda

8 Unpacking the Shifting Landscape of Music Evaluation in Indaba Music Contests

Hiesun Cecilia Suhr

INTRODUCTION

Music evaluations have often been fraught with controversy. Since generating consensus about music's value and quality has been challenging and contentious, the various methods, criteria, and standards related to music's qualitative value have been underexplored, if not generally ignored, in the cultural studies discipline. Echoing this observation, Frith (1996) notes that "the importance of value judgment for popular culture . . . seems obvious, but it has been quite neglected in academic cultural studies" (p. 8). This neglect deserves to be studied more carefully because with the rise of digital media, the evaluation methods for music are constantly evolving. For instance, during MySpace's heyday, the number of "friends" that musicians had on their profiles undoubtedly played a dominant role in launching the professional careers of various popular music artists (Suhr, 2012). Other sites, such as YouTube, continue to be forceful factors in musicians' careers, since the value of musicians is often determined by the number of views their videos receive. Despite some concerns about the impact of music contests on the productivity and value of music (Miller, 1994), competitions and contests are ubiquitous in digital environments, where they influence the rankings and hierarchies connected with the value and popularity of works produced by both amateur and professional musicians. Overall, digital environments have become a *contested terrain,* echoing Warf and Grimes's (1997) view that "the internet is neither inherently oppressive nor automatically emancipatory; it is a terrain of contested philosophies and politics" (p. 259). Indeed, musicians often earn recognition and manage reputations via emerging evaluation methods, which are richly embedded with social, technological, and cultural practices. Thus, today, at the height of the evaluation culture, an exploration of what surrounds these complex evaluation processes is imperative.

While many websites provide evaluative frameworks in the form of critiques, votes, and ratings, Indaba Music (https://indabamusic.com) is considered one of the prominent sites for the assessment of musicians. Since its founding in 2007, the site has evolved from promoting collaboration among amateur musicians to hosting contests that provide collaboration opportunities with highly established, professional musicians in many genres of music. Most recently the site's contests have expanded in scope by offering potential work opportunities, such as submitting music for media soundtracks. Focusing on the expanding scope of Indaba Music's contests, this chapter explores how musicians have contended with the issues of evaluation by drawing from the select findings of an open-ended survey of 255 U.S. and international musicians,[1] an interpretive textual analysis of Indaba Music's contests, and an in-person interview with the vice president of content management on Indaba Music, Josh Robertson. The goal of this chapter is to unpack the shifting landscape of music evaluation in the digital era by focusing on musicians' general views on varying evaluative criteria. As a whole, I problematize four emergent themes as extrapolated from the findings: (1) the trend against populism as a criteria of music evaluation, (2) the fraught and controversial nature of peer assessments, (3) algorithms as a new type of evaluative surveillance in the digital era, and (4) the irrationality and subjectivity of experts' criticisms.

CONTESTATIONS OF MUSIC EVALUATIONS

Prior to mapping the new ways to understand music evaluation by focusing on Indaba Music, a preliminary overview on music evaluation is necessary. Music evaluation invokes manifold interpretations that can be explored through numerous traditions/ideologies/thoughts. Music evaluation also depends on a particular context, as in educational, philosophical, social, technical, and economic contexts. Music evaluation can also be explored via the background or credentials of the people involved, such as experts. Thus, the creation of a comprehensive mechanism whereby one can ascribe to or align oneself with a specific evaluation mode is challenging. The capricious nature of music evaluation not only depends on an institutional context or on individual subjectivity, but it also relies on different disciplines and schools of thought. As a further complication, live performances, as well as recordings, are evaluated, and the criteria and standards for both types of performances are often different. While reconciling the differences is not the main priority here, I wish to briefly touch upon the diverging, yet overlapping, philosophical and sociological views related to the evaluations, and to then segue into my study of the music evaluations taking place on Indaba Music.

I broadly conceive the different ideological emphases in music evaluations into three categories: music's value in terms of ethical operations, music's relationship to listeners' feelings, and music's value in the context of quantity (i.e., hit music). Various scholars in the philosophy of art (Carroll, 1987; Gaut, 1998) have underpinned the link between aesthetics and ethics, exploring the concept that good-quality art possesses an ethical dimension based on the formation of good character, morals, and consciousness. Carroll (1987) states that much of this view of aesthetics as ethics was not accepted or embraced in the past. As autonomism argues, "artworks . . . are valuable for their own sake, not because of their service to ulterior purposes, such as moral enlightenment or improvement" (p. 351). However, in defense of the negative charges made against an ethical framing of aesthetics, Gaut (1998) notes that "ethicism does not entail the casual thesis that good art ethically improves people" (p. 183). Despite the controversial outlook on art's value stemming from ethics, the influential writings of Adorno and the Frankfurt theorists on the value of the arts embed this outlook in the context of capitalism. In their seminal essay, Horkheimer and Adorno (2002) hierarchized art's value based on the high/low art dichotomy. They further argued that only autonomous art, devoid of capitalistic features, could empower individual and social progress. On the other hand, formulaic and repetitive music only yields regressive listening behaviors (Adorno, 1978).

An ethical approach to understanding music and aesthetic tastes intersects with the second perspective related to the evaluation of music, which is based on listeners' relationships to music. In short, the question arises here: What does the music listener experience? Is it qualitatively good or bad? The interconnection between feelings and aesthetic experience is noted by Langer (1966) when she states that "the arts objectify subjective reality, and subjectify outward the experience of nature. Art education is the education of feeling, and a society that neglects it gives itself up to formless emotion. Bad art is corruption of feeling" (p. 12). For Langer, the aesthetic experience one feels can be categorized into the good/bad dichotomy; good art is supposed to yield good feelings, as bad art logically produces bad feelings. Therefore, the ethical factor is connected with the feelings related to the aesthetic experience. However, for Levinson (1996), pleasure versus displeasure cannot be a qualified measure of art's value:

> Many artworks unmistakably offer us rewards that do not naturally cash out as pleasure, or enjoyment at any level, rewards that are at least distinct from and independent of any pleasure or enjoyment that may attach to them
>
> (p. 12)

Echoing the notion of Kant's (1952) "disinterestedness," where pleasure is linked with sensuality and lower forms of aesthetic experiences, does good music supposedly create displeasure? Shumway (2008) asserts that values and pleasures are linked to the judgment of arts and aesthetic quality. However, he further notes that there is a distinction between two types of pleasures: "The way in which the idea of the aesthetic is most often used is to maintain that pleasure in beauty is fundamentally different from the pleasures of the senses, or the 'lower pleasures' " (p. 107).

Reflecting earlier discussions on the symbiotic relationship between music and feelings, Frith (1996) also notes how the assessment and evaluation of music inevitably intersect with one's personal feelings about music.

> [W]hat's really at issue is feeling. In the end 'bad music' describes an emotional rather than an ideological judgment. We don't like a record; we then seek to account for that dislike. . . . Feelings, particularly feelings of like or dislike—for music, for people—are often surprising, contradictory, and disruptive, they go against what we're supposed to feel, what we'd like to feel.
>
> (pp. 72–73)

This outlook produces a significant binary that must be wrestled with in the context of music listening. If somehow music provides us a pleasurable experience, then music must be, by nature, good. However, there is still one unsettling question to answer: Whose experience matters? Is it the experience of an "authority" or of the masses? This leads us to the third evaluation method based on the dichotomy between quantity and quality.

The highest recognition in music evaluations in capitalistic societies has often been considered the concept of "hit" music. In this view, quantity speaks volumes about a specific song's or work's quality. Within this framework, the more people consume a song, the better its value is deemed to be; therefore, the goal for any song should be to be liked by many individuals. Adorno, as one of the most outspoken scholars to critique hit music, defines a hit as commodified music that results from industrial mass production and that seeks to increase profit margins. Hit music is most incisively critiqued for its standardization (Adorno, 1998), as music becomes imitative of other works that were previously proven to be successful. However, despite the argument that the masses may desire familiarity in music, "standardization in radio produces its veil of pseudo-individuality" (Adorno, 1945, p. 216). In other words, repetition and familiarity do not exist overtly but are masked by the pretense of originality and uniqueness, thereby creating an illusion that consumers have a choice: "The less the listener has to choose, the more is he made to believe that he has a choice" (p. 216).

Considering the music industry's interest in profitability, the "hit" song has been a central aspect across all genres, including country music (Jaret, 1982). Hit music in the commercial music industry is clearly recognized through the ranking system of the charts. To this end, the music charts are considered "useful decision support tools that influence the visibility and success of artists, as well as help calculate their financial rewards" (Bhagwan, Grandison, & Gruhl, 2009). As Parker (1991) also notes, "The charts define, the most popular of popular music, the goal, the pinnacle of success"

(p. 205). While the *Billboard* chart epitomizes commercial success, the metric is not without controversy. In the week of January 20, 1990, *Billboard* magazine introduced a new system of technology that measured a detailed profile of listeners (Breen, 1990). As Breen sharply pointed out, this so-called scientific system only "represents the refinement of the commodification of popular music" (p. 370). Even today, the effort to distinguish and rank musicians has not diminished; in fact, in the age of social media, the metric has simply been reconfigured. A case in point is the inclusion of YouTube rankings into the *Billboard* charts (Sisario, 2013), as well as the introduction of the *Social 50* chart that tracks the popularity emerging from social media (Billboard.com). Although it no longer exists, BBC's *Sound Index* was once a comprehensive evaluation mechanism that accounted for multiple types of data, such as the number of listens, plays, downloads, sales, and comments (Bhagwan et al., 2009).

As such, the evaluation mechanisms in social media have adopted the format of the charts from the mainstream industry. In the online context, the need to order and rank music is imperative due to the decentralized nature of digital environments. Because of the valorization of quantity, it is no wonder there has been a surge in services that aid in helping the mechanical increase of these numbers through the paid use of various programs, the learning of social protocols, etc. (Suhr, 2010). In this vein, Baym (2013) also makes a sharp observation about the deceptive meaning of social media metrics in music audience analysis:

> Even if we set aside the possibility of social media metrics being skewed by algorithms that foreground some content over other content, incomplete emphasis on the positive, non–representative partiality, and deception, they are still problematic in that their meanings—seemingly so obvious—are inherently ambiguous.
>
> (para. 50)

Related to the myopic standards of the number games and their ambiguity of meaning, another emerging trend of evaluation is online music contests through which the evaluative criteria supposedly function as more substantive evaluation processes. Unlike other formats of social media charts, where the criteria are often based on a simple measure of the number of views, plays, likes, or friends, Indaba Music's system is slightly different because despite voting procedures, winners are selected by industry experts or Indaba Music staff, while the peers play the role of gatekeepers prior to the final outcome in providing feedback and voting. To further contextualize the Indaba Music community's evaluation systems, I explore how music evaluation in the digital era has evolved, taking into account peer and professional critics, who combine the roles of new and traditional gatekeepers.

THE EMERGENCE OF PEER/PROFESSIONAL CRITICS IN THE DIGITAL ERA

In digital environments, a new type of cultural intermediary consists of a variety of people. Unlike the older category of cultural intermediaries (i.e., the mass consumers who stepped in to raise popularity and recognition), the activities of professional critics often collide with peer opinions on Indaba Music. Reflecting Negus' (2002) recognition of the expanding scope of cultural intermediaries, Indaba Music proves that evaluations are no longer solely generated by select people of influence and power but are, rather, being produced by four different types of individuals: professionals, peers, cultural producers' personal networks, and everyday consumers.

In this vein, Lieb (2013) discusses the role of niche gatekeepers, who exist "in the form of bloggers, podcasters, Facebook friends, and song and album recommenders on iTunes and Amazon" (p. 79). Lieb notes that despite these newly emerging gatekeepers, "conventional music industry gatekeepers are still abundant and powerful in the role of building and popularizing artists and music" (p. 79). Much of this claim directly applies to Indaba Music, because while peer critics are part of the site's group of cultural intermediaries, the primary attraction to this site and its contests are potential connections with the traditional gatekeepers in the music industry.

Lieb further elaborates on the emergence of cultural intermediaries, both from the production and the consumption sides. From the consumption side, the gatekeepers include radio station owners, programmers, and television station and film owners and producers. It is noteworthy that previously gatekeepers influenced the type of music that consumers were exposed to through a tight control of access as arbitrated by A&R (artist and repertoire) representatives and business executives (Frith, 2000). However, in the digital era, consumers increasingly seek their own gatekeepers, individuals they trust in the context of social networking sites and music sites:

> [The] new niche of gatekeepers has the potential to dilute the power of the traditional gatekeepers by showing artists that there are new ways of attracting a following and becoming popular without them. But still, those interviewed could not come up with examples of significant artists who had broken big without the support of traditional gatekeepers, which itself is telling data.
>
> (Lieb, 2013, p. 80)

As revealed by Lieb, in the digital era, niche cultural intermediaries and traditional cultural intermediaries are not acting independently but in collaboration with each other. Given that ultimate commercial success (as in "breaking big") is still aided by conventional gatekeepers, the older power structures continue to be maintained. This is a critical point to remember, since the intricate interplay between the traditional gatekeepers and the niche gatekeepers inevitably has symbiotic effects, although there are different interests at stake (i.e., for mainstream artists, the promotion and marketing of new releases from the labels; on the other hand, grassroots artists seek opportunities for work/exposure). To this end, it is not surprising that a site like Indaba Music attracts aspiring musicians, as many opportunities center on collaboration with a variety of traditional and niche gatekeepers. While traditional gatekeepers are present, Indaba Music mainly operates as a niche gatekeeper. With this in mind, I would like to demarcate another category of sub-niche gatekeepers comprising peer critics on music websites. In the case of Indaba Music, the sub-niche gatekeepers are the musicians who compete on the site while also serving as initial gatekeepers for other users, driving much of the traffic to the site and creating "buzz."

INDABA MUSIC

Indaba Music's website was launched in 2007, and as of 2014, this online community boasts over 800,000 musician members. Previously, Indaba Music held many contests that involved remixing already established popular musicians' new releases. In surveying the landscape of Indaba Music's contest archives from 2012 to 2013, the contests on Indaba Music have evolved over time, and now there are many new types of contests on the site. While remix contests continue to be prominent on Indaba Music, other types of unique opportunities range from educational to strictly work-for-hire situations that provide music for catered themes and television and film soundtracks. In return, contest winners received monetary rewards and different types of exposure.

Other contests provide opportunities to interact with the new cultural intermediaries. According to the Indaba Music site, "Et Musique Pour Tous" is a music and culture blog dedicated to quality, not traffic. It has built a reputation as being influential among music supervisors and other tastemakers. Chosen musicians were featured by the blog for promotion and exposure, which functioned, to a certain extent, as a seal of approval. Similarly, the *Electronica Oasis* contest asked musicians to submit original electronic dance music for the opportunity to be interviewed and featured on the popular "Electronica Oasis" music blog. The blog boasts thousands of visitors a month, and Indaba Music noted that the site has "become a go-to destination for electronic dance music lovers to get their fix." In March 2013, *Artist Search* gave its winner the opportunity to have Indaba Music produce a record. The *Emerging Artist* contest awarded the chosen musician with studio time either in Los Angeles or New York City, along with gear from the Blue Microphones. In addition, *MusicXray* invited musicians to submit music for evaluation by the music industry in terms of potential fan appeal. While I have highlighted only select contests to showcase how widely and uniquely varied many contests are on Indaba Music, at certain times, there may be as many as almost 30 contests going on within a given month.

Against Populism as Evaluation: Amateur Critics

The first emerging theme with regard to contest and evaluation was the rejection of populism as means of evaluation. On Indaba Music, "Honorable Mention" badges are given to contestants who accrue the most votes by the end of the contest. Although Honorable Mentions are not winners, they still receive recognition and "honor" within the community.

In the digital era, the issue of populism deserves some close scrutiny, especially when applied to the evaluation of music. In line with Holbrook, Lacher, and LaTour's (2006) assertion that nonexperts and ordinary consumers' standards are based on popular appeal rather than on the experts' standards, musicians have expressed concern with ordinary people determining music's value. One survey commentator put it quite bluntly: "I don't believe in self promotion, I leave the decisions and stuff like that to judges, I don't actually care about how much votes I got and so on".

The notion of populism is generally imbued with negative connotations by music journalists, since it implies a lack of serious talent or artistic merits, or it is connected with selling out to commercialism (McGuigan, 2002, p. 2). In tandem with this view, many musicians on Indaba Music resent the trend of social media popularity being turned into a prevailing mode of criteria: "Musicians could easily send swarms of friends to vote, regardless of quality. Sometimes I feel like my lack of a group of fans can't compete with that" (Indaba Survey). Another musician noted: "I think social media plays too much of a role: musicians with less Facebook friends are instantly at a disadvantage to those with many, regardless of the quality of their music. We can only hope that voting from other Indaba members [is] able to offset this imbalance but I fear that this is often not the case" (Indaba Survey). One participant also pointed out that Indaba Music is not *American Idol* and vehemently reacted against the measure to determine performances' value based on the masses. The criticism here invokes issues related to the televised singing talent show *American Idol,* and the survey commentator questioned whether or not music contests should be based on popularity. However, it is important to point out that Indaba Music does not operate on the same rules as *American Idol*; the voting power of peers and masses does not determine the winners, unlike on *American Idol.* The only gatekeeping takes place in the preliminary round of *American Idol,* and after that, public voting determines the winner. Surprisingly, Amegashie (2009) notes that the voting process does not necessarily serve as a distracting or undermining factor for contests. Rather, in some instances, voting could increase a finalist's efforts and motivations to sing better: "By allowing the votes of viewers to count, sufficient noise is introduced into the contest since the viewers tend to care more, relative to the judges, about factors other than a contestant's singing ability or performance" (p. 268). Yet, a sharp difference also lies in that Indaba Music contests are not based on live performances but on recorded music; the music submitted to the contests is fixed. Thus, voting cannot function to improve the submissions, but the contestants are able to listen to others' submissions prior to submitting their own tracks for evaluation. To this extent, the issues of popularity tied to the public viewers and those linked to the peer networks are quite different. Popularity emerging from *American Idol* reflects instant feedback after a performance, but on Indaba Music, popularity is accrued after the submissions are closed and the voting procedures begin.

Furthermore, this inherent unfairness is heightened by Indaba's new Facebook craze. According to another survey participant:

> I don't use Facebook because of its Big Brother tendencies and neither do my friends, so we can't vote anymore just because we like to keep some sense of privacy. How stupid is that? I know, I just told you that winning wasn't my primary motive but still, it would be nice if those of us who refuse to bow to a totalitarian machine were treated at least equally with the sheep.
>
> (Indaba Survey)

As noted above, the consequences of self-promotion on social media have major implications for those musicians who wish to retain their privacy and avoid the issues of surveillance and privacy related to Facebook. One inevitably faces a dilemma if he or she is unwilling to succumb to the social media craze, which can potentially pose a threat to personal privacy.

Peer Assessments on Indaba Music

Besides a simple method of voting, peer assessments and criticisms are also an integral part of Indaba Music contests. To this extent, the second emerging theme that I explored was how peers assessed one another via criticisms and feedback. During contests, musicians are able to comment on specific parts of a track by clicking on the timing section of the track. Peer evaluation is not just unique to online contest settings, since understanding how peers assess one another's work has long been an interest of music education researchers (Blom & Poole, 2004; Hunter, 1999; Lebler, 2008). The benefits of learning from other peers have been studied, in particular, by Jones and King (2009), who illustrate how this can be achieved in a recording studio through "surrogate teaching" and "proctoring."

Although strengths in peer mentoring have been noted in music pedagogy, peer assessments in the context of reputation mechanisms raise concerns. Marti and Garcia-Molina (2006) posit that peer-to peer reputation systems include the consideration of incentives and punishment, while

Papaioannou and Stamoulis (2006) focus on the issue of exploiting reputations: "It appears that a high-performing peer is thus unfairly 'punished' " (p. 565). In noting this bias and inequality, the authors problematize how these "incentives lead to a market of 'lemons' and possibly to the gradual collapse of the peer to peer system" (p. 565). For Indaba Music, a mixed and contradictory response was noted in the evaluation of the benefits and challenges of the peer-to-peer system.

On Indaba Music, although the voting procedures do not determine the winners, voting has some merit, since through this process, musicians gain additional exposure during the contests and may end up receiving honorable mentions. It is noteworthy that ascribing value takes place through hype generated within the community. Musicians often point to the problematic nature of peer assessment. One user, who had been positively received during a contest, also pointed out the bias during judgment process:

> As an individual who has received Honorable Mentions and success on the Indaba website, I can say without bias that the tracks on this site which receive the most acknowledgement are not the deserving tracks, but the ones that are marketed the most sufficiently. Also the winners are chosen not by trained judges who base their opinions and decisions on multiple sets of established criteria, but merely the subjective opinion of the artist who is the Judge for each particular contest.
>
> (Indaba Survey)

On Indaba Music, the system in which musicians are ranked is based on multiple measurements, such as how many peers have taken interest in listening and critiquing fellow contestants. Anyone can listen, comment, and provide feedback. Nonetheless, contrary to the common belief that feedback on music by peer musicians should be helpful, many musicians stated that feedback was only a means to an end, not an end unto itself. In short, positive feedback was given with the expectation of reciprocity—many peers were serving as what Hearn (2010) calls "feeling intermediaries," whose goals are to give and receive positive feedback.

> A lot of musicians on Indaba go around spamming (leaving good comments on other people's songs while politely asking for good comments back). I've seen lots and lots of really bad and mediocre music placing itself as a hot track and in the leader board because of this system and it's ridiculous and not fair that musicians get ranked by their own rivals. On the other hand I think the songs chosen by the judges as winners of the contest are always very deserved, so I think there should be no popular vote winner and all the winners should be chosen by the judges.
>
> (Indaba Survey)

In this context, being candid with one's criticism or feedback often does not seem to be feasible, because peers fear that it could potentially have a negative impact on their own competitions.

> There is no way one will get honest feedback on their songs because, as we depend on votes from our peers and if we have negative critics for someone, they are unlikely to vote for us. Therefore the whole commenting experience becomes insincere, sugar-coated B.S.
>
> (Indaba Survey)

Although there is a growing concern over the inauthentic nature of peer feedback, not all comments can be viewed as nonconstructive criticisms. Some survey participants argued that Indaba Music's competitions had some learning value, insofar as one could gain a better appreciation of individual fortes and areas in need of improvement: "Hearing competition give[s] oneself a good understanding of where one's strengths and weakness are" (Indaba Survey). The other useful aspect was the chance to learn about professional-quality sound and mixing techniques: "It is a great opportunity for me to learn a lot more about production and mixing by analyzing and working with the commercial tracks provided in the contests" (Indaba Survey).

The Meeting of Peer Assessment and Algorithm

While peer assessment offers a platform for the users to give each other feedback and vote for one another, the activities of peer assessment also affect the algorithm called the Hottest Track (see Figure 8.1).

The Hottest Track is displayed on the leaderboard, which shows all of the contestants' entries to a given competition. Hottest Track, determined through an algorithm, allows the contestants to easily discern which music is gaining the most recognition during a contest. Upon asking what aspects the algorithm takes into consideration, Robertson (a vice president of content management at Indaba Music) noted that it takes into account the number of comments a musician receives and whether the submitter had previously won a contest, because previous achievements can be a potential indicator for determining future success. However, he noted that the configuration of the algorithm is not revealed to the users, nor did he specify entirely what it entails. Nonetheless, it is clear that the Hottest Track algorithm functions as a way to generate collective value through increased visibility among others. Users can click on the Hottest Track tab and can instantly be seen and heard. To this extent, Indaba Music's evaluation mechanism creates a "regime of visibility," echoing Bucher's (2012) study of the Facebook algorithm. She argues that the greatest fear in the digital era is not necessarily the threat of being observed and monitored incessantly: "The problem as it appears is not the possibility of constantly being observed, but the possibility of

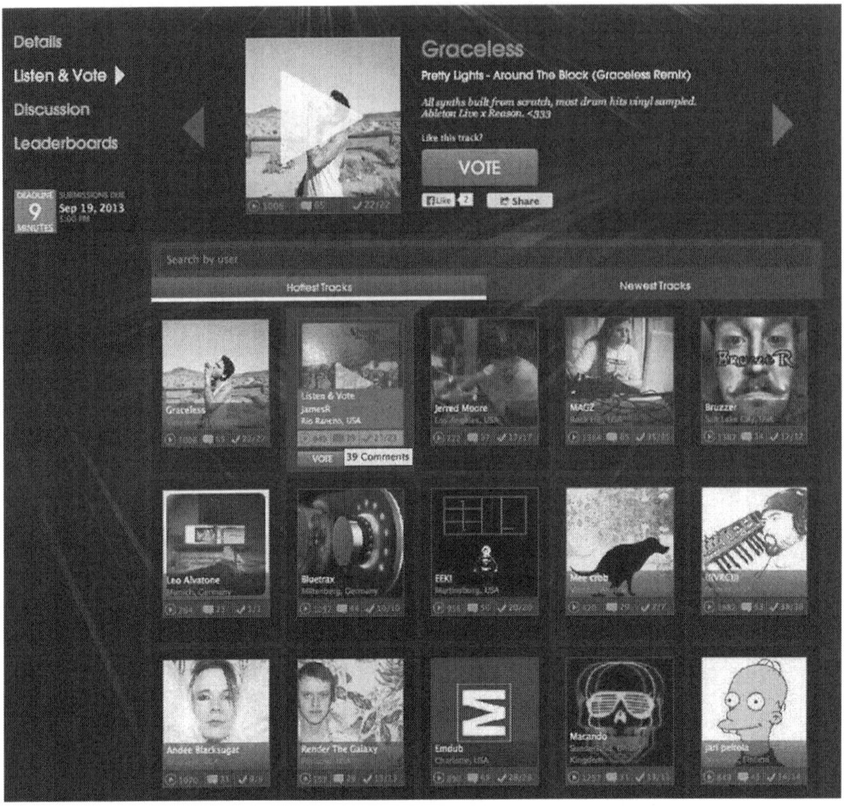

Figure 8.1 Hottest Track and New Tracks

constantly disappearing, of not being considered important enough" (p. 7). Much of this analysis also applies to the Hottest Track designation. Inasmuch as the winners are not being determined by these records, visibility and exposure are critical factors that cannot be ignored in relation to the popularity of the tracks.

Algorithms are also "knowledge logic" (Gillespie, 2014, p. 168). In the case of music, algorithms reflect public endorsement, and such knowledge represents a collective musical standard of what is "hot" and popular. To some extent, this feature echoes Lash's (2007) observation that "in a society of pervasive media and ubiquitous coding, at stake is a third type of rule, algorithmic, generative rules" (p. 71). Although for Lash, these generative rules in the software are "pathways through which capitalist power works" (p. 71), in the case of Indaba Music, to view its algorithm as an asymmetrical, top-down power dynamic is a bit reductionist. One cannot simply ignore peer assessments and the intricacy of social dynamics. A particular logic applicable to the social media needs to be considered, such as programmability, popularity, connectivity, and datafication (van Dijck & Poell, 2013). In particular, the aspect of programmability is salient to the current discussion: "Content is not just programmed by a central agency, even if this agency still has considerable control. . . . Users themselves also have the ability to shape these algorithmic mechanisms. They can either 'go with the flow' or they can manipulate coded interaction" (van Dijck & Poell, 2013, p. 6). Thus, users hold a certain degree of agency in terms of manipulating or interacting with the pre-configured architectural foundation.

In this vein, a comparable analysis could be made by problematizing algorithms as an evaluative surveillance, since algorithms monitor users' activities and these data further help generate the Hottest Track category (see Figure 8.1). Although the configuration of the algorithm is not transparent to the users, it provides a way to track users' activities, even picking up negative comments and potentially displaying misleading data. To this extent, algorithms cannot be solely interpreted as the products of inanimate technology. Gillespie (2014) incisively points out that "a more fruitful approach will turn as much to the sociology of knowledge as to the sociology of technology—to see how these tools are called into being by, enlisted as part of, and negotiated around collective efforts to know and be known" (p. 169). However, surveillance in the digital environments defies a top-down, monolithic power operation, unlike Foucault's analysis of the panopticon. Haggerty and Ericson (2000) reconceive Foucauldian surveillance, since it does not address the contemporary context in which the surveillance technology has been developed (p. 607). Instead, they draw from Deleuze's notion of assemblages, whereby the focus is not placed on creating a sharp bifurcation between the powerful and the powerless: "[A]ll this, lines and measurable speeds, constitutes an assemblage" (Deleuze & Guattari, 1987, p. 4). Haggerty and Ericson (2000) contend that from a Deleuzian context, "surveillance [becomes] rhizomatic, it has transformed hierarchies of observation, and allows for the scrutiny of the powerful by both institutions and the general population" (p. 617). In this case, the general population includes everyone who engages in evaluation on Indaba Music, including peers and others.

The influence of peers implies a number of interesting paradoxes about the nature of evaluations. By redistributing power to peers to make preliminary decisions, evaluation appears, on one hand, to be democratic, but on the other hand, it creates a new power structure among those who seek the same outcomes. To this extent, the potential for agencies, in this case musicians, to react against the power structure is slim, because they hold the power themselves. Essentially, because of this structure, evaluation in digital environments, even considering peer feedback, rather works not as a free-will agent, but under the greater mechanism and constant reorganization of the power structure. In this case, authority is distributed between the professional judges and ordinary people/peers. Most peer endorsement is important, since it impacts the algorithm receiving input from the discussions and comments about the contestants' tracks. Therefore, Indaba Music evaluation does not operate as a one-way power distribution, but it rather yields various power structures: the many to the many, the many against the many, and the one against the many. The constitution of multiple power dynamics is useful because it masks the injustice that may potentially arise, and it provides some level of agency through which one believes one is not competing against a powerful, monolithic oppressor. In line with this discussion, Albrechtslund's (2008) notion of participatory surveillance sheds further light upon the nature of the surveillance taking place on social networking sites. He emphasizes that on social networking sites, surveillance is not taking place in a hierarchical power dynamic but functions as a horizontal practice whereby mutuality and sociality are emphasized. Unlike the conception that one who is being monitored is powerless, in participatory surveillance, the process can empower individuals through the finding of new ways to construct identity (Albrechtslund, 2008). Similarly, in the case of Indaba Music, the activities feed the algorithms and allow for greater visibility for oneself.

The Inherent Arbitrariness of Music Contests and Experts' Judgment

Besides peer assessments and algorithms, the winners are selected by a rotating panel of judges. At times, they are artists, Indaba Music staff, or people affiliated with sponsoring the contest. Together these individuals serve as a new type of cultural intermediary. This selection process is also meant to compensate for the shortcomings of the algorithms as a way to determine music's value. Vice president of content Josh Robertson mentioned:

> Yeah, even though it's like a pretty good algorithm, it's still not as good as humans listening to things at this point. And there's an X-factor to music that you can't put into an algorithm that it will, just will, determine whether or not that a human needs to be able to hear whether or not that song moves them. And you can't do that with an algorithm.
>
> (Personal communication with Josh Robertson, April 25, 2013)

Despite this rationale, some musicians have expressed skepticism about how any established and famous musical artist could have the time to go through the hundreds of submissions.

> I like Indaba Music, but sometimes I question the legitimacy of the site. How do I know people like Barry Manilow or Disney are actually judging/listening to hundreds of remixes of their song and fairly judging them? And what odds do I got when there are 200+ other versions of a song people have done? I am back on the site now but the above reason is one thing that made me quit visiting for a while. Recently I entered a

> metal music competition where I was voted in the top nine by popular vote, the judges picked random songs that didn't even make the top 10. It's frustrating to work on music and not get anything back from it. When I try to remix/create music for Indaba it feels forced. Like I am forced to pick certain songs by certain artists and the hobby that once was something I loved to do feels like a chore that I'm not getting any recognition out of.
>
> (Indaba Survey)

While this skepticism is noteworthy and makes a critical point, exploring musicians' opinions on the evaluation of music and contests sheds further light on why these types of contests still receive numerous submissions despite underlying doubts about the legitimacy of the contest procedures.

The issue of compromised evaluation systems within the contests and competitions is not something that pertains to only Indaba Music, as it extends to other contest-driven activities. Research in the realm of music contests has already noted the shortcomings of competitions in relation to music pedagogy (Austin, 1990). In particular, Glejser and Heyndels (2001) point out a discrepancy in evaluation results in terms of the ranking order of musicians. A similar observation was made by Haan, Dijkstra, and Dijkstra (2005), who note that musicians who perform later in contests ranked better than earlier contestants, thus revealing the bias and inefficiency in the system. However, the issues with the competitions are not exclusive to certain genres of music. Classical music competitions echo the problematic nature of evaluations, confirming the findings connected with Indaba Music. In her observation of classical music contests, McCormick (2009) notes three major findings from the contestants: (1) "Competitions are inherently arbitrary and unfair"; (2) "competitions failed to discover the next generation of great artists"; and (3) "competitions did more harm than good" (pp. 13–14). In particular, the first finding was echoed by many Indaba musicians. In this regard, the issue was not just who should be the judge of music or if one could solely blame the corporate system that credentializes musicians for profit; the main underlying question pertains to *whether* music can be judged in a fair, objective way at all. In the case of music, the issues of subjectivity of tastes and aesthetic standards are prominent, which makes it challenging to establish fair criteria and assessment systems:

> Everything is based on the judges in these contests and how open they are to new ideas for the winner. The rest of the winners are subjective to how many places they link their songs with. So the people with more computer time have a better audience for the votes.
>
> (Indaba Survey)

In general, musicians find that when it comes to evaluations of music, neither the quantity of popular votes nor the evaluations by the judges fully indicated a work's value. The issues brought up by most musicians were related to the subjectivity of tastes.

> [I]t is impossible to rank, rate or evaluate music from the beginning. [A]ccuracy, justice and so on in this matter are pointless to talk about. [H]owever, these still are contests we are talking about. [S]omeone has to win, but it does not mean it is the best music created. [I]t was just the right piece for the judges.
>
> (Indaba Survey)

Another survey participant echoed the earlier comment, albeit more philosophically:

> Sound doesn't exist, it's just vibrations. With that said, it's my brain telling me if the music is good or not. It's all down to one's subconscious. Memory will also play a major role. So it's down to that one individual and that one piece of music at that given point in time.
>
> (Indaba Survey)

Music was also perceived, not as a form of a commodity, but rather in affective terms, tapping into the personal interior: "Good music is something that comes from the heart that resonates with people who are listening to it. It evokes a feeling of calm, gratitude, happiness or is a catharsis of some sort" (Indaba Survey). The subjectivity of musical standards was echoed by many members: "Music is subjective. It usually tells us what the judges were looking for, and how to gain votes in the future" (Indaba Survey). Another musician noted: "There is no such thing as 'universal criteria' when it comes to an inherently subjective art. Anyone who says otherwise is either misinformed—or an asshole" (Indaba Survey).

One musician commented that even when the judges make a decision, the judges' own perceptions about good music are flawed and biased because they themselves are influenced by how the public is reacting to a track.

> Well, we can't speak of fairness when the criteria is completely subjective. Although I suspect that the judges often make decisions based on what they *think* [the] general public will like rather than on what "good" music is. As for the contests decided by votes—those are completely skewed towards people with most friends/connections.
>
> (Indaba Survey)

Upon gathering various viewpoints on music evaluations and the role of personal and subjective tastes on the judgment of winners, one noteworthy comment can be made. For contestants, music evaluation lacks universalism, and subjectivity has multiple dimensions. To this effect, contestants, in general, express that no fair evaluation can be made regarding music's quality. In other words, they believe that winners may be selected by judges who are influenced by popularity and hype within the community or who may make decisions based on their own personal penchants. Furthermore, certain political maneuverings might take place without the knowledge of the other users. Overall, the underlying pessimistic views about music evaluation and contests, ironically, seem to drive the system rather than work against it. The assumption here is that there may be no loss in trying, since there is still a small hope for winning.

CONCLUSION: WRESTLING WITH THE INSTABILITY OF MUSIC EVALUATION

Music contests have long been an integral part of music evaluation culture. From television talent competitions, such as *American Idol,* to highly prestigious and elite classical music competitions, the selection of winners parallels the notion of consecrating the subjectivity of tastes into a collective seal of approval, invoking Bourdieu's (1984) notion of symbolic capital. In this chapter, I have outlined several prominent evaluative activities taking place on one online-based contest site called Indaba Music. Despite some similarities with other music contest formats, such as expert judges, peer assessments, and the valorization of popularity, several unique characteristics of social media impacted the way in which criteria have been shaped. In the Indaba Music community, populism is highly problematized. Quantifiable measures, such as the number of votes and peer judgment, are critiqued because of the resulting state of reciprocity involving the giving of positive and uplifting comments. In addition, the covert configuration of the algorithm has created additional exposure for some contestants' submissions as the Hottest Track. The algorithm that generates the Hottest Track is development in digital environments. However, the underlying logic is that every action counts on Indaba Music; the more one participates and receives comments, the higher one's visibility becomes on Indaba Music. Experts' judgments, on the other hand, were considered arbitrary, random, and irrational. This is because the legitimacy of expert critiques was questioned due to the large number of submissions. Furthermore, in this community, the judges' activities took place behind the scenes, unlike on some television talent shows that provide immediate feedback and delivery.

In problematizing the diverse components that affect music evaluation on Indaba Music, one must also keep in mind that music evaluation is metaphorically an underground process. This situation is unstable, since it is shaped by mutations and metamorphoses caused by both extrinsic and intrinsic factors. The intrinsic factors point to the subjectivities of personal and collective aesthetic tastes, while the extrinsic factors refer to the domain or territory connected with digital platforms and environments. Both factors are facile and fluid, because unpacking taste as it relates to evaluation is a highly complex endeavor; although seminal works by Bourdieu (1984) and Gans (2008) have delved into the discussion of tastes in relation to social class and popular and high cultures, the nuances of these distinctions are obfuscated in social networking sites, where one's cultural tastes are often displayed in a decentralized network (Liu, 2008). These representations, regardless of intention, can function like a virtual curator (Hogan, 2010). The digital environments, such as social networking sites, evolve over time. Given the way people interact and share their tastes, it is not an overly exaggerated view that the new ways to share and display preferences may influence others' taste formation.

Hence, another aspect unique to online music contest sites, such as Indaba Music, is that evaluation methods operate as a hegemonic process between site users and site developers; changes can happen rapidly (or gradually) due to the influence of concerns or complaints. In the summer of 2013, Indaba Music attempted to rectify its problematic voting methods. Although the site has not indicated its rationale, the leaderboard, which displays all contest submissions and votes, now exhibits the sources of the votes (see Figure 8.2).

This allows the leaderboard to track the origins of popularity and to demarcate the votes coming from Indaba (peers) and the networks of random Facebook friends. This change indicates how evaluation can be revised, and how new rules and policies can be made. Taking the temporal and dynamic aspects into account, evaluative metrics can be clearly shaped through the influence of participants.

In digital environments, the astatic nature of social media interactivity, the emergence of social norms, and the advancement of technology can profoundly affect the evaluation criteria. While focusing on evaluation may initially seem to be a task primarily suited to music theorists, music educators, sociologists, and philosophers, as more contests and evaluations take place in digital environments, the need to study these evaluative processes from an interdisciplinary framework is imperative. Through this effort, we can challenge the prevailing mode of inquiries, which have previously been limited to binary formats, such as quantity versus quality, powerful versus powerless, high versus low art, machine versus human, and good feeling versus bad feeling.

Although the online evaluation of music on Indaba Music has benefits in terms of creating a global community of musicians who can share music and connect with potential collaborators, as far as evaluations are concerned, the criteria hardly focus on just music alone. Emerging social norms and protocols, as well as other techniques, such as algorithms, impact the categorization and ranking of musicians. Thus, as the culture of music evaluation evolves in tandem with the advancement of technology, the evaluation process should be rethought outside of the comparative standpoint through the acceptance of the fact that these meaning-making practices are cultural, technological, personal, affective, subjective, and political in nature.

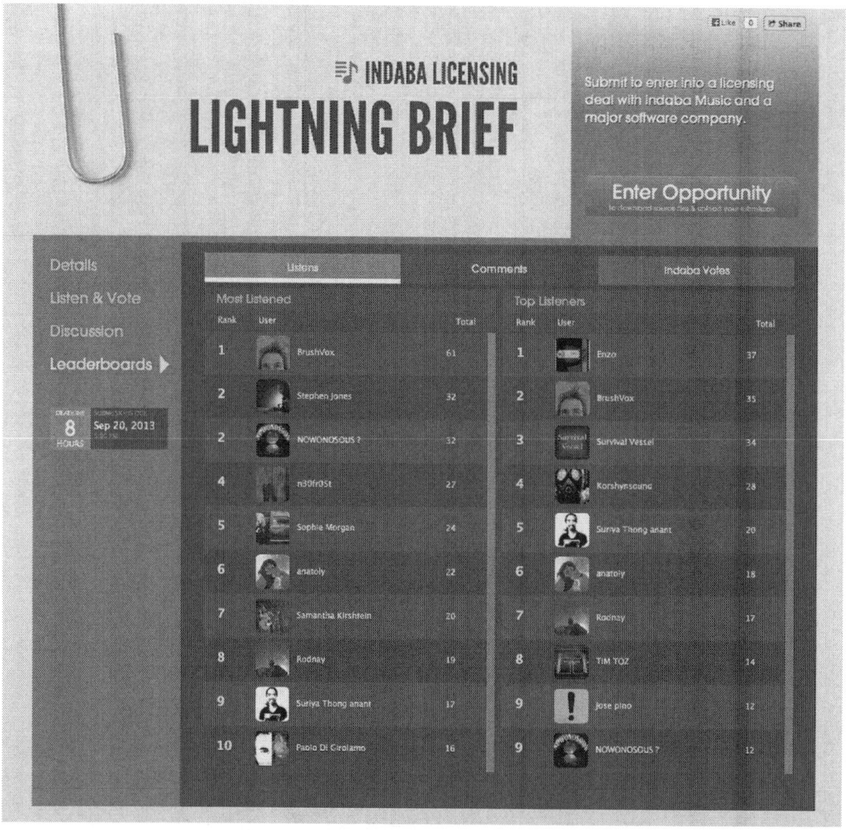

Figure 8.2 Indaba Music leaderboard

NOTE

1. The survey utilized both open-ended questions and multiple-choice questions. The online survey ran from July 2012 to February 2013, and the findings resulted in over 130 pages of survey data. In order to generate a diverse participant pool, my research assistant and I reviewed the recent contest submissions and contacted the competitors directly via email with the survey link.

REFERENCES

Adorno, T. W. (1945). A social critique of radio music. *The Kenyon Review, 7*(2), 208–217.

Adorno, T.W. (1978). On the fetish character in music and the regression of listening. In A. Arato & E. Gebhardt (Eds.), *The essential Frankfurt School reader* (pp. 270–299). New York: Bloomsbury Press.

Adorno, T.W. (1998). On popular music. In J. Storey (Ed.), *Cultural theory and popular culture: A reader* (pp. 197–209). New York: Prentice Hall.

Albrechtslund, A. (2008). Online social networking as participatory surveillance. *First Monday, 13*(3). Retrieved from http://firstmonday.org/article/view/2142/1949

Amegashie, J. A. (2009). *American Idol*: Should it be a singing contest or a popularity contest? *Journal of Cultural Economics, 33*(4), 265–277.

Austin, J.R. (1990). Competition: Is music education the loser? *Music Educators Journal, 76*(6), 21–25.

Baym, N.K. (2013). Data not seen: The uses and shortcomings of social media metrics. *First Monday, 18*(10). Retrieved from http://firstmonday.org/ojs/index.php/fm/article/view/4873/3752

Bhagwan, V., Grandison, T., & Gruhl, D. (2009). Sound index: Charts for the people, by the people. *Communications of the ACM, 52*(9), 64–70.

Blom, D., & Poole, K. (2004). Peer assessment of tertiary music performance: Opportunities for understanding performance assessment and performing through experience and self-reflection. *British Journal of Music Education, 21*(1), 111–125.

Bourdieu, P. (1984). *Distinction: A social critique of the judgement of taste.* Cambridge, MA: Harvard University Press.

Breen, M. (1990). *Billboard* goes into technological overdrive to make radio hits. *Popular Music, 9*(3), 369–370.

Bucher, T. (2012). Want to be on the top? Algorithmic power and the threat of invisibility on Facebook. *New Media & Society, 14*(7), 1164–1180.

Carroll, D. (1987). *Paraesthetics: Foucault, Lyotard, Derrida.* New York & London: Taylor & Francis.

Deleuze, G., & Guattari, F. (1987). *A thousand plateaus: Capitalism and schizophrenia* (B. Massumi, Trans., Vol. 2). Minneapolis: University of Minnesota Press.

Frith, S. (1996). *Performing rites: On the value of popular music* Cambridge, MA: Harvard University Press.

Frith, S. (2000). Music industry research: Where now? Where next? Notes from Britain. *Popular Music, 19*(3), 387–393.

Gans, H. (2008). *Popular culture and high culture: An analysis and evaluation of taste.* New York: Basic Books. (Originally published 1999)

Gaut, B. (1998). The ethical criticism of art. In J. Levinson (Ed.), *Aesthetics and ethics: Essays at the intersection* (pp. 182–203). New York: Cambridge University Press.

Gillespie, T. (2014). The relevance of algorithms. In T. Gillespie, P.J. Boczkowski, & K.A. Foot (Eds.), *Media technologies: Essays on communication, materiality, and society* (pp. 167–194). Cambridge, MA: MIT Press.

Glejser, H., & Heyndels, B. (2001). Efficiency and inefficiency in the ranking in competitions: The case of the Queen Elisabeth Music Contest. *Journal of Cultural Economics, 25*(2), 109–129.

Haan, M.A., Dijkstra, S.G., & Dijkstra, P.T. (2005). Expert judgment versus public opinion—evidence from the Eurovision song contest. *Journal of Cultural Economics, 29*(1), 59–78.

Haggerty, K.D., & Ericson, R.V. (2000). The surveillant assemblage. *British Journal of Sociology, 51*(4), 605–622.

Hearn, A. (2010). Structuring feeling: Web 2.0, online ranking and rating, and the digital 'reputation' economy. *Ephemera: Theory & Politics in Organization, 10*(3/4), 421–438.

Hogan, B. (2010). The presentation of self in the age of social media: Distinguishing performances and exhibitions online. *Bulletin of Science, Technology & Society, 30*(6), 377–386.

Holbrook, M.B., Lacher, K.T., & LaTour, M.S. (2006). Audience judgments as the potential missing link between expert judgments and audience appeal: An illustration based on musical recordings of "My Funny Valentine." *Journal of the Academy of Marketing Science, 34*(1), 8–18.

Horkheimer, M., & Adorno, T.W. (2002). *Dialectic of enlightenment: Philosophical fragments* (E. Jephcott, Trans., G.S. Noerr, Ed.). Redwood City, CA: Stanford University Press.

Hunter, D. (1999). Developing peer-learning programmes in music: Group presentations and peer assessment. *British Journal of Music Education, 16*(1), 51–63.

Jaret, C. (1982). Hits or just heartaches: Characteristics of successful and unsuccessful country music songs. *Popular Music & Society, 8*(2), 113–124.

Jones, C., & King, A. (2009). Peer learning in the music studio. *Journal of Music, Technology and Education, 2*(1), 55–70.

Kant, I. (1952). *The critique of judgement* (J. C. Meredith, Trans.). Oxford: Oxford University Press.

Langer, S.K. (1966). The cultural importance of the arts. *Journal of Aesthetic Education, 1*(1), 5–12.

Lash, S. (2007). Power after hegemony: Cultural studies in mutation? *Theory, Culture & Society, 24*(3), 55–78.

Lebler, D. (2008). Popular music pedagogy: Peer learning in practice. *Music Education Research, 10*(2), 193–213.

Levinson, J. (1996). *The pleasures of aesthetics: Philosophical essays.* Ithaca, NY: Cornell University Press.

Lieb, K. (2013). *Gender, branding, and the modern music industry: The social construction of female popular music stars.* New York: Routledge.

Liu, H. (2008). Social network profiles as taste performances. *Journal of Computer-mediated Communication, 13*(1), 252–275.

Marti, S., & Garcia-Molina, H. (2006). Taxonomy of trust: Categorizing P2P reputation systems. *Computer Networks, 50*(4), 472–484.

McCormick, L. (2009). Higher, faster, louder: Representations of the international music competition. *Cultural Sociology, 3*(1), 5–30.

McGuigan, J. (2002). *Cultural populism.* New York: Routledge.

Miller, R.E. (1994). A dysfunctional culture: Competition in music. *Music Educators Journal, 81*(3), 29–33.

Negus, K. (2002). The work of cultural intermediaries and the enduring distance between production and consumption. *Cultural Studies, 16*(4), 501–515.

Papaioannou, T.G., & Stamoulis, G.D. (2006). Reputation-based policies that provide the right incentives in peer-to-peer environments. *Computer Networks, 50*(4), 563–578.

Parker, M. (1991). Reading the charts: Making sense with the hit parade. *Popular Music, 10*(2), 205–217.

Shumway, D. (2008). Questions of pleasure and value. In M. Berube (Ed.), *The aesthetics of cultural studies* (pp. 103–116). Malden, MA: Blackwell Publishing.

Sisario, B. (2013, February 20). What's Billboard's no. 1? Now YouTube has a say. *New York Times.* Retrieved from www.nytimes.com/2013/02/21/arts/music/billboard-makes-youtube-part-of-hot-100-formula.html

Suhr, H.C. (2010). Understanding the emergence of social protocols on MySpace: Impact and its ramifications. *Comunicar: Scientific Journal of Media Education, 17*(34), 45–53.

Suhr, H.C. (2012). *Social media and music: The digital field of cultural production.* New York: Peter Lang Press.

van Dijck, J., & Poell, T. (2013). Understanding social media logic. *Media and Communication, 1*(1), 2–14.

Warf, B., & Grimes, J. (1997). Counterhegemonic discourses and the Internet. *Geographical Review, 87*(2), 259–274.

9 Online Social Influence and the Evaluation of Creative Practice

A Critique of Klout

Alessandro Gandini

INTRODUCTION

A number of applications and algorithms have emerged over the past few years claiming to calculate the personal *influence* of a user across different social network sites, namely the capacity to engage with other users in online conversations and actions. The most established of these applications is Klout (http://klout.com), a privately owned online service that browses and scrapes the activity of individual profiles across the most important social media platforms to create an individual "influence score." Sites like Klout market their supposed ability to assess the user's capacity to influence the online behavior of others, especially in terms of sharing content and generating interactions. The rapid diffusion of such services has helped popularize the term *influencer* as a status indicating the online reputation of a user on a certain topic across a network of personal contacts, in a way that recalls the notion of opinion leadership. The present contribution discusses Klout's effectiveness at measuring influence and reputation across creative environments and networks. Does Klout really measure influence and, as a consequence, the reputation of a user across a network of contacts? Is the online influence on Klout a potential proxy for the "general" reputation of a creative professional in a network? This study will use data coming from research on freelance creatives and their professional networks in Milan and London, focusing on the extent of personal reputations within the networks. The research shows that reputation is a determinant element for the professional success of freelance creatives in these networks, as it appears to be more relevant than other factors, such as trust, skills, and the educational titles.

Data concerning online presence across creative practitioners, which are included in this paper, indicate that Klout, despite claims and slogans, does not appear to be a reliable proxy for the assessment of one's reputation in a network of freelance creatives. Rather, the overall assessment of Klout as a tool for the measurement of influence and reputation in these contexts reveals that Klout merely seems to be a quantitative elaboration of one's frequency of online activity. This argument will be framed into a wider discussion around the notion of reputation economy (Anderson, 2006; Arvidsson & Peitersen, 2013; Botsman, 2010, 2012; Hearn, 2010), which has become fashionable in recent times. The contribution will end up discussing the traits—and the risks—of a potential "Klout culture," with this term meaning the increasing fetishism toward such algorithms in relation to different forms of creative production.

THEORETICAL FRAMEWORK: THE REPUTATION ECONOMY

The most recurrent activity perpetrated by users of social media platforms takes place via the so-called social buttons, with this term indicating "likes," "retweets," "mentions," and similar tools that perform different kinds of actions on social network sites. Social buttons should be considered the elements which are critical to a social network site functioning as such, as they are the numerical and tangible representation of interactions attached to online content. The extent of these activities reflects the quantity of interactions associated with individual profiles. Drawing on Gerlitz and Helmond (2011), it may be argued that the relevance of such social buttons calls into question the relationship between the sociotechnical features of the web and the forms of value that can be generated online. Specifically, the social buttons may be taken as elements which measure the degree of *affectivity* attached to online content and individual profiles, in other words as proxies that enable an individual's *reputation* to become visible and potentially measurable on online platforms.

Take, for instance, the number of followers, mentions, and retweets on Twitter, the number of connections on LinkedIn, or, to a general extent, the number of interactions that an individual profile is able to generate through a profile page on a social network site. These may all be considered as indicators for the assessment of one's reputation in a field; the more "influential" contacts one has, the greater one's capacity is to generate interaction over content pertaining to a certain topic or practice. In the end, these numbers function as a measure of the reputation an individual user has in that field. It is from here that the idea of a *reputation economy* arises as the theoretical framework for this contribution. Reputation can be defined as the ensemble of opinions and beliefs generally held about someone or something (Marwick, Murgia-Diaz, & Palfrey, 2010). In sociological terms, it takes the shape of one among many elements concerning the notion of social capital (Lin, 2002), in strict relationship with trust. It may also be argued that influence and reputation are in direct connection, as influence may be seen as an "effect" of the personal reputation of an individual in a field or network.

The notion of a reputation economy describes the decisive role played by reputation across online platforms as a regulator for online behavior. This idea is rooted in the impact made by the emergence of the Google

PageRank algorithm, which can be considered as the first example of an online, reputation-based ranking system. Before PageRank appeared, search engines were largely unable to appropriately conduct the user to the object of the search to a sufficiently reliable degree. PageRank represented a revolution in the practices of online searches, as it made it possible to quickly find the most relevant websites on the basis of the number and quality of incoming links related to the keyword selected. The ratio of this service is based on the assumption that the more a website is in-linked, the more it is likely to be what one is looking for, according to the keyword chosen.

Following the emergence and the impact of PageRank, Masum and Zhang (2004) argued that reputation has the potential to become a central concept of a new measurement of value production in qualitative terms. Through the adoption of a Marxist framework, they sustained that this kind of reputation appears to be a form of use-value that indicates qualitative, socialized value production in contrast to exchange value, taken as a value production for quantity and profit. Reputation is considered by Masum and Zhang as the most important feature of the contemporary, network-based market structures that exist on the web. These essentially rely on socialized use-value production across widely connected environments (Masum & Zhang, 2004).

The attention granted to the role and meaning of reputation across different spheres of society has increased over the last decades. The term "reputation economy" was first coined by former *Wired* magazine editor Chris Anderson (2006). In his argument on "the long tail," in which he discusses the business model of online enterprises like Amazon and eBay, Anderson maintains that the emerging digital economy essentially represents a reputation economy, as word-of-mouth information and reputations help to foster differentiation among online businesses. This is due to the fact that through the evolution of digital platforms, reputation has increasingly become visible and, under certain conditions, even potentially measurable for purposes of valorization and economic return.

Along this line, Hearn (2010) argues for the existence of an emergent "digital reputation economy," based on the role of the "flexible" and "branded" self that inhabits offline and online environments (Hearn, 2008, 2010, 2011; Moor, 2003; Peters, 1999). At the same time, drawing from the autonomist Marxist literature on "immaterial labor," Hearn (2010, 2011) warns about the risks endemic to this new kind of society, as most of these processes represent an ensemble of exploitative practices and "free labor." This, nevertheless, remains a controversial issue considering the disputable entity and boundaries of such exploitation, as discussed in the debate over value in informational capitalism (Arvidsson & Colleoni, 2012; Fuchs, 2010, 2012).

More recently, in the discourse on collaborative forms of consumption and production, Botsman (2010, 2012) argues that the role of reputation across the online sphere configures the existence of a reputation economy, whereby online ratings and reviews are instrumental for the emergence of collaborative practices. In this sense reputation functions as a form of currency, enabling trust among strangers. Arvidsson and Peitersen (2013) suggest that reputation in this context should be considered as a potential "general equivalent" on the basis of which a new definition of value, coherent with the emerging "ethical economy" based on affectivity and use-value, can be built. This approach owes much also to the role of reputation and trust in the analysis of the economic performance of individuals and firms in different online contexts, especially consumer platforms, as assessed through online reputation systema (ORSs) (Bolton, Katok, & Ockenfels, 2004; Bolton, Loebbecke, & Ockenfels, 2007). These have been studied frequently over the past decade (Bolton et al., 2004, 2007; Dellarocas, 2003), especially in relation to social interaction and economic exchange practices on websites devoted to online commerce. An ORS uses algorithms that aggregate the users' feedback and reviews to calculate a reputation score that functions as a proxy for trust, as occurs in the cases of eBay or Amazon, where trust is needed to further economic transactions. Dellarocas (2003, 2012) argues that reputation systems across online environments should be seen as the digitization of word-of-mouth exchanges.

ORSs have been adopted by many e-commerce sites and have specific design norms which enable their functionality on the platforms, dependent on the nature of the interaction involved (for a detailed review, see Farmer & Glass, 2010). Design choices concerning the ORS profoundly affect the life and culture of their "communities" (Dellarocas, 2012). Resnick (2001) claims that reputation systems are important in the construction of sociotechnical capital, since these help establish a common ground of trust in a network through persistent interaction (Lampe, 2012). As shown by the already mentioned cases of eBay and Amazon, where economic exchanges are involved, the ORS operates as the main device by which buyers and sellers can reciprocally trust each other in a digitally mediated economic transaction (Bolton et al., 2004).

Reputation systems are, nevertheless, also subject to potential gaming. The risk of cheating and manipulation potentially affects all ORSs (Dellarocas, 2012). The main remedy to avoid this damage is to enhance the transparency of the algorithms and aggregation rules by favoring "metamoderation" to "rate the raters." This is considered an effective tool to reduce bias (Farmer & Glass, 2010) through emphasizing user-generated reputations over system-generated reputations (Lampe, 2012). In the next section, I will look more specifically at a particular type of online reputation system: Klout.

A PARTICULAR ORS: KLOUT

Klout and its most important competitors aggregate and elaborate data over the activity of individual profiles on major social network sites, such as Facebook, Twitter, LinkedIn, Instagram, YouTube, and others, including the blogging platform WordPress. The elaboration results in a score that claims to indicate one's capacity to be influential over the network of contacts in relation to content posted on different social media platforms. The score ranges between 0 and 100 (the average value is approximately 20). Taken as such, Klout represents an example of system-generated reputation scores (Messias, Schmidt, Oliveira, & Benevenuto, 2013; Schaefer, 2012), as each grade is automatically produced by an algorithm on the basis of the number of interactions on the social media platforms which have been associated to it. Klout etymologically recalls a branding of the English word "clout," meaning influence, weight, or importance. The site was launched in September 2009 by a private corporation (Klout, Inc.) as a social network site designed to generate individual "influence scores" based on each user's activity on a plurality of social networking sites. According to the typology proposed by Cascio (2012), we can consider Klout as an "emergent universal" network, where ratings are based on an algorithmic analysis of the online behaviors of an individual profile over diverse participant bases. Emergent universal networks potentially offer a high utility but are far more difficult to construct than all other types (Cascio, 2012).

One problematic point relates to the fact that the algorithm which calculates the Klout score is not open source and remains undisclosed. The user is given only a limited amount of information on how the data are elaborated and treated. In the early days of Klout, three parameters were publicly displayed on each individual profile, and these were supposedly the values used in the calculation of the score. These were: True Reach (how many people one can influence), Amplification (how much one can influence others), and Network Impact (the capacity of your network to be influential). These parameters are no longer present on the profile page. On the day this piece is being finalized, Klout claims to aggregate data from over 400 "signals" from social media activity across the web, but the full extent of how the score is constructed remains unknown. The uncertain nature of Klout's calculations is a problematic element, since different sorts of benefits are being generated from the Klout scores, with no precise clue about how the score is generated. This results in a nontransparent process overall. The methodology adopted by Klout as concerns the quantitative elaboration of data on likes, comments, and the other social buttons appears to be a sort of industrial secret which functions within Klout's business model. This model is based on "perks" and the integration of scores into a plurality of contexts for profitable return.

"Perks" are essentially gifts that Klout gives to its "influencers" as a result of their high score on a certain topic. These can vary from test products up to "first-class" airline or hotel vouchers and discount rates. Through the system of perks, the company earns money by collaborating with other companies and brands all over the world and by operating as an intermediary to deliver products and services to influencers who are then asked to perform as opinion leaders about that brand, service, or product. Klout seemingly functions as a professional service of intermediation based on the capitalization of social interaction, helping partners to get to the "most appropriate influencer" for a business and then cashing in on his or her reputation. This model is similar to what happens to successful fashion bloggers or food bloggers, when companies and brands ask them to test new products and write reviews.

The diffusion of Klout and its perks also has a series of implications, some of which have appeared in the media over the recent years. A number of hotels, especially in the U.S., require guests to provide their Klout score when making a reservation, as a proxy to assess their reliability (Stevenson, 2012). Also, the growing importance of social networking sites (SNS) is now frequently combined with the use of social media platforms for job searches, resulting in what is commonly known as "social recruitment." A number of stories have appeared in the media about the use of Klout for recruitment purposes (Meister, 2012), especially in the creative sector. Certain "creative" professional figures, such as SEO (search engine optimization) specialists, social media managers, and similar others, are increasingly required to display a high Klout score together with a capacity for handling similar tools. To a larger extent, an individual's online presence is increasingly perceived and assessed as a crucial element, such that a candidate should expect to be evaluated also according to these indices when competing for a job. "We say to brands that these are the people they should pay attention to most," Mark Thompson, Klout VP, declared (Owen, 2012).

The most advanced competitor to date is Kred (www.kred.com), which is essentially a Twitter-based application. It seems to be more transparent than Klout. Through a rich FAQ section on the website, Kred clearly operates through an algorithm based on two parameters: outreach and influence. Outreach is gauged from 0 to 10 and "reflects generosity in engaging with others and helping spread their message." It is measured through the number of retweets, replies, and mentions of others. Influence goes from 0 to 1,000 and is calculated through weighing retweets, mentions, likes, and followings. If one accepts an invitation to connect a Facebook account, the same parameters apply to posts, mentions, shares, likes, and event invitations. The average Kred score is between 450 and 600. It is evident that Kred is making a strong effort to deliver a more transparent system by displaying as much information as possible on how the score is generated and, generally speaking, by considering transparency as a valuable asset. However, Klout is able to operate across a larger number of SNSs, while Kred scores appear to be biased by the greater importance granted to Twitter accounts. Thus, the relevance of Kred scores seems yet to be limited, and this is the reason why this contribution focuses solely on Klout.

RESEARCH METHODS

The following data originated within the proceedings of an empirical research study on freelance creative professionals and their informal networks in Milan and London. The research shows how reputation across a personal network of contacts is a determinant element for the professional success of freelance creatives. The term "creatives" here comprises a broad range of multiskilled professional profiles, including illustrators, communication designers, audiovisual producers, and other similar figures, employed with freelance contracts in different sectors of the industry. The different creative "skills" and professional identities, which may vary among different participants, do not play a significant individual role in these samples, as the interviewees can be considered within the "multifunctional" definition of creatives provided by Christopherson (2002, 2008). These are professionals with similar sets of skills which are activated independently from the separate professional definitions.

The research is based on 80 interviews (42 in Milan, 38 in London) conducted with a snowball sampling approach. The focus of this mapping was on a small-size network of creatives active in the urban scene and on the individual social capital acquired in the networks. The use of the snowball sampling method allowed the researcher to elaborate the reputation scale possessed by each participant in the sample based on the number of times one was mentioned in response to the following "name generator" question: "Could you please list a maximum of five names of independent creative professionals that you consider highly in their job, notwithstanding if (a) you're a friend with them or not, or (b) you know them personally?"

The research was conducted within an overall ethnographic framework through semistructured interviews. These were conducted following the principles of the "conversational survey" (Gobo, 2011; Gobo & Mauceri, 2013), a technique which allows one to easily manage data collected in the interviews in order to use them as quantitative, survey-like data to perform basic statistical analysis. These elaborations are not to be taken as a display of causal relations, keeping in mind the shortcomings that pertain to this operation, including a relatively small sample size and the choice of a network approach. These shortcomings resulted in the violation of the assumption of independence in the samples. However, the intention is to show the existence of a number of trends, in order to cast a new light on the study of reputation across networks, especially in relation to trust.

The study also comprises specific data on the online presence of the participants, as well as their use of SNSs for professional purposes. This was organized according to the principles of "digital ethnography" (Caliandro, 2011; Marres, 2012), a methodology derived from the digital methods approach (Rogers, 2009, 2013). This approach pertains to collecting online data by "following the medium," in other words, by mapping all available data on the platform and maintaining an ethnographic framework. This is the technique used for the collection of data concerning the Klout profiles of the creatives who have been interviewed for this work.

KLOUT AND CREATIVE PROFESSIONALS

The existing literature on creative labor markets shows how the management of relationships and contacts constitutes a crucial part of the job search strategy, as well as of professionally successful careers (Blair, 2001, 2009; Grugulis & Stoyanova, 2011, 2012). In this context, the use of SNSs by professionals active in the creative and cultural industries appears to be increasingly important as practices of *personal branding* are conducted across social media. These are perceived as necessary for creative professionals in order to construct coherent professional images and marketable profiles (Hearn, 2010; Hoffman & Casnocha, 2012). These practices include a continuous and refined process of *curation* of the online image, as well as of the content posted on social media platforms, as these are elements that may significantly affect the assessment of a professional profile, either in positive or detrimental terms. As a result, the increasing importance of the content posted on social media platforms implies a greater relevance of one's *reputation* over the online sphere. The online reputation, for the realm of creative practice, is therefore made an object of the *management process* by which the curation of social media profiles becomes a working practice that combines the nature and quality of the information available online:

> Social media are fundamental, not simply for direct advantages. I don't generally get work directly from Facebook or LinkedIn . . . but it's true that if I have to meet someone, I will look at the social networks. Maybe we are meeting because someone recommended you, or I met you somewhere, but social media are a portfolio and I want to know how you work. Through social media I look for information and I use them as a 'shopping window', also on my side. If I have to work with you and I can't find you online, I won't hire you.
>
> (M., communication consultant, Milan, 24, male)

The management of online presence combined with that of offline relationships and contacts is essential to the success of the creative professionals interviewed for this study. As seen, it is considered strongly detrimental not to have a profile on the major social network sites. Thus, it is not surprising to see that a large majority of the participants have a structured social media presence based on the professional use of a wide range of platforms.

In Milan, 30 of the 42 participants have Twitter accounts, which are largely used for professional reasons; 38 of the 42 have LinkedIn accounts, 12 of whom have more than 500 connections; and 17 of the 42 also have personal blogs. In London, 29 of the 38 participants have professional

Twitter accounts; 36 of the 38 have LinkedIn profiles, 5 of whom have more than 500 connections; and 9 of the 38 have professional blogs. In both contexts, with only few exceptions, Facebook is largely considered as a private SNS, which is not used for professional curation.

> I tried Facebook more like a personal tool, and I found it quite teenage, not very useful professionally; and also something to worry about in terms of your reputation if you are a professional. I tend to post links to my website, and it actually drives a lot of people to my website, but I think it doesn't work that much.
>
> (L., arts consultant, London, 46, female)

As a result of these considerations, with the increasing visibility of Klout and the other services rising during the course of my research, I began questioning the extent of Klout as a proxy for the online influence and reputation of professional creatives across their networks. In order to do so, I mapped the Klout scores of those who participated in my study, and then I examined whether these values correlated with the "reputation scores" I had mapped in my study of the small-size samples of creative networks in Milan and London. Though the networks studied in Milan and London were small in size, the combined nature of offline and online presence in the professional practices of creative freelancers made this sample a good test for the reliability of Klout scores in more general terms, maintaining the measurement of "offline" reputation I did for my own research as a solid reference.

The Klout scores of each participant in the study were all collected on the same day in February 2013, following the already mentioned methodological principle to "follow the medium" (Rogers, 2009, 2013). In Milan, 26 of the 42 participants have a Klout account connected to at least one major social network. The average score is 50, with a maximum score of 75 and a minimum score of 17. Women show a higher Klout score than men, with an average value of 57, while the men's average score climbed only to 46. Therefore, bearing in mind the shortcomings that such an operation possesses, I have questioned whether there is a correlation between the "offline" reputation value pertaining to the participants of my study and their Klout scores collected online, in order to explore to what extent high Klout scores can function as predictors of the existence of a high reputation in a professional network. Data show that Klout values do not correlate significantly with reputational values in the sample in Milan (Table 9.1). In other words, Klout does not seem to be able to successfully mirror the "offline" values in the sample.

As concerns London, the number of participants who have active Klout accounts is 27 out of the 38. The average score is 48, and the interval goes from a minimum of 13 to a maximum of 65. As concerns gender, the sample is quite neatly split in two (14 men and 13 women) and, as it was for Milan,

Table 9.1 Klout elaboration—Milan

	REPUTATION INDEGREE	KLOUT
REP_INDEGREE Pearson correlation	1	.452
Sig. (2-code)		.020
N	42	26
KLOUT Pearson correlation	.452	1
Sig. (2-code)	.020	
N	26	26

The correlation is significant at 0.05 (2-code).

Table 9.2 Klout elaboration—London

	REPUTATION INDEGREE	KLOUT
REP_INDEGREE Pearson correlation	1	–.141
Sig. (2-code)		.484
N	38	27
KLOUT Pearson correlation	–.141	1
Sig. (2-code)	.484	
N	27	27

The correlation is significant at 0.05 (2-code).

the score is higher for women (61) than men (37). Similarly, if a correlation between the reputation variable and the Klout variable in the London network is performed within this sample (Table 9.2), the results show that Klout does not seem to be able to significantly mirror the "offline" values.

These insights provide a basic but indicative attempt to test Klout's capacity to be a good proxy for the measurement of influence and reputation in a professional network, in these cases a creative network. Though both elaborations are not significant, the correlation values appear to be very different between the two contexts, as Klout seems to largely mirror the reputational values in Milan, although it does not do so in London. This can be explained by a possible sample bias, although snowball sampling ensured a certain degree of randomness (Biernacki & Waldorf, 1981). Further research should replicate this analysis on large sets of data to see whether this is a context-dependent factor or if other issues may apply. Nevertheless, to a larger extent, despite the methodological shortcomings attached to these elaborations, data seem to show the distance between what Klout is able to mathematize and the more rounded notions of reputation and influence across networks at stake with creative practices. These imply a plurality of qualitative and quantitative elements which contribute to their construction and meaning. Klout seems to get just a fraction of this issue, and this weakness needs to be supported and rounded out with more data, such as quantitative network analysis elaborations and qualitative insights coming from interviews and observations within the networks, in order to be assessed in full.

DISCUSSION: CREATIVE PRACTICE TOWARD A KLOUT CULTURE?

Although it is branded as a "standard" for influence, Klout does not appear, at present, to be able to determine a reliable qualitative stance of its quantitative score. It seems as though we are confronted with a metric whose design determines a vague and broad estimation of online influence, substantially overlapping with activity and frequency.

Quantitative, not qualitative. The qualitative or semantic analysis provided by Klout alongside the score strives to individuate the topics on which one can be considered influential. This, however, seems to be substantially ineffective. Klout gives the user the ability to list the topics he or she talks about the most often; however, at the time this piece was written, Klout does not seem to be able to efficaciously retrieve these topics from the user's activity list and, thus, remains generalized in its scope. The only qualitative stance is the system of K+, by which a user can declare a peer to be influential in a certain field through this system of "badges." However, the actual weight of the K+ in the overall score is unknown. The system of K+, which is what we can call a "metamoderation" (Farmer, 2011) or "user-generated" individuation, blends with the "system-generated" score and may partially operate in order to mitigate potential abuse or cheating (Lampe, 2012).

Being influential is being active. A second weakness in this regard is the importance of continuous activity in the calculation of the score. Klout requires one to be constantly active on social media platforms in order for one's score to consolidate and grow, thus generating a sort of "addiction" to interaction as the score becomes an element of confrontation and play among social media "friends." More so, although Klout defines influence as "the ability to drive action," claiming that "being active is different than being influential" (www.klout.com)—in other words, one cannot become an influencer by merely being active on an SNS—the opposite may actually be argued. If we consider, in fact, that the main criterion on which the influence score is calculated is the other users' engagement, one can theoretically reach a high Klout score simply by being active and involving others in a great number of conversations and comments, regardless of the content and the quality of the information shared. A plurality of bloggers from all over the world have shown how Klout scores can be boosted by simply being active with other active members, or merely knowing the most common "tricks" of social media management and SEO, resulting in unlikely figures, as shown by Gillin (2011).

A coarse example of this distortion is given by a famous case which occurred in Italy in 2012, known as the Groupalia incident. On the day of a tragic earthquake that plagued the center of the country, the Twitter account of Groupalia Italy posted an ironic tweet saying: "Scared by the earthquake? Drop everything and fly to Santo Domingo with Groupalia." The account was flooded by negative responses, and Groupalia's Klout score boomed (Filigheddu, 2012). This shows quite radically how activity is instrumental in order to get to a high Klout score and how the measurement of influence provided by Klout has substantial issues yet to be resolved. In this sense, as a traditional online reputation system, Klout is subject to potential gaming and cheating (Sekander, 2011). As bots and automated machines proliferate around social media, the risk of alteration of these metrics is realistic (Botvich et al., 2010; Messias et al., 2013). The existing algorithms, in fact, do not distinguish whether a user is a human being or an automated machine, a "bot," thus indirectly confirming critiques of confusion between influence and recurrent activity. Particularly, Messias et al. (2013) show how Klout is at serious risk of manipulation and cheating as long as the diffusion of "bots" extends.

Does Klout measure reputation? No. To sum up, it seems as though Klout, at present, is not a reliable measure for reputation and influence. Reputation is a quantitative, as well as a qualitative, instance that takes the form of a collective or shared perception about one another, crafted over the judgments made upon the mosaic of information publicly available (Marwick et al., 2010; Solove, 2008), but also, specifically, it represents a range of opinions from good to bad. The presence of a high Klout score may signal the presence of a reputation on a topic, without making a distinction between good and bad. As a result, Klout does not seem to measure influence per se, rather how much a profile is "hot," meaning an elaboration concerning activity and affectivity which is substantially decontextualized. In other words, influence metrics, such as Klout uses, provide a quantitative assessment of likes, shares, and all social buttons as a form of digital currency to cash in and out to get beneficial outcomes (Gerlitz & Helmond, 2011). What Klout and others seem to get is not "pure" influence, but rather a fraction of influence, displayed in the capacity to disseminate viral content throughout the online sphere. These sites gauge how much one engages with other users—notwithstanding the nature and quality of such content. It appears difficult to call "influencers" the individuals with this capacity, as these, by definition, should also generally be reputed in a field.

However, as value production increases around such tools, there seems to be a necessity to take influence seriously as a sociological concept, shifting from a media-based to an actor-based perspective of social media devices and platforms. In this sense, creative practice can be seen as a perfect terrain for such a study. Creative professions show concrete elements of separation from the traditional "labor theory of value" (Marx, 1976), whereby value is extracted according to labor time and the performance of certain practices and skills. Creative practice shows a different logic, as an interviewee in Milan told me:

> A creative does not take the reference of hours worked. A creative has creative references. Recently we have been conditioned by this relation, especially in the relationship with the client. I generally mix the two things. A fraction of my fee is calculated on a supposed relation between hours worked and tasks; another fraction, sometimes 80%, sometimes even 100%, is a "creative fee." This goes beyond the hours I have worked for that specific project or task. The first part gets bigger if I do a more "technical" job which is less creative. But, I mean, true creatives should not consider the amount of hours they work: such a quantification for our jobs is meaningless.
>
> (S., art director, Milan, 50, male)

The absence of the time reference, together with the importance of social capital and reputation across networks, brings Klout-like applications, if reliable, in a strong position of being a potential "general equivalent" (Arvidsson & Peitersen, 2013) for creative professions. In a context where reputation regulates value production, the emergence of applications which make reputation visible, tangible, and measurable has invaluable potential—and increasingly risky implications.

This is what I intend by pointing out the emergence of a *Klout culture,* with this term meaning the increasing "fetishization" of influence metrics in search of a general equivalent for value production within environments, such as creativity, where valorization takes place through immaterial production. The term "Klout culture" appears to be a useful epistemological tool to grasp the cultural implications and contradictions of the diffusion of such tools in a vast number of fields, going beyond the mere adoption of such metrics within a specific creative sector or for certain purposes (as, for instance, recruitment). Rather, the risk that seems to emerge in this regard is the increasing acknowledgment of such metrics as a "natural" standard for valorization without a critical approach that assesses the issues and shortcomings affecting Klout, such as the undisclosedness of the criteria for valorization and the private nature of such measurements.

Possibly for this reason, an intense debate has ignited out of the diffusion of Klout and its competitors, both in and especially out of academia in the context of magazines and blogs. This has resulted in a polarized confrontation between those who see the potential benefits conveyed by the diffusion of such services and those who look at these instances with various degrees of criticism. Among those who argue about influence metrics in positive terms, Schaefer (2012) sustains that the emergence of such algorithms is heralding a new era of the democratization of influence, whereby one does not need to be a celebrity in order to become an influencer. He argues that influence metrics are leading to the rise of a "citizen influencer," implying a third age of the web. As happened in the early days of Web 2.0, when everybody became a publisher by producing and consuming online cultural products, now everybody will be able to pave their way to social success through what he calls a return "to the very roots of influence: conversations between real people that make something happen" (Schaefer, 2012).

In a similar line of thought, Solis (2012) argues that we are on the verge of a new age of marketing, thanks to the renewed importance of word of mouth becoming measurable and instrumentally used for outcomes and effects in, for instance, consumer choices. In his view, in order for the "influence magic" to occur, social capital is required to activate the process of influence by spreading its most important features (trust, authority, popularity, affinity) throughout the network to achieve outcomes and a measurable effect. The network, he claims, is a community of connections classified in a social graph: "Relationships in social media are evaluated based on the nature of interaction[, t]ypically . . . connections based on common interests" which form a community at large whereby words and actions are a form of currency (Solis, 2012).

The numerous critical accounts, on the other hand, generally take into consideration the essentially private nature of some businesses, as in the case of Klout, which generally do not release publicly available information on the way influence rankings are constructed. The "secret" algorithm that lies beyond the most common influence metrics is in line with warnings of cheating and manipulation that we have seen concerning online reputation systems. American psychologist Aleks Krotoski (2012) believes that influence metrics function as intrinsically deceiving "echo chambers." Such rankings, according to Krotoski, are quite far from being democratic: high scores merely reward those who spend more time and money to manipulate the algorithm and generate traffic around a profile. The notion of "echo chambers" resembles that of the "daily me" (Sunstein, 2001), which here seems to be articulated in a different form. The selective filter of the user that Sunstein argued about before Web 2.0 is now changing its morphology toward a "daily me" made of a numerical account of personal interactions, virality, and network engagement among online contacts on SNSs, without diminishing the effects of segmentation and homophily. As Marwick and Boyd (2011) similarly argue, online practices of celebrity construction are theoretically open to all but do not actually require any equalizing or democratizing discourse and, on the contrary, seem to enable newly articulated forms of power and hierarchy.

CONCLUSION

This contribution has shown how social media metrics should be seen as controversial tools to measure the online activity of the social media user. Thus, they should be approached with a critical stance. The analysis of the famous social media metric, Klout, in relation to a study on reputation among creative practitioners in two major "creative cities" shows how Klout seems to be a good predictor for the capacity of an individual to engage with others on different platforms, together with their degree of activity. However, the Klout metrics seem unable to relate directly to the influence and reputation of professionals in the creative sector to a sufficiently reliable degree, as these instances are connected to more complex dynamics of socialization of value production which are linked to "offline" interaction as an investment in social relations for economic return (Lin, 2002).

Nevertheless, applications like Klout emerge and proliferate precisely in a sector where processes of value production take place through the capitalization of the relational nature that characterizes creative production, thus bearing risks and potential distortions. It appears, therefore, increasingly necessary to reflect on the nature of value production across creative environments, and how it connects with the rise of algorithms, which are quickly being established as forms of capture and control, organization and order, value production and assessment. In this regard, the present contribution shows how it is relatively easy to misinterpret and fetishize online metrics. In fact, Klout per se "does" nothing; rather, the uses and practices which are associated with the Klout scores transform them into performative markers that operate at various levels.

To a larger extent, the rise of social network sites and their billion-figure global diffusion has generated an unprecedented amount of data now available through online platforms. These can be considered a sort of "magic box" for social scientists, especially for those who are keen on quantitative approaches, given the sudden availability of a huge number of potentially accountable observations of social activity at all levels. Discourses on big data, sentiment analysis, and micro-interaction have merged together with the diffusion of the social buttons, including a wide range of implications consisting of effective advantages or disadvantages for users according to their influence scores. However, the score makers are not just chance, neutral tools. Rather, although relatively easy to manipulate, they appear to be increasingly relevant in different contexts (Martin, 2014). Their opaque and somehow contradictory characteristics are still largely underestimated. As social researchers, we need to learn how to deal with, discuss, and assess such tools in a critical perspective.

As noted, many believe we are at the dawn of a new, revolutionary era where influence is being democratized. In fact, there are elements referenced in this paper which seem to indicate a different scenario. Klout does not provide any genuine democratization of influence; actually, it does not seem far removed from a traditional, neoliberal discourse that pushes for individual success by all means—in this case, through the gamification of rankings. Indeed, reputation management practices, together with the problematics attached to influence metrics, seem to deploy new and different kinds of hierarchies, more or less implicit or explicit, based on both offline and online relational skills. The measurement of the strength of horizontal relationships among peers reveals a vertical movement of hierarchical differentiation among the same (supposed) peers. This kind of naïve enthusiasm for online influence metrics reminds one of a similar wave of optimism surrounding Florida's (2002) idea of the creative class. This predicted a new era of wealth and success thanks to the expansion of the creative industries, together with great employment opportunities in this sector. What actually emerged was a form of massive precarization and a fragmentation of the labor market (Hesmondhalgh & Baker, 2008, 2013; Neilson & Rossiter, 2005).

To conclude, Klout (and other sites like it) is still an imperfect tool, and it is hopefully going to be ameliorated, made more transparent and clear, and enriched through effective and useful qualitative criteria. However, Klout and its competitors have already benefited from the creation of an all-in-one tool, a metric for the assessment of the processes tied to social interaction, engagement, and virality. This is constructed on numerous advancements, particularly in terms of marketing strategy. Still, as concerns reputation, eventually a potential "reputation bubble" may come to exist in the long term, based on the absence of a critical approach toward influence metrics. The renewed attention to reputation in recent years, especially in relation to creative practice, shows how reputation has a central role in value production across different contexts. Whether it will be established as a shared general equivalent for value assessments, as seems to be the case across creative labor markets, remains to be seen.

REFERENCES

Anderson, C. (2006). *The long tail: Why the future of business is selling less of more.* New York: Hyperion.

Arvidsson, A., & Colleoni, E. (2012). Value in informational capitalism and on the Internet. *The Information Society, 28*(3), 135–150.

Arvidsson, A., & Peitersen, N. (2013). *The ethical economy.* New York: Columbia University Press.

Biernacki, P., & Waldorf, D. (1981). Snowball sampling. Problems and techniques of chain referral sampling. *Sociological Methods and Research, 10*(2), 141–163.

Blair, H. (2001). 'You're only as good as your last job': The labour process and labour market in the British film industry. *Work, Employment & Society, 15*(1): 149–169.

Blair, H. (2009). Active networking: Action, social structure and the process of networking. In A. McKinlay & C. Smith (Eds.), *Creative labour. Working in the creative industries* (pp. 116–134) New York: Palgrave Macmillan.

Bolton, G.E., Katok, E., & Ockenfels, A. (2004). How effective are electronic reputation mechanisms? An experimental investigation. *Management Science, 50*(11), 1587–1602.

Bolton, G., Loebbecke, C., & Ockenfels, A. (2007). *How social reputation networks interact with competition in anonymous online trading: An experimental study.* Cesifo Working Paper 2270. Retrieved from www.ifo.de/portal/pls/portal/docs/1/1187082.PDF

Botsman, R. (2010). *The reputation economy.* Retrieved from www.collaborative consumption.com/blog-and writings/Reputation%20Economy%20BOSS.pdf

Botsman, R. (2012). Welcome to the new reputation economy. *Wired UK.* Retrieved from www.wired.co.uk/magazine/archive/2012/09/features/welcome-to-the-new-reputation-economy?page=all

Botvich, D., McGibney, J., Ostapenko, G., De Paoli, S., Kerr, A., & Keatinge, M. (2010, June). *Integrating players, reputation and ranking to manage cheating in MMOGs.* Proceedings of the Fifth ACM International Conference on the Foundations of Digital Games, Monterey, CA.

Caliandro, A. (2011). *Il lavoro affettivo dei consumatori volto alla co-creazione di valore sui social media: un'indagine netnografica* [The affective labor of consumers for the co-creation of value on social media: A netnographic research] (Doctoral dissertation). Università degli Studi di Milano.

Cascio, J. (2012). The future of reputation networks. In H. Masum & M. Tovey (Eds.), *The reputation society: How online opinions are reshaping the offline world* (pp. 185–194). Cambridge, MA: MIT Press.

Christopherson, S. (2002). Project work in context: Regulatory change and the new geography of media. *Environment and Planning, A, 34*(11), 2003–2015.

Christopherson, S. (2008). Beyond the self-expressive creative worker: An industry perspective on entertainment media. *Theory, Culture & Society, 25*(7–8), 73–95.

Dellarocas, C. (2003). The digitization of word of mouth: Promise and challenges of online feedback mechanisms. *Management Science, 49*(10), 1407–1424.

Dellarocas, C. (2012). Designing reputation systems for the social web. In H. Masum & M. Tovey (Eds.), *The reputation society: How online opinions are reshaping the offline world* (pp. 3–11). Cambridge, MA: MIT Press.

Farmer, R. (2011). Web reputation systems and the real world. In H. Masum & M. Tovey (Eds.), *The reputation society: How online opinions are reshaping the offline world* (pp. 13–24). Cambridge, MA: MIT Press.

Farmer, R., & Glass, B. (2010). *Building web reputation systems.* Sebastopol, CA: O'Reilly Media.

Filigheddu, L. (2012). Is Klout score completely irrelevant? *TechGenius.* Retrieved from www.techgenial.com/2012/06/is-klout-score-completely-irrelevant.html

Florida, R. (2002). *The rise of the creative class.* New York: Basic Books.

Fuchs, C. (2010). Labor in informational capitalism and on the Internet. *The Information Society, 26*(3), 179–196.

Fuchs, C. (2012). With or without Marx? With or without capitalism? A rejoinder to Adam Arvidsson and Elanor Colleoni. *tripleC: Cognition, Communication, Co-operation, 10*(2), 633–645.

Gerlitz, C., & Helmond, A. (2011, January). *Hit, link, like and share. Organizing the social and the fabric of the web in a Like economy.* Paper presented at the Digital Methods Initiative mini-conference, University of Amsterdam, Netherlands.

Gillin, P. (2011). The trouble with Klout. *Paulgillin.com.* Retrieved from http://gillin.com/blog/2011/09/the-trouble-with-klout/

Gobo, G. (2011). Back to Likert. Towards the conversational survey. In M. Williams & W.P. Vogt (Eds.), *The Sage handbook of innovation in social research methods* (pp. 228–248). London: Sage.

Gobo, G., & Mauceri, S. (2013). *Collecting survey data*. London: Sage.

Grugulis, I., & Stoyanova, D. (2011). The missing middle: Communities of practice in a freelance labour market. *Work, Employment & Society, 25*(2): 342–351.

Grugulis, I., & Stoyanova, D. (2012). Social capital and networks in film and TV: Jobs for the boys? *Organization Studies, 33*(10): 1311–1331.

Hearn, A. (2008). Meat, mask, burden: Probing the contours of the branded self. *Journal of Consumer Culture, 8*(2), 197–217.

Hearn, A. (2010). Structuring feeling: Web 2.0, online ranking and rating, and the digital 'reputation' economy. *Ephemera, 10*(3/4), 421–438.

Hearn A. (2011). Confessions of a radical eclectic: Reality television, self-branding, social media, and autonomist Marxism. *Journal of Communication Inquiry, 35*(4), 313–321.

Hesmondhalgh, D., & Baker, S. (2008). Creative work and emotional labour in the television industry. *Theory, Culture & Society, 25*(7–8), 97–118.

Hesmondhalgh, D., & Baker, S. (2013). *Creative labour: Media work in three cultural industries*. London: Routledge.

Hoffman, R., & Casnocha, B. (2012). *The start-up of you: Adapt to the future, invest in yourself, and transform your career*. New York: Random House Digital.

Krotoski, A. (2012). Your Klout score is meaningless. *Wired UK*. Retrieved from www.wired.co.uk/magazine/archive/2012/03/ideas-bank/aleks-krotoski

Lampe, C. (2012). The role of reputation systems in managing online communities. In H. Masum & M. Tovey (Eds.), *The reputation society: How online opinions are reshaping the offline world* (pp. 77–88). Cambridge, MA: MIT Press.

Lin, N. (2002). *Social capital: A theory of social structure and action*. New York: Cambridge University Press.

Marres, N. (2012). The redistribution of methods: On intervention in digital social research, broadly conceived. *The Sociological Review, 60*(S1), 139–165.

Martin, J. A. (2014). Does your Klout score matter? *Cio.com*. Retrieved from www.cio.com/article/747159/Does_Your_Klout_Score_Matter_

Marwick, A., & Boyd, D. (2011). To see and be seen: Celebrity practice on Twitter. *Convergence, 17*(2), 139–158.

Marwick, A. E., Murgia-Diaz, D., & Palfrey, J. G. (2010). *Youth, privacy and reputation (literature review)*. Berkman Center Research Publication No. 2010–5; Harvard Public Law Working Paper No. 10–29. Retrieved from http://papers.ssrn.com/sol3/papers.cfm?abstract_id=1588163

Marx, K. (1976). *Capital: A critique of political economy*. Vol. 1. Harmondsworth, UK: Penguin/New Left Review.

Masum, H., & Zhang, Y-C. (2004). Manifesto for the reputation society. *First Monday, 9*(7). Retrieved from http://firstmonday.org/article/view/1158/1078

Meister, J. (2012). Will your Klout score get you hired? The role of social media in recruiting. *Forbes*. Retrieved from www.forbes.com/sites/jeannemeister/2012/05/07/will-your-klout-score-get-you-hired-the-role-of-social-media-in-recruiting

Messias, J., Schmidt, L., Oliveira, R., & Benevenuto, F. (2013). You followed my bot! Transforming robots into influential users in Twitter. *First Monday, 18*(7). Retrieved from http://firstmonday.org/ojs/index.php/fm/article/view/4217/3700

Moor, E. (2003). Branded spaces. The scope of "new marketing." *Journal of Consumer Culture, 3*(1), 39–60.

Neilson, B., & Rossiter, N. (2005). From precarity to precariousness and back again: Labour, life and unstable networks. *Fibreculture 5*. Retrieved from http://journal.fibreculture.org/issue5/neilson_rossiter.html

Owen, L. H. (2012). High Klout score? Expect airport perks and hotel room upgrades. *Paid Content*. Retrieved from http://paidcontent.org/2012/04/25/high-klout-score-expect-airport-perks-and-hotel-room-upgrades

Peters, T. (1999). *The brand called you*. New York: Random House.
Resnick, P. (2001). Beyond bowling together: Sociotechnical capital. In J. Carroll (Ed.), *HCI in the new millennium* (pp. 247–272). New York: Addison Wesley.
Rogers, R. (2009). *The end of the virtual: Digital methods*. Vol. 339. Amsterdam: Vossiupers UvA.
Rogers, R. (2013). *Digital methods*. Cambridge, MA: MIT Press.
Schaefer, M. W. (2012). *ROI. Return on influence. The revolutionary power of Klout, social scoring, and influence marketing*. New York: McGraw-Hill.
Sekander, Y. (2011). Here is how you can game Klout. *ElevateLocal*. Retrieved from www.elevatelocal.co.uk/blog/here-is-how-you-can-game-klout-22094835
Solis, B. (2012). *The rise of digital influence and how to measure it*. Retrieved from www.briansolis.com/2012/03/report-the-rise-of-digital-influence
Solove, D. (2008). *Understanding privacy*. Cambridge, MA: Harvard University Press.
Stevenson, S. (2012). What your Klout score really means. *Wired US*. Retrieved from www.wired.com/business/2012/04/ff_klout/1
Sunstein, C. (2001). *Echo chambers*. Princeton, NJ: Princeton University Press.

Contributors

Brooke Erin Duffy is Assistant Professor in the School of Media and Communication at Temple University.

Alessandro Gandini is Postdoctoral Research Fellow at the University of Milan.

Helen Kennedy is Senior Lecturer in New Media at the Institute of Communications Studies, University of Leeds, UK.

Ramon Reichert is Professor of Media Studies at the University of Vienna.

Joseph Reagle is Assistant Professor of Communication Studies at Northeastern University as well as a Faculty Associate at the Berkman Center for Internet and Society.

Hiesun Cecilia Suhr is Assistant Professor of Digital Media at Miami University–Hamilton and Affiliate Faculty in the Department of Art at Miami University–Oxford, OH.

Aaron Trammell is a Doctoral Candidate and Lecturer at the Department of Journalism and Media Studies, Rutgers University.

Linda Vigdor received her Ph.D. from the University of Illinois–Urbana-Champaign in Education Psychology. She is an independent scholar and artist.

Index